JHS C
(Hol)

Handbook for
Newly
Qualified
Teachers

011 702 6484

Handbook for

Newly Qualified Teachers

the definitive guide to your first years of teaching

Elizabeth Holmes

London: The Stationery Office

Second impression 1999

The right of Elizabeth Holmes to be identified as Author of this Work has been asserted by her in accordance with the Copyright, Design and Patents Act 1998.

Illustrations by Nigel Paige.

British Library Cataloguing in Publication Data

A catalogue record for this book is available from the British Library.
ISBN 0 11 702648 4
Printed and bound by The Stationery Office, Parliamentary Press, London
J95398   C15   10/99   456520   19585

Published by The Stationery Office and available from:

The Publications Centre
(mail, telephone and fax orders only)
PO Box 276, London SW8 5DT
General enquiries / Telephone orders
0870 600 5522
Fax orders 0870 600 5533

www.tso-online.co.uk

The Stationery Office Bookshops
123 Kingsway, London WC2B 6PQ
020 7242 6393 Fax 020 7242 6394
68–69 Bull Street, Birmingham B4 6AD
0121 236 9696   Fax 0121 236 9699
33 Wine Street, Bristol BS1 2BQ
0117 9264306   Fax 0117 9294515
9–21 Princess Street, Manchester M60 8AS
0161 834 7201   Fax 0161 833 0634
16 Arthur Street, Belfast BT1 4GD
028 9023 8451   Fax 028 9023 5401
The Stationery Office Oriel Bookshop
18-19 High Street, Cardiff CF1 2BZ
029 2039 5548   Fax 029 2038 4347
71 Lothian Road, Edinburgh EH3 9AZ
0131 228 4181   Fax 0131 622 7017

The Stationery Office's Accredited Agents
(see Yellow Pages)

and through good booksellers

Contents

Introduction

Rewarding and stimulating as it can be, teaching is an extremely complex career requiring high-level expertise in many skills areas. It is also a career in an area in which the nation is permanently interested. You only have to glance at a newspaper or listen to the news to see how frequently education issues are, sometimes inaccurately, discussed. Add to this the pace of change in education, and you could easily find yourself confused, however satisfying your job is.

The purpose of the *Handbook for Newly Qualified Teachers* is to provide NQTs in primary and secondary schools with a valuable resource for their first few years in the profession. It includes ideas on easing your way into your new career and draws from the Standards for the Award of Qualified Teacher Status, the Induction Standards and OFSTED guidance, as well as dealing with the other needs of new teachers and those returning to the profession after a career break, such as finding a job, how to deal with work-related stress and union membership. It is packed with the information you are likely to require during your first few years, and also gives useful addresses and hints for further reading.

Teaching can seem a lonely career, with many new teachers feeling that they must cope with the job alone. This book is designed to help you accept that you don't have to muddle through – that there are lines of support that you can follow and lean on. Your first few years of teaching should not be about surviving the profession; surviving is only a marginal improvement on barely existing and no one can teach effectively under those circumstances. Your induction year is about building on your sense of security in your job, as well as enjoyment.

The *Handbook for Newly Qualified Teachers* is not an academic textbook, relying heavily on teaching and learning theory or 'hoop-jumping' tips. It doesn't attempt to tell you how to teach, a skill that you will continue to perfect throughout your career, neither is it a digest of academic papers and texts.

It does, however, draw together good practice and a heavy dose of common sense in an easily accessed way. It is a practical, functional guide for everyday use – for you to reach for whenever you need an idea, support or inspiration. It seeks to enable rather than preach, to help you guard against misinformation and dogma and to encourage you to develop your own ideas about the best way of managing your job with integrity.

Checklists

For ease of information retrieval, many hints have been organised into lists. It is not intended that you should follow each list slavishly; rather use them as a springboard for your own ideas. They are designed to be a time-saving device for you. Simply dip in, select the information you need, and go.

Action features

These have not been written around hypothetical issues, requiring you to spend time on hypothetical answers. Rather, they are intended to draw from your own wealth of resources for problem solving. Again, there is no need to work through them slavishly.

Example boxes

All of the examples have been drawn from the real experiences of teachers, although some of the names have been changed. They have been included to illustrate points in the text, and some deal with relatively unusual situations.

About boxes

These boxes contain succinct information covering the many issues and situations that face new teachers.

No book is perfect, and there are bound to be comments and ideas that you, as an NQT, would wish to make about the material presented here. If you would like to make your thoughts known, then you can e-mail me at: ea.holmes@virgin.net. Finally, I offer my good wishes to all of you working through your first few years of teaching and sincerely hope that the *Handbook for Newly Qualified Teachers* will be an important companion, helping you to find your job valuable, rewarding and, at times, exhilarating.

Acknowledgements

This book could not have been written without the input of the many people who freely offered time, ideas, support and encouragement. In particular, I would like to thank:

- Charlotte Howard of the Fox and Howard Literary Agency
- Sally Downes, Emma Martin, Michele Staple, Jayne Wilkinson and everyone else at The Stationery Office who was involved in this book
- Gillian Watson, Helen Fretwell and all those at the Teacher Training Agency who responded to my many enquiries
- the staff of the Department for Education and Employment and the Department of the Environment, Transport and the Regions who assisted with technical details
- Tim Brighouse (Birmingham Education Authority), Matthew Hansen-Kahn (East Sussex Education Authority), Redmore Church, Howard Bottomley and Anne Fenton (West Sussex Education Authority) and the many other education authority staff across the country who offered insights into local practice
- Rosa Drohomirecka and Meryl Thompson of the Association of Teachers and Lecturers and staff of the other teaching unions who contributed information
- Roger Deeks and Maureen Mobley of Bristol University for permission to quote from *The Bristol Guide*
- Sue Abbott of University College, Chichester Careers Service
- Ann Greatorex of Bishop Luffa School, Chichester; Lyn Fryer and Martin Quaiffe of Worthing High School; Sara Spivey of Littlehampton Community School; Claire Taeger of Plumstead Manor School, Greenwich; the many other teachers and pupils who gave their time; and all the people in the global education community who responded to my newsgroup postings.
- Kevin McCarthy of Re:membering Education

- Andy Hudson and Chris Watkins of the Institute of Education, London
- the Penny family and all my other family, friends and colleagues whose encouragement along the way has been greatly appreciated
- my parents and David and Carolyn.

E Holmes

July 1999

Publisher's note

Any advice given in this book concerning the health of a reader is for information and guidance only and is not intended to replace the advice of a qualified health care practitioner. Neither the author nor the publisher can be held responsible for any consequences incurred by those following the guidance herein.

For my parents, Dorothy and Tony

CHAPTER 1

Finding jobs in education

Where do you want to teach?

Completing your initial teacher-training (ITT) course leaves you with many decisions to make. Not only do you have to decide whether you would like to continue your teaching career in education but, also, in which type of school you would like to work – independent or state, community or voluntary-aided, mixed or single-sex, inner-city or rural. You may even decide you would prefer to work in a profession related to teaching.

Rather than falling into the first vacancy that comes your way, it is worth considering all the options available to you. What kinds of experience do you want to gain? Do you want to consolidate your training in a school similar to, or the same as, your teaching practice school? Are you eager for a complete change?

JOINING THE MAINSTREAM

By far the largest percentage of all schools falls into the category of mainstream education, including state and independent schools, voluntary-aided schools and colleges of further education.

The independents

These invariably involve the payment of fees, although the parental burden can vary tremendously as some children will be eligible for bursaries, scholarships and sponsorships. They do not come under the guidance of a local education authority and are free to develop the curriculum and teaching styles as they see fit. That said, most do use the National Curriculum as a framework and offer the opportunity for pupils to prepare for and take national qualifications.

In direct contrast to the state system, the headteacher of an independent school usually has the final say over the way in which the school is run, with a board of governors adopting an advisory and ratifying role.

TEACHING IN INDEPENDENT SCHOOLS

Pros	Cons
Misbehaviour is generally less common.	You may not be able to serve an induction period.
Class sizes are considerably smaller than in most state schools.	Teachers can be expected to perform duties outside the teaching day, e.g. sports training, clubs etc.
Parental support for the school can be greater.	Independent schools are exclusive on the grounds of the fees payable.
Independent schools can sometimes offer a wider variety of subjects, which may suit your interests.	You may not be paid on the same scale as your state colleagues.
An anti-staff sub-culture is relatively uncommon.	The pension arrangements may be down to you.
Holidays are longer in an independent school.	It can prove difficult to move from the independent sector into the state

For the teacher, working in an independent school is a different experience from working in a state school. Although, in both kinds of establishment, an educational package is being offered to both parents and pupils, in the independent sector, market forces do seem to play a more central role. Naturally, when parents are choosing which product to buy, they are going to be conscious of the quality of education on offer. This can create a culture of exceptionally high expectations being placed on teachers by:

- the school management (wanting to keep the standards high enough to attract more clients)
- the parents (who are aware of value for their money)
- the pupils (who often understand their relatively powerful position at the centre of these dynamics).

ABOUT

WORKING IN A BOARDING SCHOOL

Boarding schools are unique educational establishments in that all staff can find themselves playing the roles of mother, father, teacher and guardian. Certainly during term time, teachers at boarding schools are fully immersed in the life of the school (which extends way beyond the usual teaching day) and may even be required to live on site. Working in a well-run boarding school can be like working within a commune, the intensity of which can be balanced by the unusually long holidays.

Vacancies for jobs in independent schools are advertised in the educational press. Gabbitas Educational Consultants (see Appendix 7 for useful addresses) recruits at all levels on behalf of independent schools both home and abroad.

If you do decide to apply for a job in the independent sector, ask for answers to these questions before accepting an offer:

- Does the school adopt the same pay spine as the state sector?
- Is your contract comparable to one you would receive in the state sector?
- Under what circumstances could your contract be terminated?
- What are the arrangements for your pension?
- Will you be able to serve a statutory induction period at this school?
- What expectations will be made of you in terms of extra-curricular activities?

State schools

The structure of state schools varies tremendously from county to county and looks set to continue to change in the foreseeable future. As an NQT, you need only be aware of whether the institution you join is maintained by the local education authority – a community school (with the LEA as the employer) – or is a voluntary-aided/foundation school (with the governing body as the employer).

Community schools

The LEA is the contractual employer of teachers working in these schools. There are also community special schools.

Voluntary-aided schools

The LEA maintains these schools, but a foundation (usually religious) appoints most of the governing body, which is responsible for all aspects of the working of the school, including the appointment of staff and dealing with complaints and grievances; it is the contractual employer. The next level of authority above the governing body in such schools is the Secretary of State for Education and this is worth serious consideration.

Foundation schools

Some of the schools that were previously grant maintained (GM) will be run as foundation schools. It is anticipated that this will be very close to the way in which voluntary-aided schools are run now. The governing body is the contractual employer. There are also foundation special schools.

Other considerations

- *Church schools* While all schools have to have an element of spiritual teaching, joining a church school carries specific obligations on the part of the teacher. You will usually be expected to live according to the doctrines and tenets you teach and, as with most religions, degrees of tolerance vary.

- *Special schools* It is possible to gain employment in a special school for your first post and if you are sure that this type of teaching is for you, then all is well. However, it is often a good idea to consolidate your experience in mainstream-ability ranges first, before specialising. You can use this time to become involved in special educational needs (SEN) at your school and gather skills and experience.

- *Post-16 colleges* These are very tempting for those with a real love of their subject. However, do think about how committed you are to this age range, because it could be difficult to adjust to secondary level once you have worked with the 16–19s, should you subsequently decide to work in a school. Another consideration is that post-16 colleges receive their funding from the Further Education Funding Council and are totally independent of the LEA. Many require staff members to teach evening classes as well and the salary you can expect may be slightly lower than that of an NQT teaching in a school.

- *Single-sex schools* Opinion about single-sex education seems to change with great frequency, as do ideas on the merits of working in such a school. Girls' schools are very different places from boys' schools and it would be worth spending a few days observing in each to assess whether single-sex teaching is for you. You may also like to consider the fact that you are likely to be in the minority if you teach in a single-sex school of the opposite sex to your own.

- *Specialist schools* These are schools offering particular expertise in one of four areas: technology, languages, sports or the arts. They receive extra funding and some offer master classes to challenge the brightest pupils. The aim is that by 2001 there will be 500 specialist schools. If your particular interest falls under one of the above headings, it could be rewarding working in a specialist school.

WHAT'S THE ALTERNATIVE? PROGRESSIVE EDUCATION

This is your opportunity not only to choose the type of school in which you want to work, but the philosophy of teaching you want to pursue. Progressive education is almost exclusively offered by 'Small Schools'. These are schools in which the learning environment specifically aims to allow for the creative, spiritual, psychological, intellectual and physical aspects of each child to be nurtured. Unlike the USA and the rest of Europe, where progressive education is part of the package of choice on offer to pupils, parents and teachers, in the UK it is almost entirely in the private sector and parents will be required to contribute to the cost.

ABOUT

HUMAN SCALE EDUCATION

Human Scale Education (HSE) is a pressure group set up to promote the education being offered by Small Schools. Its main belief is that teachers, pupils and society all benefit from the opportunities that Small Schools offer children for active, participatory learning in groups small enough for solid interpersonal relationships to be built. HSE wants children to be educated to develop purpose, imagination and a sense of truth, and for personal development skills to be nurtured.

At the heart of progressive education lies the teacher/pupil relationship, which is based on mutual trust and respect. Pupils are usually instrumental in decision-making in these schools, made possible because of the relatively low pupil populations and high teacher/pupil ratios.

Some Small Schools offer their pupils the National Curriculum; others select from it what is most appropriate for their students, as learning intentions can be influenced by both the curriculum and the other needs of each child.

The ideas of the Small School movement are filtering into mainstream schools, with some reorganising themselves into a collection of mini-schools. Flexi-schooling has also been adopted in some areas, which allows for pupils to be educated at school and in the community as appropriate.

Small Schools offer new teachers some distinct advantages:

- It is believed that if children can make decisions about their education on some level, they are more motivated academically.
- Teaching groups are often very small – about ten pupils.
- Such small groups allow teaching skills to be developed and confidence gained.
- Fewer curriculum constraints allow for more creative teaching and the easy dissemination of good practice.

However:

- In Britain progressive education is almost entirely in the private sector, so the same considerations need to be made when accepting a job in a Small School as in any other independent school.
- Teachers attempting to move from the private sector to the state sector may have to contend with negative discrimination.
- Salaries are usually lower than those in the state sector.

USING PROGRESSIVE IDEAS

You don't have to work in a Small School to use progressive ideas in your teaching and develop your own philosophies as an educator. There is no reason why you cannot pull threads of progressive education through to the mainstream setting in which you work. The organisation, Re:membering Education, promotes the teaching of awe and wonder at the world and the ability to reflect on events and raise self-esteem. It suggests that teachers look at relationships on all levels: between learner and subject, between learner and teacher, and between subjects. Educating about and through the emotions is something that all teachers can attempt. Aim to visit Small Schools in your area.

ACTION: Spend at least a day when you actively implement some of the ideas of progressive education. Perhaps set aside some time in a lesson for pupils to decide on their own targets for learning or focus on how emotional intelligence may affect the absorption of the subject(s) you teach.

TEMPORARY CONTRACTS – IS SHORT-TERM SHORT-SIGHTED?

'A verbal contract isn't worth the paper it's written on.' Sam Goldwyn – a phrase of caution to be heeded, although verbal contracts may not be as ineffective in law as is generally believed.

The type of contract you have been offered may not seem important when you have just secured your first teaching job, but it is important to be circumspect when accepting anything other than a permanent contract.

The main two temporary contracts concerning NQTs are:

- Fixed-term contracts. These allow schools to plan for falling rolls, or other foreseeable situations that will result in fewer teachers being required.
- Specific-task contracts. These allow schools to cover particular events, such as maternity and sick leave.

Such contracts should never be, but sometimes are, used by a school as insurance against a new teacher who may turn out to be unsuitable. It is sometimes believed that it is easier not to renew the contract of a 'weak' teacher than provide the necessary professional support.

However, a temporary contract can be appropriate in certain circumstances. You may want to gain experience in a variety of settings before committing to one particular type of school, or you may need to move your home mid-year, making a permanent contract less important.

The references you can pick up from your employment on a temporary contract are far more detailed regarding your skills once in post than anything your tutors are in a position to write. In that respect they add greatly to the value of your CV. Don't forget, there really is no such thing as a job for life!

If you do accept a temporary contract, keep these points in mind:

- Regardless of the type of contract you accept, as an NQT you are entitled to an induction programme and should be offered the same opportunities as NQTs on permanent contracts. Don't miss out. You need to find out when you will be deemed to have completed your induction period if you take a temporary contract.
- Taking over from another teacher mid-year can be difficult, especially if the pupils know that you are not a permanent member of staff. Support from your school at this stage is crucial. Make your mark on each class you teach; you are not simply a babysitter and can do things 'your way'.
- Make sure you know the termination date of your contact, its type and the reason why it is temporary.

TAKING CARE OVER CONTRACTS

It can feel as though you are being unnecessarily meticulous if you question the finer details of your contract, but it is important to protect yourself against possible future disputes, which can drain your energy and place a negative focus on your career. There is no reason why a contract that is fair to you and the school cannot be negotiated. Your union and LEA education personnel office are able to offer contract advice and some lawyers will also do this free of charge. Make sure you clearly understand your contractual obligations, so that you are free to commence your career from a position of knowledge and security. Above all, do not sign or agree to anything unless you are happy with the implications – if not, your first job could be your worst job.

Disputes over contracts seem to be common, and for this reason some unions are fighting for national standards.

- 'Fixed-term' contracts carry more employment protection than 'specific-task' contracts. If you are employed on a series of fixed-term contracts, your employment rights regarding unfair dismissal and redundancy accrue after two years. However, this looks set to be reduced to one year and current legal thinking is to act as if this is so. Seek advice from your union if you feel you have been treated unfairly.
- If your post will be open beyond your termination date, you should be offered a renewal of contract without the post being re-advertised.
- Make sure you will be receiving the correct remuneration – some schools calculate bizarre combinations of salary and supply rates in order to save money, especially if your contract takes you over a long holiday.

PART-TIME TEACHING

Recent legislation now means that there is no such thing as a part-time employee – all employees are equal regardless of the hours they work each week. This means that part-timers have the same holiday and sick pay entitlements (pro rata) as full-time employees. For this reason, part-time teaching can be attractive to some teachers, providing you can afford to accept the necessary reduction in salary! It also offers these benefits:

- It gives you the chance to pursue other career options.
- It can allow you to continue your career at a time when you have domestic pressures such as child-rearing or caring for a relative.
- It frees time to concentrate on further professional development such as obtaining additional qualifications.
- There is usually flexibility to increase your working hours, often through covering for absent staff.

However, even if it has been possible to negotiate part-time hours at your school, there are always disadvantages that should be considered:

- It can feel as though you are not fully involved in the life of the school when you only attend at certain times.
- Liaising with colleagues can become difficult because of your work patterns.
- Part-time teachers invariably spend more time than their pay suggests preparing for lessons and marking/assessing.
- Career progression can become difficult (and in some schools, impossible).
- Depending on how efficient your school is at disseminating information, it can be very difficult to stay fully informed of the latest changes.
- You will probably spend a disproportionate amount of time travelling to and from school if you do not work full days.

Job-sharing

As the work profile of the nation changes and increasing numbers of people are looking for more flexibility in their work, job-sharing seems to have become an interesting option. Many schools have job-sharing schemes in place, which can offer all the advantages (and disadvantages) of part-time teaching, as well as the added bonus of having ready-made cover should you need time off for any reason. You should, however, be aware of these factors:

- Job-sharing can be an extremely good deal for the school – the sum of two half-teachers is often greater than one!
- Time must be spent liaising with your colleague for the purposes of planning, marking and assessment.
- Difficulties can arise if one side of the partnership leaves and good working dynamics have to be established quickly with a newcomer.

As with any job, full-time, part-time or shared, always check the finer details of your contract, and consider the implications for your pension.

CAREERS RELATED TO TEACHING – EDUCATED CHOICES

Receiving Qualified Teacher Status does not mean that you are obliged or committed to take a job as a teacher, or to teaching in this country. There are many opportunities for qualified teachers – in fact, people with teaching qualifications are often sought by industry because of the transferable skills they possess. These include skills such as the ability to multi-task, to work to extremely tight deadlines, to relate to a variety of different people within each working day and to adjust the time spent working each day as appropriate.

Here are just some ideas you may like to consider.

Choices within teaching

You may not want to take a permanent job in a British school, but there are many other ways of earning money from teaching.

SEEKING CAREERS ADVICE

Careers advice is available from many sources now, but since the privatisation of the Careers Service, you are more likely to have to pay for the advice you receive. The Careers Service used to come under the remit of LEAs and privatised services are still organised with county boundaries.

Most institutes of higher education offer students and ex-students careers advice specifically for people with higher-education qualifications free of charge. This is probably the best place to start. An agreement of 'mutual aid' means that you will probably be able to get careers advice from the university/college in your home area as well as the university/college you attended. You may, however, have to wait for an appointment as university careers services will put their own students first. You can also get advice from independent careers offices but it is a good idea to use a county service that employs trained careers advisors. There is usually a charge for the advice they give, but the time, resources and follow-up care you are given can be worth the investment. Other sources of careers advice for teachers are the Teacher Training Agency and the Internet (look at the 'Prospects' site).

Teaching English as a Foreign Language

Teaching English as a Foreign Language (TEFL) can offer excellent opportunities to work with students of all ages and even travel around the world. Some language schools insist on specific TEFL qualifications, which can be gained by attending various courses, either full-time or part-time. Training is advisable, as it will enhance employment opportunities, particularly if you go through the British Council. There will always be a world market of people keen to learn English, either as a second or third language, or for specific purposes such as business.

Teaching in developing countries

Voluntary Service Overseas (VSO) can offer opportunities for graduate teachers to teach overseas, normally for at least two years. Payment is at local rates. Some aid agencies and Christian organisations also employ teachers to work abroad. Embassies and the educational press often have details of overseas teaching opportunities.

Other work abroad

Opportunities in the USA, Canada, Australia, New Zealand, and non-European Union countries are limited, but European Union (EU) countries offer some possibilities. Again, the relevant embassies or high commissions will be able to advise as to how to obtain employment. Also, the careers section of your local library will have information on job opportunities in EU countries.

ABOUT

RETURNING AFTER WORKING ABROAD

If you spend time in your career teaching abroad, there will inevitably be some employers who do not value the extra experience you will have gained. In order to capitalise on your breadth of experience, carefully select elements of your work abroad that have specific application to teaching in this country. Find ways of working this information into any interviews you have on your return. Unfortunately, some schools may not recognise work abroad as a justification for an additional point on the salary scale.

It is worth noting that you will have to complete an induction period if you have not already done so in order to be eligible to teach in a maintained school or a non-maintained special school.

Private tutoring

There are often advertisements for teachers to work as private tutors in families, both in this country and abroad, in the educational press. Some teaching agencies maintain registers of private tutors, although obtaining work through such agencies can result in having to pay a fee for the introduction, or a percentage of any earnings you receive from work through the agency.

For this reason it can be more lucrative to advertise your teaching services in your local press. Such advertisements usually cost less than £20. If timed well, for example around Easter time to catch the exam crammers and the beginning of September for those students whose parents want them to improve on their performance in the previous year, you can quickly recoup your expenses. Do remember that any earnings from private tutoring form part of your taxable income! For further information contact your local Training and Enterprise Agency. You will find details in the 'Yellow Pages'.

Many teachers find private tutoring extremely rewarding as it allows an opportunity to focus on teaching and interacting, without the need to consider the dynamics of a large group. Your union will be able to advise on what is the current rate for private tutoring.

Supply teaching

Supply teaching is quite a tough route to take as a newly qualified teacher. As you move from school to school covering for absent staff, your abilities to adapt to different institutions, subjects and age groups will need to be well honed. However, there seem to be increasing opportunities whereby supply teaching could lead to a temporary contract which could, in turn, become a permanent one.

Supply teaching makes it virtually impossible to gain a valuable induction into the teaching profession if you are not based in one school, and this has grave implications for your chances of satisfying the requirements of what should be your first year of teaching. Professional support is likely to be patchy too, at a time when behaviour management will be at its most challenging. For this reason, supply teaching should only really be considered in extreme circumstances.

The best way into supply teaching is through your own contacts. If you have connections with a particular school, ask the headteacher for an informal interview with a view to being added to the school's list of supply teachers. Alternatively, if there is a school you would like to work in, doing some voluntary work as a precursor to paid employment is a great way of convincing the powers that be of your skills and abilities.

All LEAs maintain a list of teachers available for supply work that is distributed to schools within its remit. Contact the appropriate LEA's education personnel office for details.

In some areas, supply agencies operate and this can be a slightly safer way of working in what is an area of teaching totally unprotected by employment rights. Your union will be able to advise you on agencies in your area.

Choices outside the teaching profession

You're not selling your soul if you decide to go for work outside the teaching profession. There is tremendous scope for using your qualifications and the profession will invariably welcome any experience you gain should you decide to return at a later date.

Project work

Look in the education press for advertisements for trained teachers to take part in projects. These are usually research-based, fixed-term contracts, which offer the chance to become involved in a specialist area of education.

Resource development

Most teachers write their own materials on occasion (if not all the time) and there are opportunities within publishing to become involved in book and resource package projects. Either approach suitable publishers directly with a brief synopsis of your idea (the *Writers' and Artists' Yearbook* is invaluable for information on publishing companies) or look out for 'creative' and 'media' advertisements in the quality press.

Multi-media educational-resource development is another growth area and one in which it would be wise for most teachers to become involved.

Education administration

There are opportunities at many levels in local education administration from planning and budgeting to policy implementation and problem solving. Vacancies will usually be advertised in the local press, but it is also worth arranging some work experience or talking to key personnel in your local education authority. Many local government education administration jobs still allow for close contact with schools.

Education officer posts

Most museums, heritage and conservation sites, large companies and major charities have education officers whose job it is to liaise with visitors and generally inform the public of the work of the organisation. This may be through writing worksheets and newsletters or organising exhibitions and fund-raising.

Often, such jobs are advertised in the education press but, again, if there is a particular organisation you would like to work for, make your own introductions through speculative applications, work experience and voluntary work.

Training in industry and commerce

The training department of any company performs a vital role, especially now that the pace of change within the workplace is so rapid. The skills you would need for a job in training are very similar to those needed in the teaching profession, i.e. good communication, motivation, organisation, analysis and problem solving.

As training departments in companies are often part of the human resources services, you may need to do some further study to acquire the relevant professional qualifications.

Caring work

This general term covers all jobs involving caring for others such as social work, youth and community work, educational welfare and residential care. Caring work often allows you to develop solid relationships with those you are working with over a long period of time and will demand many skills.

Jobs in other areas

These job areas are also worth considering:

- retail management
- public relations
- marketing
- librarianship
- broadcasting
- research
- leisure
- careers advising
- counselling
- writing
- journalism.

Applying for teaching jobs

Unless you fall into the relatively small category of beginning teachers who are offered a job in their teaching practice school and want to accept that job, you will have to apply to an unfamiliar school for a teaching post at some stage. Although this may seem daunting, when you view the challenge as a project that can easily be broken down into stages, you could not only be successful in receiving a job offer, but also in ensuring that it is suitable.

TUNING YOUR VACANCY RADAR

Somewhere, your ideal job will be advertised and, if you are not looking in the likely places, it will be offered to someone else.

The best way to start the great hunt is to decide on the geographical area in which you are prepared to work. Obviously, the smaller your chosen area the more limited your search, but that is no reason to force yourself into applying for jobs in areas about which you have doubts. Once you have a list of places in which you would be happy to work, pursue every lead in the hunt for the ideal vacancy.

Covering every option

Resignations of teaching posts are made to three deadlines throughout the year; 31 October, 28 February and 31 May, although these deadlines may be waived if both parties agree. Naturally the few weeks following these deadlines are particularly good times to search for job advertisements.

The national press

The vast majority of vacancies in the teaching profession are advertised in *The Times Educational Supplement* which comes out on Fridays. More specifically, look out for the first appointments sections published three times a year, usually in October, January and May. These are packed full with vacancies and features geared towards new entrants to the profession.

Other newspapers to scour are the *Guardian* (on Tuesdays), the *Daily Telegraph* (on Wednesdays) and the *Independent* (on Thursdays) all of which have interesting education sections usually including several pages of vacancies.

The local press

As only vacancies for heads and deputies have to be advertised nationally, it is well worth scrutinising the local press. If you are not living where you would eventually like to be working, contact the appropriate local paper and they will arrange to send you the copies you require.

LEA bulletins

These are invaluable to the job-searching NQT, as vacancies will often be advertised here before they go into the national press. Arrange with relevant LEAs to have newsletters posted to you. Contacting the appropriate education personnel department is usually enough to get this set up.

The Internet

Many LEAs have channelled resources into creating sophisticated web sites where current vacancies, amongst other things, may be posted. Either phone for specific web site addresses or browse through to see what you can find. *The Times Educational Supplement* has a good web site (http://www.tes.co.uk) and will e-mail you every Friday with details of appropriate vacancies. Simply visit the site and register what you are looking for. It is also worth scanning the education newsgroups as they are a good source of contacts and you may pick up advance information on interesting vacancies.

Contacts made during teaching practice

Don't underestimate how valuable networking can be when you have the opportunity during training to visit a variety of schools. Utilise any contacts you have made and you may be privy to information about a vacancy before it is advertised to the general public. Such contacts could be mentors, heads and deputies, course tutors (who invariably retain close links with local schools) and any inspectors and advisors you may have come across in the course of your studies. A phone call

WHAT TO LOOK FOR IN A VACANCY

Although it is important to be enthusiastic and have high aspirations, you should never accept extra responsibility points in your first year of teaching. Leave the promotions until you have completed your induction period.

Go for vacancies that either specifically refer to NQTs or are advertised as core pay scale (CPS). A school that is prepared to offer an NQT extra responsibilities is probably thinking more of the budget than your abilities to cope, and the additional support you will need is unlikely to be forthcoming.

or letter could provide you with a specific piece of information that puts you at an advantage.

DECIDING TO APPLY

Actually deciding to apply for a teaching vacancy is a commitment to a fair amount of work and, therefore, not to be undertaken lightly. Minimise the possibility of pulling out at any stage by finding out as much as you can about the school.

The job advertisement will give limited information and if this sounds tempting, request an application form and job description. It is essential not to apply for a job unless you have been sent both.

The job description should contain at the very least the following information:
- the title of the post (e.g. class teacher, history teacher etc.)
- the salary
- details of the person to whom the post is responsible (e.g. head of department)

- what the responsibilities are
- any extra duties
- an indication of the timetable
- an applicant profile.

Vacancies can be advertised on the basis of a verbal resignation. Whilst retraction of the resignation is extremely unlikely, do bear in mind that this could, in theory, happen right up to the interview stage. Before sitting down to complete the necessary forms, do some mental questioning to establish whether, based on the information available to you at this stage, you would accept the job if offered. The questions below will be helpful here.

Questions to ask:
- Is it an NQT post?
- Would the job allow you to live in an area in which you want to live?
- Is it in the type of school you would like to be a part of?
- Would you be teaching subjects you have specialised in?
- Would you be teaching an age group you have specialised in?
- Is the school in an Education Action Zone (EAZ) (see Chapter 2)?

SPECULATIVE APPLICATIONS

If you have set your heart on a particular school but have not seen an advertisement for a vacancy, send a speculative application, or 'broadcast letter', so called because you are announcing your availability.

Points to remember

- Plan your letter carefully, being sure to include any achievements and outstanding skills. Keep it punchy and use bullet points as appropriate. One side of A4 paper should be ample, as you will be sending a current CV with the letter. Remember, don't plead; the idea is for the school to feel that they can't function without you!

- Write or type on good quality paper.

- First state what kind of vacancy you are interested in.

- Match your skills and experience to what you know of the school.

- State some attributes that you can bring to the school.

- Ask for an interview – offer broad suggestions for possible dates.

- End with the expectation of a reply, e.g. 'I look forward to hearing from you', and include an SAE.

- If you don't hear within a week, make a follow-up call – ask to speak to the person to whom you wrote.

ACTION: What are your unique selling points? This can be hard to think about without some feedback from other people. Talk to at least two trusted friends (preferably ones who have worked with you). Ask them what your outstanding skills are and you should end up with a list that will get you started.

COMPLETING THE NECESSARY FORMS

The method of application varies among schools and LEAs, so it is essential to follow any guidance given carefully, especially if you are making applications in different authorities. The minimum you will have to do is fill in an application form including a supporting statement in which you have the opportunity honestly to sell your skills. Some schools require a medical form as well.

It is a good idea to have a current CV printed and ready to send at short notice. Your training institution will be able to offer advice on how it should be set out. However, even if you are employed on the basis of your CV, most personnel departments still require a completed application form for your records. Before you put your mark on the form, take a photocopy so you can have a dry run.

Selling your skills

The application form is designed to elicit basic information about you, your education and employment history. This alone will not make you stand out from the crowd, but your real opportunity to shine is in the supporting statement.

Your main goals when writing your supporting statement must be to match your skills to the job description and to include your unique selling points. Don't simply write about the experiences you have had. There are many experienced teachers, but are they necessarily skilled? Inform your future employers of your achievements. Your leading sentence must engage the reader immediately, giving a sense of your personality. Always optimise your positive aspects and end with something memorable.

Although the supporting statement is by far the most trying part of the application process, don't be tempted to reproduce it for all your applications, without relating it directly to respective job descriptions.

Checklist for writing a supporting statement
- Before starting, write a list of key points from the job description (e.g. year 3 class teacher, class contains pupils with special

needs, high display standards, strong singing tradition in the school etc.).

- Write a list of your unique selling points, ensuring that they relate directly to your first list (see above).
- Begin with impact and end unforgettably!
- Convey a sense of your personality.
- Fill the main body of the statement with your skills and achievements, always optimising the positive.
- Use impeccable grammar throughout, avoiding lengthy sentences and aimless paragraphs. Brevity is the key.
- Express what your teaching practice has taught you.
- Include information on any travel, hobbies and voluntary work that you have done, and how this equips you for the job.
- If possible, or unless requested otherwise, type your statement.

ABOUT

REFEREES

Think carefully about whom you appoint as a referee. Employers will look closely at their status and how recent your contact was, so your favourite primary teacher or best mate from the pub are probably bad choices! Choose referees who will be in a position to match your qualities and capabilities to the job's requirements and be as supportive as possible. Perhaps a past employer and your tutor from your ITT institution would be good choices. Make sure you have their permission before appointing them as referees.

SENDING IN YOUR APPLICATION

Always use an A4 envelope for your application so that it does not have to be folded. Write down a checklist of items that need to be included, e.g. the application form, CV and medical form, and tick them off as you put them in the envelope. Send in the originals, but keep a photocopy of everything so you can refer to it before an interview.

If at all possible, deliver your application to the school. If you do have to post it, include a stamped, self-addressed postcard that can be sent to you as acknowledgement of receipt. Schools rarely do this unless you provide the stamp. Now all you have to do is sit back and wait for an invitation to an interview!

ABOUT

NOT BEING INVITED FOR AN INTERVIEW

If you are not asked to attend for an interview, try not to think about it as a disaster. It is certainly frustrating that your hard work has not apparently paid off, but there are always positive aspects in any situation. Cultivate the attitude that perhaps the job was not as suited to you as you first thought, and that the experience has been a valuable one. Think how much easier future applications will be now that you have gone this far. Do, however, take the opportunity to reassess your application to see if there are any obvious weaknesses that can be tightened up in future.

If you suspect ageism may be the problem, contact the Association of Teachers Against Ageism, a pressure group formed in September 1998 to deal with this issue. Statistics show that those over 45 are twice as likely to be unemployed six months after training than those in their twenties.[1] The reason for this is almost certainly financial.

ATTENDING FOR AN INTERVIEW

'If you think you can or you think you can't you're right.' Henry Ford.

'Failure to prepare is preparing to fail.' John Wooden.

The interview is an opportunity for both sides to gather the additional information needed before a commitment can be made. At this stage, a positive attitude is at least as important as any other factor in securing a job offer.

Preparing for the day

While it is important to be prepared for an interview in terms of physical appearance, knowledge of the job and the school etc., there is something to be said for maintaining a balance. Over-rigorous preparation can lead to excessive anxiety that will inevitably limit your chances of success.

As soon as possible after receiving your invitation to an interview, send a reply confirming the arrangements. Only in extreme circumstances would you be justified in attempting to change the arrangements suggested by the school.

You should have been sent a map and information on the level of expenses payable and advice on accommodation, if you will be travelling a long distance, together with additional information about the school, such as a description of the surrounding area, site and buildings, an outline of the staffing structure and details of the governing body along with the interview format.

What are the interviewers looking for?

- the person who matches the job criteria most closely
- the person who will fit in with the existing staff
- the person who will be able to make a valuable contribution to the work of the school
- your attitudes to the role of management and governors
- your personal philosophy of teaching
- your motivations, satisfactions and dissatisfactions.

That said, the success of the interview in terms of extracting this information depends on the skills of those asking the questions.

Dressing to win

'Nothing succeeds like the appearance of success.'
Christopher Lasch.

It sounds totally irrational, but instant judgements will be made of you based on your appearance. For this reason, there are some basic ground rules to follow when deciding what to wear on the big day.

Schools vary tremendously in their dress codes. From jeans and T-shirts to suits and ties, there is a school at every point on the spectrum. As far as is possible, try to find out what the dress code is for your school. If it is local, catching a glimpse of staff is useful, or arranging an informal visit will settle the matter. Otherwise, ring the headteacher and ask if there is a dress code. This enables you to establish whether you need to wear a suit, or toning separates. Feeling inappropriately dressed, be it too formally or otherwise, will not boost your confidence on the day.

Use these guidelines:

- Darker, co-ordinated colours are most appropriate.
- Avoid extremes in style – e.g. nothing too short, baggy, striped or patterned.
- Go for comfort. Your clothes should be an extension of your body, i.e. you shouldn't have to think about them.
- Get your hair trimmed and wear it in a style that won't need constant adjustment.
- Be moderate in your use of jewellery, make-up and perfume or aftershave. It's not a date!

Before the big day

It's so easy to get anxious about events like job interviews, especially if your heart is set on a positive outcome. Yet this anxiety can rapidly backfire and severely affect performance on the day if you don't actively strive for balance. For this reason, physical and mental preparation needs to begin a few days in advance.

Here are some ideas on maximising your chances:

- **Do** eat sensibly. A diet high in fresh fruits and vegetables will provide you with the extra energy you need to sail through the interview.
- **Do** focus on your breathing. Slow, deep breaths are instantly calming in stressful situations.
- **Do** plan your route to the interview and aim to arrive about 30 minutes early. This will not only give you extra time in case you are delayed, but also, the chance to freshen up when you arrive, familiarise yourself with your surroundings and practise some deep breathing if you are nervous.
- **Do** read the education press to ensure you are familiar with current developments and popular jargon.
- **Don't** let negative thinking spoil your day. Say to yourself that the interview will be a success and the outcome will be the best possible one.
- **Don't** smoke anywhere near your interview clothes.
- **Don't** drink alcohol for 24 hours before the interview. It affects physical appearance, not to mention wits!
- **Don't** worry about potential problem areas in your application such as gaps in employment or a long period of illness. Work out ways of expressing this in positive terms, e.g. what adversity taught you.

ACTION: If anxiety can be a problem, you need to be able to control it with your breathing. This can be done surreptitiously. Relax your jaw by unclenching your teeth, placing your lips lightly together and teeth slightly apart. It's virtually impossible to retain tension in your face in this position. Then start 4-2-4-2 breathing, i.e. breathe in to a count of four, hold for two, breathe out to a count of four, pause for two. Keep going until you feel noticeably better.

Interview scenarios

Interviews for teaching jobs generally involve a tour of the school, possibly some food or a drink and questioning by a panel comprising the headteacher, a deputy, head of department or year and at least one governor. Each member of the panel should be introduced to you and their position in the school made clear. If not, you are justified in tactfully asking. Although the governors of a school are technically your employers, they will draw heavily on the expertise of the senior management team. There are distinct advantages in panel interviews as personal biases are less likely to be strong deciding factors.

The practice of asking interviewees to perform a task or teach a sample lesson has become the norm in most schools. This can be of limited value in terms of determining which candidate will be most suitable in the long run unless your interviewers are highly skilled in their interpretation of results.

If you are asked to perform in your interview you should have been given plenty of advance warning. Anything sprung on you unexpectedly, besides the usual panel questioning, is not acceptable practice and you may even consider the implications for your possible employment at the school. Do you want to work for this type of management team?

Assuming you have been given prior warning of anything you might have to do, you owe it to yourself to prepare thoroughly, asking advice from tutors and mentors and gathering resources where appropriate. View it as an exciting challenge.

Remember, if you feel that to continue with the interview would weaken your confidence thus jeopardising future interviews, or you simply don't want to work at the school, you may politely withdraw from the proceedings at any stage.

Seating arrangements

Be prepared for a wide variety of creative seating plans. Ideas on the optimum arrangement are changing all the time and you could find yourself either:

- facing the panel across a desk
- sitting around a table with the panel

- in comfortable chairs around a coffee table
- in comfortable chairs with no table, or
- most oddly, sitting in front of a panel, the members of which are seated in a row with no desk – formal informality!

EXAMPLE: *Armena was surprised to get all the way through her interview to the stage of being offered the job without being introduced to her future head of department. Be extremely suspicious if you are not given the opportunity to meet the key personnel with whom you would be working. Ask yourself (and your interviewers) why you have not been introduced and draw your own conclusions.*

Questions to answer and questions to ask

Every interview offers the opportunity to show your appropriateness for the job through the answers you give and the questions you ask. However, there are two golden rules that should always be remembered:

- Listen carefully to every question and answer so you don't misinterpret what is being said.
- Never begin your answer until you know how you intend to end.

If you do find you have not understood a question or have allowed your mind temporarily to wander, there is no harm in asking for it to be repeated. Likewise, if you begin an answer and lose your thread, own up as soon as possible to avoid an embarrassing ramble.

When putting your answers together, try not to use vague, tentative, colloquial language like 'sort of, you know what I mean, right?'. At the same time, avoid appearing to be dogmatically fixed in your beliefs to the point of becoming argumentative with questioners. If you're flappable with adults, what is going to happen in the classroom? A balance must be struck through the use of appropriate language delivered at a steady pace and moderate pitch and volume.

BODY LANGUAGE

'Mortals can keep no secret. If their lips are silent, they gossip with their fingertips; betrayal forces its way through every pore.' Sigmund Freud.

Body language can shout louder than any other form of communication, so utilise it and make it work for you. Without being aware of it, we are all experts at reading body language, but often allow it to give away our innermost thoughts. When greeting your interviewers, use a firm grip for handshakes, and smile. This indicates co-operation and friendliness. Be aware of your posture when walking and when invited to sit, keep your back straight. Avoid crossing your legs.

Eye contact is essential. Maintain it without letting it deteriorate into a staring contest! A calm, steady gaze that follows the speakers hands when a point is being made will be read as confident. If you need glasses or contact lenses, wear them.

Other positive signals are to lean forward slightly and smile or nod in agreement. Aim to keep your hands lower than your elbows and limit your movements. This will give you at least the appearance of calm serenity.

Negative signals to be avoided are folding your arms or holding something in front of your body, clasping your hands behind your head, putting your hands in your pockets, fidgeting with fingers or things (holding your fingers in a 'steeple' can control active digits), adjusting hair or clothing and slouching.

Be yourself and be honest. Don't say anything that can be challenged or contradicted (worst of all by you!) at a later date. Cut the blather – if you get the job you're going to have to live with your words!

You will be asked two different kinds of questions. The key is to know the difference.

TYPES OF QUESTIONS

OPEN QUESTIONS	CLOSED QUESTIONS
Example You had the opportunity to teach A Level at your TP school. Was that something you enjoyed?	*Example* How long have you lived in Sussex?
These require more than short, factual answers.	These require short, factual answers. They are not trick questions!
Advantages	**Advantages**
These give the opportunity to add depth to your answers and expand on ideas.	These don't demand creativity or the ability to 'think on your feet'.
These offer the chance to reveal aspects of your character.	These allow the interview to move on at a pace.
Disadvantages	**Disadvantages**
These can trip you up if you have misunderstood the question and lead you to 'waffle'.	These don't allow you to expand and justify answers you give.
These could show that you can be side-tracked off the key issues and that you haven't thought your answer through.	These can make you feel as though you were on a programme like 'University Challenge'.

Although you will be expected to do most of the talking in an interview, apparently the more your questioners talk, the more likely it is that

REVEALING PERSONAL AND PROFESSIONAL SKILLS

There are key skills that employers want to see in applicants and these fall into two broad categories, personal and professional. Under the heading, 'personal skills' expect to find drive, motivation, communication abilities, energy, determination and confidence. Under 'professional skills', fall reliability, honesty and integrity, loyalty, pride and skills of analysis and listening. Formulate your answers to reveal these characteristics.

they are impressed with you. So if you can't get a word in, you're doing well!

The following lists of general questions and questions for recent graduates contain some of those that are being asked in teaching interviews today. A list of tricky questions has also been included, with some suggestions on how to tackle them.

Expect to be asked a variety of questions. You will also be asked specifically about your year or subject specialisms so be up to date with recent developments. Tutors and mentors will be invaluable here.

General questions you may be asked

- Give examples of methods of teaching you have used.
- How would you deal with potential problems, like difficult parents, or troublesome pupils?
- What are your major accomplishments?
- What are your career aspirations?
- Describe your worst experience on teaching practice.
- What interests you most about this job?
- How do you handle stress?

- What do you feel about taking work home?
- Are you a team player?
- What is your greatest strength?

And even:
- What was the last book you read?
- What film did you last see?

Questions for recent graduates
- Why do you want to be a teacher?
- So many teachers leave the profession, what makes you think you'll stay?
- Tell me about your dissertation work.
- What issues in education interest you?
- What are you looking for in your career?
- What direction do you think your career will take?
- What have you done that shows initiative?
- What motivates you?

Tough questions you may be asked
- Tell me about yourself.
  This is a tricky question. 'How long have you got?' might be on the tip of your tongue. Rather than begin a soliloquy on your best characteristics, it might be better to ask, 'Is there a particular aspect that interests you?'
- What did you dislike about the last school you taught in?
  This is the one situation when honesty may not be the best policy. 'I hated the head – he was amoral' is probably not going to win you favours. Even if your experience of the school showed it to be run by mavericks and attended by thugs, say something tactful about what you learned there and express your desire to expand your horizons.
- Why did you take a job ... strawberry picking?
  Every job, no matter how apparently menial, has given you experience and taught you some skills. Formulate an answer that reflects this and shows that you can extract positive benefits from

every situation. If you can possibly relate it to teaching, then do so.

- Why did you choose to train at … institution?
Avoid answers like, 'Because my Dad went there', 'Because it was the only one that would have me' or 'It meant that I didn't have to leave home'. You have spent at least a year there so speak about its strong points and how much you enjoyed being a part of the institution.

- Why do you think you would like this post?
Regardless of the truth, you must relate your answer to the job specification. Tell the panel what they want to hear. When you have done that, there is no harm in injecting a little humour into the proceedings and admitting, for example, that it would allow you to live on the doorstep of your favourite football team. At this stage they will have made a decision and you can afford to reveal more aspects of your character.

- What do you know about this school?
Be honest about what you know. Do not be tempted to bluff. If you have to think on your feet, mention aspects you have learned since being at the school for the interview. Outsiders' perceptions are always very helpful for a school to understand how it is viewed by the world. The key words here are honesty, tact and diplomacy. There is also a great amount you can find out from a school's web site. (Even if they don't have one, that tells you something!) Also look up their OFSTED report on the Internet, available through the OFSTED site.

- What aspects of the job are most crucial?
Do not focus on the parts you would most like to do. They are looking for tendencies towards task avoidance and your abilities to prioritise.

- What are your energy levels like?
Everyone goes through periods when their energy levels are low; it is in our nature to experience these fluctuations. However, prospective employers, some of whom think that because you are (probably) young, you will be able to keep a consistent pace indefinitely, do not always understand this. Rather than speak about how you have a tendency to get tired if you work too hard, focus on what you do to maintain good health, such as eating sensibly, taking regular exercise, going to a relaxation class etc.

ILLEGAL QUESTIONS

Interviewers have a moral and legal duty to avoid unfair discrimination on the grounds of disability, race, ethnic background, religion (with the exception of church-aided schools), marital status, political preferences (including trade-union membership), sexual orientation and gender. In order to ensure that this is adhered to as far as possible, it is illegal for you to be questioned on any of these areas.

However, many candidates are asked such questions and are happy to answer. The best policy if you are asked a forbidden question is to take one of two options. Either answer it, taking care to remember the context in which the question was asked for future reference, or politely explain that you would rather not answer that question. Only if your interviewers persist should you offer further explanation of your decision.

Questions you may like to ask

At some stage in the interview you should be offered the opportunity to ask some questions. It is wise to have some ready to show how well you have prepared and your interest in the school and the job. Alternatively, if absolutely everything has been discussed and you can think of no further comments to make, say that you are happy that all of your questions have been covered. This implies that you had thought of some in advance!

The following should give you some ideas:

- Has the school had an OFSTED inspection? What was the result?
- Who would be your employers, the governing body or the LEA?
- Will you be a form tutor? What pastoral support will there be for you as a tutor?

- Will you have to teach personal and social education, or does a specialist teach that?
- Will you be offered the chance to come into school before starting work if you are successful?

EXAMPLE: *'One of the reasons for the smooth progress of my first few days at Stafford was the knowledge that I had gained during a number of visits to the school before the summer holiday. These proved to be invaluable, particularly as they allowed me to familiarise myself with the basic layout of the school, its routines and its policies and schemes of work.*
I was particularly pleased to have the opportunity to meet my future class and to discuss their progress with their present teacher. It was extremely reassuring to discover that they were not the class of horrors that I had dreamed of over the past few nights.' Lee, NQT, East Sussex.[2]

- What would your starting salary be (if this has not been made clear)?
- Does this school have plans to become part of an EAZ? If so, what would be the implications for you as a teacher?
- Is there an active parent/staff association?
- Do parents come into the school to help?
- Does the school put on any drama throughout the year?
- Is there information and communications technology (ICT) support for staff?
- What outings do pupils go on?
- Have there been any other NQTs at this school recently? Did they successfully complete their induction periods?
- What are the main strengths of the induction programme here?
- Will there be consortium arrangements for the induction of NQTs (e.g. clusters of schools getting together to deliver support)?

DELIBERATIONS

When all the candidates have been interviewed, you will have to wait for the panel to reach a decision on whom they want to employ. This decision is usually reached on the same day and you will probably be informed of the outcome before you leave the building.

While the panel is deliberating, use the opportunity to make some judgements of your own. Listen to your gut reactions when you consider the school's ethos, size, physical environment, discipline and style of management. If offered the job, would you be happy? Can you visualise your first day?

Possible outcomes

- You are offered the job. Congratulations! Make sure the offer is unambiguous – 'Are you in a position to accept this job?' does not constitute an offer. Providing you are happy to accept, some schools may want you to start before the end of term, even if only as a classroom assistant. If this offer is made, you would be wise to accept. It will make the start of term far less daunting. When your offer letter arrives, write a brief letter of thanks, confirming arrangements for your first day if appropriate.

- You are unsuccessful. Although this is disappointing, it can be a blessing in disguise. You should be offered a debriefing that will be invaluable for future interviews. If you are turned down but desperately want to work there, it is worth sending a letter saying how much you enjoyed the interview, how impressed you were with the school and that you would like to be considered for future vacancies.

THE POLICE CHECK

All teachers have to be checked by the police for previous convictions. The only offences allowed are minor motoring ones. This check can only be done after selection, not on all of the candidates for a job; therefore all verbal job offers are subject to this check.

ACTION: Regardless of the outcome of your interview, take some time to evaluate what happened and your interview strengths and weaknesses. This will be useful to review before future interviews.

MOVING TO A NEW AREA

Any home move involves a tremendous amount of organisation and, sometimes, important tasks such as registering with a dentist and doctor are left until you are forced to act.

Registering with practitioners

Aim to get this sorted out before you start your first term at your new school. This will avoid any unnecessary delay in getting treatment when you need it.

Getting a GP

Every public library carries a list of GPs in the area. Use it to identify the practice nearest your new home. When you make an appointment to register with a new doctor, take into account any preferences you may have for either a male doctor or a female one, and any specialisms the GPs at the practice may have.

Most GPs carry out a mini-medical as part of the registration process, including weight and blood-pressure checks and blood and urine tests, so be prepared for a slightly longer initial consultation.

Finding a dentist

Don't leave it until crippling toothache forces you into a dentist's chair before registering. Although few and far between, there are still some dentists taking on NHS dental work, which is by far the cheapest option for newly qualified teachers. Your GP's surgery should maintain a list of NHS dentists in your area, as should your local library.

Other health-care providers

Many people now combine conventional medical treatment with complementary therapies. The availability of such therapies on the NHS is increasing rapidly as the medical profession starts to embrace their success in treating many of today's common ailments. Ask your GP what complementary therapies are available on the NHS. Otherwise, your local health-food store or 'Yellow Pages' will be sources of information on private practitioners. The professional body of a particular therapy can put you in touch with local practitioners and, as ever, personal recommendations are always valuable.

ABOUT

SETTLING IN A NEW AREA

It can be difficult to settle in a new area, especially if you have moved away from the place you consider to be your home. If there are other NQTs at your school, take the opportunity of going out with them socially. Utilise the local leisure facilities such as cinema complex and theatre, library or sports centre. Joining a class of some sort will enable you to make friends as well as ensure you have some time away from work. Local radio and newspapers will also give information about what's on in your area. Becoming familiar with your local community will help you place your school in its wider context. However, you may have to get used to bumping into pupils at any time – at the hairdresser, swimming pool, and even the local pub.

Choices facing an in-service teacher

'In the beginner's mind there are many possibilities. But in the expert's there are few.' Shunryu Suzuki.

Depending on the way you want your career to go, you could face choices at every stage of the way. For this reason, it is essential to keep a current CV ready and a good record of your skills and achievements.

ABOUT

THE PROCESS OF GATHERING EVIDENCE

The whole exercise of gathering evidence of your skills and achievements should not become a chore. It is a necessary part of moving through any profession and should therefore be considered as an aspect of the maintenance of your work. Aim to update your records on a regular basis (perhaps once a month) so the time you spend is minimised. Don't wait until the end of a term when your energy and enthusiasm is likely to be at its lowest.

GATHERING EVIDENCE OF SKILLS AND ACHIEVEMENTS

The phrase 'lifelong learning' is one which all teachers are being encouraged to embrace. Linked to this is the fact that all professional experiences form a valid part of your development; it is possible to learn something positive from every eventuality.

Many schools have devised their own Individual Professional Development Record that teachers can fill in and add to throughout the year. These are intended to supplement the Career Entry Profile for NQTs. If your school does not have such a system of individual record keeping, use the following framework to keep track of significant achievements and milestones. It will make any inspections and appraisals you experience significantly easier to prepare for. Acknowledgements for this must go to Ann Greatorex at Bishop Luffa CE School in Chichester, and Davison CE School in Worthing.

Individual professional development record

There only needs to be a maximum of three parts to this record – the final part of which could be replaced by the Career Entry Profile as appropriate. Create a file that you can add to easily.

Start with a current CV including all your qualifications, both academic and otherwise, the institutions that awarded them and when. Also include your full employment history (not just in teaching) and brief outlines of previous job descriptions.

The second section should include your professional development experiences, and how they have impacted on your work and understanding. Such experiences need not simply be courses you have attended, but may include anything that has contributed to your professional skills and knowledge. Think about these suggestions:

- curriculum and departmental meetings
- advice passed on from other staff members
- INSET
- lesson observations
- visits from LEA advisors
- secondments and exchanges
- visits to other schools
- conversations with teachers from other schools
- job shadowing
- ICT training
- Cross-curricular meetings, e.g. SEN and ICT.

The impact of such experiences could initiate changes in the way you work, the way you respond to colleagues and the way you perceive your own professional development. You could put your findings under three headings: date, event, and impact.

How to record professional development

Date 3 November 1999

Event Observation of Bob Hill's ICT lesson with year 10

Impact By not attempting to have all 30 pupils on task 100% of the time, Bob utilised the skills of the more able pupils to assist those who needed extra help. In this way, all pupils were able to maximise the learning potential from the lesson. The way the hour flowed showed me that children appreciate the opportunity to test what they have learned.

If your school requires you to complete In-Service Training (INSET) reports, you could file them in this section too. Alternatively, report on INSET courses using the above format. By recognising how much you can learn from a variety of sources, you can realise how much you are able to help others.

The final section should cover your professional targets. For teachers with a Career Entry Profile, this part is unnecessary, but for others, this is a good opportunity to draw together your personal goals and those that have been identified from assessments and appraisals. You could use this format for each goal:

How to record your goals

Target   **Timescale**

Proposed activity   **Success criteria**

Evaluation of outcome

CHANGING POSTS WITHIN YOUR SCHOOL

'Well is it known that ambition can creep as well as soar.'
Edmund Burke.

It can be possible (but not always advisable) for NQTs to move up the career ladder during the first year of teaching, or in preparation for the second year. While it is important to consolidate, there are many opportunities for taking on responsibilities of varying degrees. For the greatest chance of success, always think about *why* you want to progress.

Possible areas for promotion

For those keen to develop their work in a particular subject area, the obvious choice is to work up the departmental ladder. This could mean taking a second or third in command post in your subject area, or, if your school is small enough, it could mean taking a head of department post.

If you don't want to take on a different post, but would like to take on more responsibility, talk to your line manager about working on a specific project such as writing exam papers, or the development of a scheme of work. This can be a gentler route into middle management.

Outside your subject area, there are many opportunities to enhance your responsibilities. All schools have a pastoral team, and there are usually posts of varying degrees of importance to be had, such as head of house, head of year or head of school. Again, if this is your chosen route of promotion, don't feel you have to achieve it in one step. Shadow the person who is already in post to see if there is an aspect of his/her job you would like to take on. Alternatively, there will be opportunities to co-ordinate many cross-curricular aspects of the school such as special needs, IT, literacy and numeracy, citizenship and personal and social education. The Teacher Training Agency has documents on the standards required of personnel in key middle-management positions that will give you a clear idea of what is involved in those areas in which you are interested.

ABOUT

WANTING TO CONSOLIDATE

With the current trend in the teaching profession to progress, diversify and push for professional development, it can be easy to be swept along, assuming that onwards and upwards is where you really want to be. There is nothing wrong with consolidating your position for a few years before even thinking about the next step, rather than leaping into a promotion simply because 'you would be foolish not to'.

However, the Standards for Qualified Teacher Status do highlight the need for teachers to 'take responsibility for their own professional development and to keep up to date with research and developments in pedagogy and in the subjects they teach'.

MOVING TO ANOTHER SCHOOL

If you have decided to move to another school to continue your career, remember that you are in a more secure position now than you were as an NQT starting your first post. Consider what you have learnt in your first year, and the resources you have developed – all of this can be transferred to your new job.

Although your new school will have its own schemes of work, handbooks and ways of functioning, it is the movement of teaching personnel around the country, along with the ideas that they bring, that prevents schools from stagnating. Remember to take these items with you to your new school:

- all the resources you have produced during your first year
- copies of other resources you have used
- all records of your professional development
- copies of any handbooks you feel may be useful.

Don't be tempted to re-invent the wheel every time you join a new school!

ABOUT

FACING NEW CHALLENGES

Although you have a whole year of teaching experience under your belt, it can be easy to feel like the 'youngster' again when you join a new school. There will be new ways of working and probably a new school day that you'll have to become familiar with, not to mention new classes to get to know. Don't expect that just because you don't have the excuse of being an NQT that you have to know everything. You should still be assigned a mentor and be given a thorough induction programme. See these new challenges as learning opportunities and don't expect to absorb everything at once.

A happy Easter? A holiday appraisal

One potentially negative aspect of working within the teaching profession is that moves between jobs tend to take place at set times through the year, and most often in time for the start of the new academic year. This can lead to teachers feeling trapped in a job for years at a time, if they don't take the opportunity to move at the appropriate times in the year. For this reason it is important to do regular personal appraisals of the way you feel about the profession and your job, to ensure that you give yourself the opportunity to move on if you want to.

During your first year of teaching, the best time to do one of these appraisals is during the Easter holidays. This gives you time to move if that is what you want. In subsequent years of teaching, this appraisal can be done earlier in the year, allowing you longer to make changes.

My Easter holiday appraisal
- What have been the best events of my first two terms?
- What have been the worst events of my first two terms?
- What job satisfaction do I get?
- What would I like to change about my job?
- What factors make it difficult for me to achieve my duties?
- Does my current job allow me to move in the direction that I want my career to go?
- What other opportunities does my job offer me?
- What could I do to help me to achieve my objectives?
- What could my managers do to help me to achieve my objectives?
- Am I thriving on the demands of my job?

ASSESSING YOUR FIRST TWO TERMS

This appraisal is for your eyes only. Don't spend more than an hour on it and treat it, not as another aspect of your Career Entry Profile or a formal school appraisal, but as your private opportunity to assess your position.

Is this the job for you?

It is quite usual for new teachers to go through a period of doubt about their chosen career. This can be compounded by feelings of exasperation at the length of time it takes to qualify and the amount of energy it takes to perform the functions of a teacher. Don't feel disheartened if you have these thoughts. It is virtually impossible to prepare for the emotional and physical investment you will put into your job, which is why it is so important to ask yourself at regular intervals, 'Is this the job for me?' The answer may not necessarily be 'No'.

Unfortunately, nobody can help you answer this question. Family members and friends may encourage you one way or the other, but only you will be able to understand the thrill you get from a teaching day going well (when others may say to you, 'How can you bear to do all that preparation every evening?') or the exhaustion you feel when, after a disappointing day, you still have 60 books to mark (when others say, 'You lucky thing. A job for life and all those long holidays!').

Put yourself first, use your personal appraisal, and know that you are making the decision that inspires you most.

Options to choose

'Still round the corner there may wait,
A new road or a secret gate.' J. R. R. Tolkien.

If you conclude that teaching is the career for you, your only considerations are your future professional consolidation and development. Use your personal appraisal and your Career Entry Profile to discuss with mentors and colleagues how you can progress.

However, if you feel you would like to move on from teaching, there are several steps you can take.

If teaching is not for you

Under no circumstances should you consider this decision to be weak or negative in any way. There are very few people who stay within the same career all their lives, and fewer still that this will genuinely suit.

There are three options open to you at this point:

- Decide to stay on at your school for another year. After the upheavals of joining a new institution and completing the induction year, not to mention all the materials you have had to devise from scratch, the next year may be significantly easier. It may be possible to negotiate some changes that could ease your way, or ensure that you are teaching the same year groups, to minimise the time you will have to spend on resource development. Talk to your induction tutor/mentor or confidante about the best way to go about this.

- Reduce your teaching load to part-time to allow you time to pursue other career options.

- Start to make steps to leave. Take advantage of any careers counselling that may be on offer from your LEA and county careers service and utilise the information on careers in your local library. Be aware of your emotions while you are doing this. Don't slip into despondency or feelings of failure. As you close one door, another has to open.

---

1 The *Independent*, 25 February 1999.

2 *A Teaching Career in East Sussex,* East Sussex Council.

CHAPTER 2

Joining an institution

···AND THERE'S THE STAFF INITIATION CEREMONY WHERE YOU END UP TIED NAKED TO THE SCHOOL RAILINGS COVERED IN TREACLE AND CHALK DUST.

Becoming a professional

Once you have gained Qualified Teacher Status, you are no longer a student and doing the job for real can be a frightening prospect.

ABOUT

ACKNOWLEDGING YOUR NEW STATUS

You are now a qualified teacher, but don't expect too much of yourself. David Berliner has identified four stages of teacher development: novice; advanced beginner; competent; proficient. Don't expect to sail from novice to proficient in the summer months between qualifying and starting your first job. That said, your rate of growth throughout your first year of teaching will probably be rapid.

The 'National Standards for Qualified Teacher Status' (see Appendix 1) clearly define what is expected of you and the way you should work within the wider context of the school community.

ESTABLISHING YOUR POSITION IN THE SCHOOL

If you have joined a new school, you will have to start from scratch as far as establishing your position with staff and pupils is concerned. They will expect you to fit in and work with shared values and a corporate purpose, and may even look to you to convince them you should be respected. You will have to set up your own routines and expectations and, above all, be consistent at a time when many of your pupils will be more familiar with the working of the school than you are.

- Make sure you have read and absorbed the appropriate staff handbooks so you know the professional procedures of the school, including information on special educational needs, sport and discipline. Also read other documentation relating to health and safety, resources, harassment, equal opportunities, child protection, first aid, emergency procedures, security (e.g. in the event of an assault or intruder), accident reporting and school visits.
- Make learning names (of both pupils and colleagues) a priority. Employ techniques such as making seating plans, spending time on name games and introductory sessions, handing out books yourself or taking pictures of your pupils to display on the wall of your classroom. Relating a piece of work to the image of a pupil is also effective.

EXAMPLE: *NQT, John, knew how effective it had been to learn the names of his pupils on teaching practice and decided to ease this task once in post by taking a photograph of each pupil he taught. He asked three students to sit together for each photograph to reduce costs and once the film had been developed he cut the photographs up, stuck them to a piece of card and put the name of the child under each picture. He then had an excellent resource to use when marking work, allowing him to make direct connections with each child.*

- Do all you can to become familiar with your pupils' personalities. Their abilities will flourish (and fester) throughout the school year, so it is a good idea to avoid making rash judgements that pupils then have to live up (or down) to.
- Aim to build on what you have achieved in your training in the first crucial weeks. Do not try to 'build Rome in a day'.
- Be aware of your levels of self-confidence and how others might see you. Do not neglect your relationships with other members of staff. If *you* consider yourself to be fully immersed into the team so will they.

ABOUT

VIEWING YOURSELF THROUGH THE EYES OF YOUR PUPILS AND COLLEAGUES

Everyone you meet, from pupils to fellow teachers to parents, will be aware of the fact that you are new. They will wonder what you are like. Are you strict or soft, funny or boring, better or worse than your predecessor? Most people will assess you in your first meeting and these impressions are hard to change. Bear this in mind as you meet new people and try to view your classes and colleagues as groups of individuals you will enjoy getting to know.

You should also consider that some members of the profession view NQTs with a sense of caution. The training you have undergone and professional expectations that are made of NQTs are now very different from previous years. It is worth being aware that some colleagues may not be familiar with current terminology.

- Take opportunities to become involved in the whole of school life. For example, attend school concerts and plays, PTA fundraisers and staff social events. If time permits, there are usually extra curricular activities that you can contribute to.

- Be aware of the many areas of school life where you will have to make your presence known. You will need to interact with many groups of people so aim to build solid working relationships with each group. This is now a requirement of Qualified Teacher Status.
- Aim to keep links with your ITT institution.

ABOUT

BEING IN THE MINORITY

It is possible that you may experience additional difficulties settling in if the majority of staff members are of the opposite sex. This can happen to males particularly in the primary sector, and both males and females in single-sex schools.

While your gender may not seem relevant when it is equally represented on the staff, if you are the only male or only female, gender identity can suddenly take on new significance. Try these tips to prevent loneliness:

- Establish a class link with a teacher of the same sex from another school.
- Create friendships and links when on INSET courses.
- Encourage speakers of the same sex as you to visit your school. The pupils will also benefit from the attempt at gender balance.
- Keep discussions with colleagues open about the issues you face as a member of a gender minority. This may encourage sensitivity on the part of your co-workers.

If you find yourself in a minority for another reason and you are not happy in your situation, talk to your induction tutor/mentor. Your union may also be able to offer support and Internet newsgroups can be a good way of making links with other teachers in the same position as you.

But it's only me

Many new teachers go through a confidence crisis as they make the transition from student to qualified teacher. It is common to wonder why classes *should* listen to you and pupils respect you. Never forget that there is a whole culture and tradition of education and teaching of which you are about to become a part and, to a certain extent, you can lean on that as you start your career.

When you take your first class as a qualified teacher, it is not 'only you'. It is you, the teacher, in whom many people – not least your tutors and the team of professionals who employed you – have a tremendous amount of faith.

ACTION: Think about the reasons why you became a teacher. Now think about how you can incorporate those ideals into your new post, using the opportunities that your job will give you. Allow yourself to indulge in a little positive thinking on how eminently suitable you are for the task that lies ahead of you.

Becoming part of a team

'None of us is as smart as all of us.' Japanese proverb.

As an NQT, you will be part of several teams, not least the team that makes up the staff at your school. Within the team(s) of which you are a part, it is essential that good relationships are created so that work can be completed, values shared and progress made. Good staff relations also have a knock-on effect throughout the school – a cohesive team will be less open to pupil manipulation ('I didn't do my homework because Miss Jones told me that if it was too difficult I should leave it') and more receptive to the dissemination of good practice. They also allow a sense of collective worth and direction to be felt by all staff members.

Ask yourself how effective you are as a team member:

- Do you listen well to others?
- Do you contribute your ideas in good time?
- Do you fulfil your share of the tasks?
- Are you aware of the balance of the distribution of tasks?
- Do you accept assistance from other members of the team?
- Do you offer assistance when you can?
- Are you able to assert your own needs as an NQT? For example, you may have a slightly reduced burden of work within the team because of your other commitments.

Too often, teachers are working hard at creating resources that may be improved by a little collective creativity. There is no doubt that this is the most effective way of coping with the rapidly shifting ground on which teachers work. Effective teams don't carry dead weight in the form of teachers who are not willing to share.

ABOUT

OWNING YOUR PROFESSION

'What do I say when people ask me what I do?' is a question that many NQTs ask. The assumption is that people will view your profession with a sense of ridicule. Not only that, but the question implies that some NQTs themselves have doubts over the validity of their chosen career. The only answer is to be honest. Explain what kind of teacher you are (e.g. history teacher, primary teacher etc.) and follow up your answer with something positive, e.g. 'I really enjoy working with teenagers' or 'I'm lucky to have a job that offers such variety'. Be proud!

Your responsibilities and rights

Any form of employment involves obligations and duties on the side of both employer and employee. The difficulties related to understanding this in the teaching profession are that a teacher's responsibilities are outlined in several separate documents. This means that you will have to read around to ensure you know the particular responsibilities and rights associated with *your* post.

The following documents will be invaluable:

- your contract and job description, which may not be given to you before you begin work
- the TTA document, 'Standards for the Award of Qualified Teacher Status' (annex A of DfEE Circular 4/98), available from the TTA Publication Centre
- the Induction Standards (annex A of Circular 5/99)
- the latest DfEE Circular entitled, 'School Teachers' Pay and Conditions of Employment', and the current 'School Teachers' Pay and Conditions Document' (known as the *Blue Book*, issued under the School Teachers' Pay and Conditions Act 1991, available from the DfEE Publication Centre and your school's office for reference)
- the 'Conditions of Service for School Teachers in England and Wales' (known as the *Burgundy Book*), available for reference from your school's office, which sets out non-statutory conditions of employment. It is not a legal document, but a set of collective agreements, which can of course be over-ridden under certain circumstances
- *The Bristol Guide*, 'Teachers' Legal Liabilities and Responsibilities', available from the University of Bristol
- any documentation from your union regarding your professional duties.

The relevant contact information has been included in Appendices 7 and 8.

UNDERSTANDING YOUR RESPONSIBILITIES AND RIGHTS

It may seem as though you are wasting valuable time by reading so much about your legal liabilities and a chat with a fellow teacher may reveal that he/she has never bothered looking into this area of employment. However, knowing what you are obliged to do gives you an understanding of what you should *not* be doing, and will minimise the chances of you becoming involved in a dispute related to your employment. It is also required of Qualified Teacher Status. Spend a little time now reading the relevant documents for added peace of mind in the classroom.

The information that follows is designed to explain *generally* what the responsibilities and rights of teachers are. It should not be considered to be a definitive guide in the event of a dispute or contractual issue. In fact, no document should, unless it is a complete and authoritative statement of the law. Even then, you should also seek advice from your union on *any* aspect of your employment that concerns you.

ACTION: Throughout the first few weeks of your first term, aim to look through one of the above documents each evening. Make a note of anything that you would like clarified by your induction tutor/mentor.

YOUR RESPONSIBILITIES

Before you were awarded Qualified Teacher Status, certain standards were satisfied. Those standards have been reproduced in Appendix 1. All the sections of the 'National Standards for Qualified Teacher Status' are equally important, but it is essential that the implications of Section D, which covers 'other professional requirements' are fully understood. Part (a) of Section D of the standards will be considered here. Parts (b) – (h) of Section D, as well as aspects of the other sections, have been covered under the appropriate headings elsewhere in this book.

Teachers' professional duties

The Bristol Guide summarises a new teacher's professional duties as follows:

Teaching (having regard to the curriculum of the school)
- *planning and preparing courses and lessons*
- *teaching the pupils assigned to the teacher (according to their educational needs) and setting and marking work to be carried out by the pupils in the school or elsewhere*
- *assessing, recording and reporting on the development, progress and attainment of pupils.*

Other activities
- *promoting the general progress and well-being of individual pupils and of any class or group of pupils assigned to the teacher*
- *providing guidance and advice to pupils on educational and social matters and on their further education and future careers, including information about sources of more expert advice on specific questions; making relevant records and reports*
- *making records of, and reports on, the personal and social needs of pupils*
- *communicating and consulting with the parents of pupils*
- *communicating and co-operating with persons or bodies outside the school*
- *participating in meetings arranged for any of the purposes described above.*

Assessments and reports
- *providing or contributing to oral and written assessments, reports and references relating to individual pupils and groups of pupils.*

Review: further training and development

- reviewing methods of teaching and programmes of work (from time to time) and

- participating in arrangements for further training and professional development.

Educational methods

- advising and co-operating with the headteacher and other teachers on the preparation and development of courses of study, teaching materials, teaching programmes, methods of teaching and assessment, and pastoral arrangements.

Discipline, health and safety

- maintaining good order and discipline among the pupils and safeguarding their health and safety both when they are authorised to be on the school premises and when they are engaged in authorised school activities elsewhere.

Staff meetings

- participating in meetings at the school which relate to the curriculum for the school or the administration or organisation of the school, including pastoral arrangements.

Covering for absent colleagues

- supervising and 'so far as is practicable' teaching any pupils whose teacher is not available.

  An individual teacher is not required to provide cover after the colleague who is absent has been so for three or more consecutive working days unless the relevant authority has 'exhausted all reasonable means of providing supply cover without success'. (This also applies if the fact that such absence would occur was known to the relevant authority two or more working days before it commenced.)

  The DfEE's guidance (Circular 9/97) makes the point that some teacher absence is inevitable and therefore the relevant authorities 'should have regard to the need for the efficient organisation of supply cover'. In particular, they should give priority to providing sufficient resources within school budgets for the estimated levels of supply cover likely to be needed during the school year.

Public examinations

- *participating in arrangements for (i) preparing pupils for public examinations and (ii) assessing pupils for the purposes of such examinations*
- *recording and reporting such arrangements and*
- *participating in arrangements for pupils' presentation for, and supervision during, such examinations.*

Administration

- *participating in administrative and organisational tasks related to the duties described above including (i) the management or supervision of persons providing support for the teachers in the school and (ii) the ordering and allocation of equipment and materials*
- *attending assemblies, registering the attendance of pupils and supervising pupils, whether these duties are to be performed before, during or after school sessions.*

Discrimination on the grounds of sex and race

In areas of both sex and race discrimination, you should be aware of the direct and indirect ways in which teachers can (sometimes inadvertently) act in a discriminatory way.

Direct discrimination involves treating one particular sex or race in a deliberately unfavourable way. Indirect discrimination refers to any discrimination that takes place as an effect of apparently fair and equal treatment.

The Bristol Guide has identified and summarised the situations in which it is illegal to discriminate against a pupil. These are when:

- *deciding whether to admit a child to the school (except for single-sex schools)*
- *providing teaching or allocating pupils to teaching groups (e.g. woodwork for boys and cookery for girls)*
- *applying standards of behaviour, dress or appearance (but it is not necessarily illegal to have different dress rules for boys and girls)*

WORKING TIME

If you are employed as a full-time teacher, you are required to work on 195 days of a year, 190 of which you may be required to teach. Over those 195 days you will be required to work at least 1265 hours (called 'directed time') – although the burden of your workload should be reasonably distributed. Your headteacher is at liberty to determine how much directed time is spent on teaching and how much is spent on other duties. In addition to the 1265 hours of directed time, you are obliged to work the additional hours needed to perform your duties. For example, you will have to spend additional time on marking, preparation, planning, training and report writing.

The European Working Time Directive, which came into force in October 1998, limits the working week to a maximum of 48 hours, averaged over 17 weeks. This means that teachers are prevented from benefiting from the legislation. However, this does not mean that you should ever agree to be excluded from the working-time limit. There are grave concerns about the effectiveness of people who work consistently long hours as well as the implications for health and safety issues. This is an extremely difficult area for teachers, many of whom, when faced with the choice of going over the 48-hour limit in order to be prepared, or staying under the limit but teaching 'cold', would opt for the former. Seek advice from your union if working time issues are affecting you.

- *making decisions on exclusions*
- *allocating resources*
- *providing other benefits, facilities or services that the school covers (except for single-sex boarding accommodation in co-educational schools).*

A paper by the Equal Opportunities Commission and the Office for

Standards in Education (OFSTED), entitled *The Gender Divide*,[1] reported that

About one secondary school in five is weak in meeting the particular needs of one or other sex. In these, some or all of the following characteristics obtain: one sex might be seriously under-performing in lessons or in examinations; the books and resources used might not take appropriate account of gender issues; pupils might not be being prepared well for opportunities in working life.

The paper suggests that the following issues (among others) be considered to help improve the quality of learning in both sexes. It would be worth bearing them in mind as you prepare and deliver your lessons.

- *To what extent are pupils' attitudes to learning, their confidence in particular subjects, and their eventual success affected by their gender? Is it possible to establish meaningful generalisations without constructing stereotypes?*

- *How do pupils' gender-related attitudes change as they mature and why are some more influenced by their gender than others? Why do some pupils put barriers to progress in front of themselves? What role is played by social class, culture and geographic location?*

- *It appears that one reason why girls often achieve more than boys in school is that they more often demonstrate diligence, good behaviour and enthusiasm for learning. If this is so, how can schools encourage boys to acquire these qualities?*

Do remember that when OFSTED visits your school, inspectors will be looking at *all* equal opportunities issues in the school. It is worth thinking about how your personal prejudices (and everyone has them) may affect your teaching. Are equal opportunities at the forefront of your mind when you speak, present information and organise the class? An open focus on equal opportunities helps to encourage acceptance of others and tolerance.

ACTION: Write down at least three ways in which you can introduce an awareness of equal opportunities to your pupils, whatever the age group you teach. This may be through a discussion, illustrated examples, or a question and answer session. This will help you to get in the habit of focusing on equal opportunities in your teaching; you may even want to jot down in your planner how equal opportunities are met in your lessons.

Common-law duty of care

All teachers have what is called a 'common-law duty of care'. The only problem with this is that exactly what it means is not properly defined. Consequently any judgements made regarding the duty of care are based on case law.

As an NQT, you should understand the 'common-law duty of care' to mean that you will do 'what is reasonably practicable' when caring for pupils. This means that carrying out ongoing risk assessment is probably wise so as to minimise the number of potential hazards. *The Bristol Guide* suggests that teachers bear these factors in mind when assessing risk:

- *the stage of the children's cognitive development and skill acquisition*
- *their physical strength, size or shape*
- *their motor skills and sensory perceptions*
- *the school environment (i.e. its size, shape, contours and construction)*
- *the ethos of the school (i.e. the nature and background of the pupils and their families and the school's behaviour and discipline policy).*

As long as you demonstrate reasonably careful standards while at work, you will not bear any liability for accidents.

Safeguarding or promoting children's welfare

There may be occasions when you and members of the pastoral team in your school will have to liaise with social service departments over the possible abuse that one of your pupils may be suffering. This is an extremely problematic area for teachers and, as an NQT, you should always talk to the member of the pastoral team who has been designated as the receiver of information about possible abuse *as soon as you suspect neglect or any form of abuse.* Under no circumstances should you wait to gather more evidence, or talk to the child about your suspicions, before voicing your concerns to the appropriate person. Your school will have set procedures for this situation and will pass the information on to the Social Services Department. Only then can investigations begin, which will probably require the co-

ABOUT

RECORDING YOUR CONCERNS

Protecting children from abuse is a teacher's legal obligation and part of that duty must be to protect yourself from allegations of negligence in the future. Always document every conversation you have about suspected abuse. You could also keep a diary in which you keep track of the development of your concerns. Such information can be invaluable at a later stage, especially if there are court proceedings. Remember, record:

● whom you spoke to
● what was said
● what was decided
● the date and time.

Above all, make sure anything you commit to paper is strictly confidential and cannot be accessed by any child or adult other than the person designated to deal with suspected abuse.

operation of the school. For this reason it is vital that you keep a record of every conversation you have regarding the possible abuse of a child, including details of whom you spoke to, what was said, what was decided and the date/time.

Appropriate physical contact with pupils

A common misconception is that teachers can have no physical contact with pupils. Pupils have sometimes exploited this belief so it is important to know the legal situation. Physical contact can be appropriate under several circumstances, mostly dictated by common sense, e.g. to prevent an accident, or physical harm being done to a child.

The Bristol Guide has summarised the DfEE's guidance on appropriate physical contact as follows:

Circular 10/95 states clearly that 'It is unnecessary and unrealistic to suggest that teachers should touch pupils only in an emergency … it is inevitable … particularly with younger pupils'. For example, teachers may have to touch pupils in PE lessons or when administering first aid and it may be appropriate to do so in order to give reassurance or to comfort a child. In addition, physical contact may be a necessary part of teaching some children with special educational needs such as those with visual or hearing impairments, and those with mobility difficulties. However, teachers should never touch pupils, however casually, in ways or on parts of the body that may be considered indecent.

This acceptance that teachers may make physical contact with children is accompanied by the rider that it must be appropriate. This means appropriate not only to the situation but also in its manner. Therefore, teachers should always bear in mind that perfectly innocent actions can be misunderstood and so may lead to accusations of professional misconduct or even child abuse. This applies particularly in situations involving a teacher and pupil of the opposite sex – especially in one-to-one contacts, extra-curricular activities and/or when pupils reach adolescence.

Teachers should also be aware that there are some children, including some from minority groups, who are particularly sensitive to physical contact. If a child's reaction shows that s/he is uncomfortable with being touched, teachers should adjust their behaviour accordingly.

The DfEE advises that schools should develop clear common practice about what constitutes appropriate behaviour and professional boundaries. They should draw up a code of conduct, perhaps in consultation with the LEA or the Area Child Protection Committee, in order to reduce the risk of allegations being made against teachers. This should be known to parents, and all teachers should be familiar with its guidelines.

The physical restraint of pupils

There are situations when it would be perfectly appropriate for you to 'reasonably' restrain a pupil, although you should always be aware of your own safety. However, the word 'reasonably' is again open for interpretation in the absence of a clear definition. Many considerations need to be made, such as the age and size of the child, how serious the situation is (for example, is a vicious fight going on, or is it simply a case of rudeness or insolence) and what could happen without intervention (i.e. might someone get badly hurt?). Of course, corporal punishment is not legal under any circumstances in schools in the state sector.

The DfEE has left it to individual schools to draw up clear policies on the restraint of pupils so make sure you know exactly what you can do and under what circumstances.

RESTRAINING A CHILD

The Bristol Guide identifies the following situations when physical intervention may be necessary or appropriate:

- *pupils are fighting*
- *a pupil is engaged in, or about to commit, deliberate damage or vandalism to property*
- *a pupil is causing, or at risk of causing, injury or damage by accident (e.g. by rough play or the misuse of dangerous materials/objects)*
- *a pupil is running along a corridor or on a stairway in a way which might cause an accident or injury to him/herself or others*
- *a pupil peristently refuses to obey an order to leave the classroom*
- *a pupil is behaving in a way that is seriously disrupting a lesson*
- *a pupil absconds from a class or tries to leave the school* and could be at risk if not kept there

It goes without saying that a calm approach is more effective than anger or frustration. At all times you should think of your own safety and, immediately after the event, record exactly what happened with a senior member of staff. Describe who was involved (including pupils, staff and witnesses), what action you took to end the situation without restraint, how the pupil responded and why you took the action you did. Try to remember as accurately as possible exactly what every party said. Keep your own copies of any reports that are written.

Personal property

'Opportunity makes a thief.' Francis Bacon.

Every teacher takes personal property to school with them, which may or may not be valuable. An item such as a handbag, containing money and credit/debit cards as well as keys etc., will be extremely tempting to some pupils. To a certain extent, you should consider that it is your responsibility to avoid placing pupils in positions of temptation, however much you feel you can trust them. This approach usually guards against potentially unpleasant situations arising. For this reason, schools should ensure that teachers have somewhere to secure valuables, such as a lockable desk drawer or a locker. Some teachers prefer to keep valuables on them all the time in a 'bum-bag' or small handbag worn across the body.

- Find out what insurance cover you have for loss of, or damage to personal items. Check your own home contents insurance and any cover your union may provide. It may seem unfair, but your school and LEA have no legal obligation to protect your property.

- In the event of loss or damage, report the incident to your headteacher and ask what may be done about it. You could also approach your LEA's education personnel department and your union, depending on the seriousness of the loss.

- If ever you suspect that something has been stolen, don't deal with the situation alone. Ask for assistance from your line manager. Never accuse a pupil, however sure you may be; for many people, a false accusation will seem a worse crime than the theft itself.

- If you are asked to look after a pupil's personal property for any reason, do so as though it was your own – lock it away. Always return the property personally. Don't give it to another child to pass on, or give your keys to the child so they may help themselves. However, children should be discouraged from bringing valuables of any kind to school.

- Be sensitive about what you ask pupils to bring in for lessons. It may seem perfectly fair to ask year 10 to bring their own cricket bats in for PE, but do think about the implications of this for your colleagues!

YOUR RIGHTS

This is a far more difficult area to quantify. It's not that you do not have any rights as an NQT, far from it, but the rights you have are, in the main, moral rights such as the right to dignity at work which is open to varied interpretations.

Education law is incredibly complicated and can change at a fast pace. Do not assume, therefore, that your rights are being deliberately flouted if you are not granted the rights discussed below. It could be that your school has acted inadvertently. Seek advice from your union, Redress (see Appendix 7) and the documents mentioned above if you feel you have been treated unfairly at any time.

What follows is what NQTs can consider to be the minimum in terms of rights at work. It is not intended to be definitive and you should refer to your own conditions of employment documents and local practices for more details of your specific situation. Rights associated with induction and professional advice from outside your school have been dealt with in the appropriate sections.

The right to correct pay

At the time of writing, the minimum an NQT with a first or second class honours degree or equivalent can be paid is spine point two on the national pay spine. There are five other headings under which you may be awarded additional points or half-points:

- **experience** (both from within and outside the teaching profession – your school's salaries policy will outline exactly what qualifies as experience – up to seven points making a total of nine)
- **responsibilities** (unlikely and inadvisable for NQTs – up to five points)
- **excellence** (particularly related to classroom teaching – up to three points, to be reviewed each year)
- **recruitment and retention** (in positions which have proved difficult to fill in the past – up to two full points, and three full points in Inner London, to be reviewed every two years)

- **special educational needs** (for teaching wholly or mainly pupils with special educational needs (SEN) – not simply having SEN pupils in your class – at least one point and up to two full points extra).

Check with your union *and* LEA education personnel office that you have been placed on the correct spine point. From that starting position, the Circular 9/98 states that every teacher must have a salary assessment *every* year as well as whenever the need arises, for example if you take on an additional responsibility mid-year. Your governing body will usually calculate your salary.

Unless your LEA or governing body decides that your teaching experience has been insufficient, or you have been employed for less than 26 weeks in any one year (not necessarily in the same school or consecutively), you are entitled to an additional full point every year, up to a total of nine points (including the two received for a good honours degree or equivalent). Holidays and periods of sick and maternity leave count as time in service for the purposes of the 26-week rule. In the future, exceptional performers may be awarded two points in a year.

If your performance has been unsatisfactory for any reason, you must be told in good time (in writing) if one of these experience points is going to be withheld. It would be most unusual for a point to be withheld without incompetency procedures being followed. You must also be given suitable help and additional training to help improve performance and, as soon as it is deemed to be adequate, the additional point should be awarded, regardless of when this is in the school year.

If you work in the London area you are entitled to an additional allowance. At the time of writing, there are three areas of London for which different rates apply. They are:

- Inner London
- Outer London
- Fringes of London.

Not only are you entitled to correct pay, but also to being paid on time. This is usually the responsibility of your LEA's payroll department. Do be aware that the day you receive your pay slip may not be the day you can start to draw on the money. Some LEAs issue pay slips the day before.

The right to equal opportunities

While issues relating to equal opportunities will need to be addressed in your teaching, you also have entitlements as an employee. Most LEAs have their own equal opportunities statements. These will aim to ensure equality of opportunity for all employees on the grounds of:

- gender
- race
- religion or creed
- colour
- disabilities and medical conditions
- nationality
- ethnic origin
- marital status
- sexual orientation
- social class
- living with HIV and AIDS
- political belief
- age
- dependants
- trade union membership and affiliation.

This usually entails a commitment on the part of employers to review selection criteria and procedures so that those who can best perform the duties of the job fill vacancies. That way, the focus can remain on abilities and merits as opposed to anything else. This could mean that in order to remain true to an equal opportunities policy, you may be entitled to extra training so that professional progress can be made.

AFFIRMING YOUR RIGHTS TO EQUAL OPPORTUNITIES

Part of an effective equal opportunities policy must be the provision of facilities for complaint and appeal for any employee who feels they have been treated without due regard for the policy. Make sure you know what the procedures are for lodging a complaint about unfair treatment under your school's equal opportunities policy. To ease the process, document any situations that you feel flout the standards set out in the policy, and talk to a trusted colleague or mentor and a representative from your union about your experiences before making a complaint. Input from others helps you to retain perspective.

The right to take leave

There could be many situations when you may need to take leave. The most common reason is for ill health, but you may also need maternity/paternity or compassionate leave. The exact arrangements and entitlements for leave vary from LEA to LEA, but there are some minimum standards that you can expect.

Sick leave

As an NQT you are entitled to a minimum of 25 working days of sick leave on full pay, followed by 50 working days on half pay, on completion of four months of service. Your sick leave entitlements increase with years in service to 50 days on full pay and 50 days on half pay in your second year, 75 days on full pay and 75 days on half pay in your third year and the maximum of 100 days on full pay and 100 days on half pay which is reached in your fourth year.

- Any sick leave you take which covers holidays is not counted as part of the number of days available to you. For example, if your GP signs you off work for two weeks, one week of which is a half-term holiday, you will use just five days of your sick leave entitlement and not ten.

- You are entitled to self-certificate for seven working days of absence due to ill health. This means that you can return to school on the eighth working day after the start of your absence and not have to produce a certificate from your GP. You will have to complete a self-certification form on your return to school. However, if it is necessary for your absence to go beyond about four days, you should consult your doctor anyway.

- Keep copies of any letters and certificates that your doctor gives you for your employers. After 28 weeks of sick leave, during which time you will have been receiving Statutory Sick Pay as part of your salary, you will have to start claiming State Incapacity Benefit. Your employer will send the necessary forms to you.

- It goes without saying that you should keep your school informed at every stage of your illness.

Maternity/paternity leave

- If your school has adopted the agreements in the *Burgundy Book*, you are entitled to at least 18 weeks of *maternity* leave regardless of whether you are a full-time or part-time teacher or how long you have been in service.

- Your entitlements beyond 18 weeks depend on the length of your service and local arrangements.

- If maternity leave is an issue for you, contact your union as early as possible for the latest information on your entitlements.

- Regarding paternity leave, this again is decided locally. Most employers allow at least two days and sometimes more, although not always paid. Again, as soon as you know you will need paternity leave contact your union for details of local arrangements. You may find that this is where the time you invested in building good working relationships comes to fruition. Do sort things out as early as possible so you are not trying to negotiate time off at the last minute.

> EXAMPLE: *Andrew's wife was expecting their baby any day when he was called in to speak to his headteacher. He was told that it would be convenient for the school if she gave birth on the Friday evening as that would allow Andrew to spend two full days with her without needing to take time off!*

Compassionate leave

- You do not have an automatic right to compassionate leave, but, on the whole, employers understand the occasional need of employees to take compassionate leave in the event of the death of a close family member or friend. This is sometimes extended to cover some time in the event of the serious illness of a close family member.

- You will need to keep your school informed of your requirements at such a time, and under no circumstances should you feel guilty about taking time off.

- Your GP will be able to sign you off if you both decide you should have some more time. As soon as your compassionate leave turns into sick leave, your sick leave entitlements kick in.

- Compassionate leave is extended in some areas to allow for a day for moving house. Obviously, at such a stressful and busy time, you need to be aware of easing your situation. Moving on a Friday or even in the holidays would be the ideal, but clearly this is not always possible.

- Other reasons for taking leave may include weddings, christenings, funerals etc. There will be local arrangements, which your union and LEA can inform you of. Such rites of passage can be incredibly important, so don't assume that you won't be able to take time off. It could be that you only need a half-day, which may well be accommodated, but may not be paid.

The right to knowledge of agreed duties and codes of conduct

You have a right to be fully informed of your duties before you begin work at a school. This should include *every* aspect of the expectations that will be made of you, including such things as break duties etc. If you don't know fully what your duties and obligations entail, you cannot be held responsible for their non-fulfilment.

You also are entitled to be told of the individual codes of conduct at your school, so that you do not have to suffer embarrassment when you inadvertently break one. Such codes of conduct are often unwritten rules such as standing up with your class when the headteacher enters your room, or wearing a tie etc.

The right to be treated in accordance with education law
Although this should be assumed, it is surprising how often teachers find themselves victims of treatment that is either not in accordance with education law, or only *just* within the legal framework when interpreted literally. Advice from your union, Redress and your LEA will be useful here.

The right to knowledge of a clear line of authority
You have entitlement to guidance on the power structure in your school and your position therein. This should include information on which personnel you should consult under which circumstances, e.g. in the event of discipline problems. Much of this will be covered in the early days of induction. Without such knowledge, you may be in danger of ignoring the lines of authority that are already established in your school.

The right to knowledge of disciplinary and appeal procedures
Before any disciplinary action needs to be taken, you should be informed as to where you can find details of disciplinary and appeal procedures. The chances are you will never need to refer to such information, but you do need to be in a position of knowledge.

Such procedures are usually a matter of local agreements and your governing body or LEA should give you a copy of the procedures. If ever you are involved in a disciplinary matter, it is essential

---

that you consult Redress and your union. There are usually informal ways of addressing disciplinary matters and formal ways. If formal procedures are invoked, you have the right to representation, full information as to the timing and schedule of the process and protection from unnecessary delays.

The right to dignity at work

Dignity at work covers many different areas, but holds equal importance to other rights you have. Some of these rights to dignity at work stem from written laws; others are moral rights that you are entitled to assert in a civilised society. For example:

- the right to work in a safe environment with due recognition of health and safety legislation – this includes all safety at work issues and the right to appropriate medical assistance if/when needed
- to work in a clean environment – this especially covers the state of your immediate work space as well as staff kitchen areas and toilets
- to appropriate treatment from peers and superiors without harassment or bullying.

EXAMPLE: Ann was suffering from a mild kidney infection, which her doctor had advised her to treat by drinking glasses of water throughout the day. When her headteacher visited her classroom and saw her take a sip of water in front of the pupils, he announced, loud enough for the class to hear, 'We don't drink in front of the class do we Miss Smith?' This is an example of a headteacher not granting a member of staff dignity at work and undermining her authority in the class by publicly reprimanding her. However, Anne could have prevented this from happening by explaining the situation to her headteacher in advance.

ACCOUNTABILITY

Questions on to whom teachers are accountable have been asked since the start of formal education in this country, and will, no doubt, continue to be asked. It is an inherently complicated issue. When thinking about your accountability as a teacher, consider your pupils, their parents, society generally, the teaching profession, your managers, the governors of your school and your LEA.

Accountability isn't all bad! There are elements of accountability in all aspects of business and industry and knowing you are accountable can certainly help to maintain high professional standards.

The education power structure

As a teacher, you are part of the whole structure of education, not simply of your school. It is useful to appreciate this not only to gain an idea of your place in the grand scheme of things, but also to gain awareness of the roles of the many tiers within your local education authority and your school's power structure. There are interactions and interdependencies with which to become familiar. With a little skill, you will be able to turn this knowledge to your advantage.

THE LEA

The local education authority is essentially the county, or borough council. Rather than try and deal with such a large area of the council's responsibilities *en masse*, the council usually delegates responsibility for the education provision in the county or borough to an education committee. This education committee then delegates some matters for discussion to sub-committees. Many of the officers working in a LEA will have been teachers in the past and will be familiar with the issues facing teachers in the classroom today.

The LEA has responsibilities to provide for all maintained schools (e.g. community and community special schools) as far as running costs and buildings are concerned. The arrangements for voluntary and foundation schools are slightly different, as their governing bodies hold more responsibilities.

The following model is not the rule, but is often the case:

- The LEA is led by a director of education (sometimes called a chief education officer or county education officer) who is usually assisted by a deputy and assistant directors. These positions are non-elected and non-political.
- The assistant directors usually share the responsibilities of all the different aspects of the education service on offer in the county including pupil services, buildings and the Advisory and Inspection Service.
- Senior education officers then look after matters delegated to them by the assistant directors. In turn, assistant education officers help them.
- There is then a tier of administration staff to support all of the above.
- Depending on the geographical size of the LEA, there may also be area education officers working in local offices (often where Teachers' Professional Centres are based), but reporting to the main LEA office (usually County Hall).

The education committee

The education committee is the place where many of the decisions regarding the LEAs' provision of education are made. Education is invariably the largest local government responsibility and it often accounts for over half of the authority's total budget. It is not compulsory for a council to run an education committee, but the practical need to have a strategic body with power over policy, capital investment and budget control makes such a committee a necessity.

The bulk of the committee usually consists of elected county councillors, the political composition of which will reflect the balance of power in the council as a whole. Religious denomination nominees, teacher nominees, a parent governor and co-opted members including representatives from local business usually form the remainder.

The impact of the education committee on all teachers (particularly in community schools) is direct and far-reaching. It has vested in it all the powers and duties of the council in relation to education. Some of the decisions taken by the council may mean significant changes for you in the classroom; changes that your senior management teams may be powerless to resist.

The vast majority of the elected members of an education committee will also be serving as governors at schools in the area.

Take the opportunity to witness how decisions that affect your working life are made. Attend a meeting as a member of the public and ask your headteacher to go through the minutes at a staff meeting, or make them available for teachers to read.

EXAMPLE: One NQT attended a meeting of his local education committee and was pleasantly surprised by the extent to which the teachers' cause was being fought. For him it was a good way of becoming familiar with the local decision-making process and the extent to which the needs of teachers are considered.

School organisation committees

The School Standards and Framework Act, 1998, sets out the requirements for every LEA to establish a school organisation committee (SOC) for their area. This committee will be a specific statutory entity and separate from the LEA and any education committees that the LEA runs.

Its main function will probably be to agree school organisation plans for the LEA. It will also look at changes to the character of a school, for example, the introduction of a sixth form, or nursery. The SOC will make decisions on school organisation that were previously made by the Secretary of State for Education, therefore strengthening local decision-making abilities.

It is likely that each SOC will comprise representatives from these six groups:

- the LEA
- schools (probably governors, although not LEA ones)
- the Church of England Diocesan Board
- the Roman Catholic Diocese
- the Further Education Funding Council
- an optional group – possibly an ethnic minority representative of the area.

It could be that there are opportunities for teacher involvement under the second category, although only for teacher-governors.

The LEA's education personnel department

While each education personnel office is set up differently across the country, there are basic services that they all provide. Its function is like that of any other personnel department, apart from the fact that teachers also have staff in the school where they work who will be able to advise on personnel issues as well.

Most education personnel departments would like to think that they offer a friendly, supportive service. They also offer the advantage of being open for advice at times when schools are not, such as in the holidays. Here are some examples of the services you can expect from your education personnel department as an NQT:

- in some cases, a free, confidential helpline for teachers and other council employees covering issues such as HIV and AIDS, stress and anxiety, personal finances, drugs and alcohol abuse and relationship problems

- vacancy lists for jobs in the area
- county housing for short-term letting, or help securing appropriate accommodation if you are moving to a new area
- advice on salaries, contracts and some legal issues
- references for banks and letting purposes
- advice and support through sick leave – some even offer home visits.

The advisory and inspection service

Each LEA has an advisory and inspection service (AIS, sometimes called an advisory, inspection and training service – AITS). As the name implies, this team of people advises and inspects teachers in the LEA (see the section on inspection in Chapter 4). There will probably be an advisor with responsibilities for NQTs and you will meet advisors and inspectors when you take part in your school and county induction programme. Your school will have to buy the services of relevant advisors and you may well be invited to sit in with your head of year or department when they have an advisor in. If you are given this opportunity, take it.

The AIS not only offers support to teachers, but also to headteachers, and again, many advisors and inspectors used to be teachers. It also offers in-service training, which can cover general topics such as school improvement and the curriculum, or specific focus courses such as behaviour management and, for example, teaching history to year 3. However, do not be surprised if the person delivering INSET and advice one week is the person inspecting you the next. It would be a good idea to find out where the AIS in your LEA is based. It will not necessarily be in the main buildings of the LEA.

THE GENERAL TEACHING COUNCIL

When it is established (expected to be September 2000), the General Teaching Council (GTC) will be the new professional body for teachers, to listen to their views and regulate their profession. It is thought that the GTC will have an important role to play in advising the Secretary of State and local authorities among others.

YOUR SCHOOL PERSONNEL

'Always be nice to secretaries. They are the real gatekeepers in the world.' Anthony J. D'Angelo.

Many of the personnel in your school will hold responsibilities above and beyond what their title suggests. For example, there will probably be someone with responsibilities for staff development, examinations, resources, ICT, and assessment. There must also be:

- a special educational needs co-ordinator (SENCO)
- a headteacher of careers and guidance
- a named person to deal with child protection issues
- a health and safety officer.

The general staff structure in your school is likely to be as follows.

Management and teaching staff

- the board of governors
- senior management team usually comprising a headteacher and one or more deputies depending on the size of the school (responsible for formulating and implementing policies on the approval of the governing body, managing the school's work and administration and organising the school's curriculum)
- heads of school or heads of year in the pastoral structure

- faculty heads in the academic structure
- heads of department and their assistants
- classroom teachers
- paid classroom assistants (some of whom may be given the opportunity to take on extra responsibilities and possibly train as teachers).

Non-teaching staff

Non-teaching staff are by no means the least important members of your school's team. It simply could not function without these people:

- unpaid classroom helpers
- secretaries
- bursar
- reprographic staff
- technicians, e.g. science, ICT and art
- mid-day meal supervisors
- premises officer/caretaker/site manager
- lollipop men and women
- cleaners, caterers and gardeners.

The governing body

Every school has a governing body. In the state sector, these governing bodies have far-reaching powers and responsibilities, especially in voluntary and foundation schools. It is worth knowing that, in these schools, the only person to whom you can make a complaint about a governor is the Secretary of State for Education.

The nature of governing bodies varies from school to school. Some governors are rarely seen in the building between meetings, yet others are fully integrated in the work of the school, often helping in classes and with school events. Most schools welcome the help and support that is freely given by those governors *who have no personal ambitions and who are generous with their time and skills.*

Governors are volunteers and are responsible for a school's budget. They are central to the running of your school, and must steer it through all eventualities in accordance with the law, the school's articles of government and the policies of the LEA (in community schools).

A school's governing body consists of appointed, elected and co-opted governors. There will be parent governors and teacher governors, partnership governors (in foundation schools) as well as representatives from the non-teaching staff too. The size of a governing body is dependent on the size of the school it serves, and it runs on the basis of collective responsibility. There does not need to be a chair of governors.

The role of governing bodies

The Standards for Qualified Teacher Status require that all NQTs are aware of the role and purpose of school governing bodies. At the time of writing these are as follows:

- The main role of governing bodies is to aid in the raising of standards in a school, including creating plans for the school's development. This entails ensuring that pupils at the school are offered the best education possible, through effective management and correct delivery of the National Curriculum and religious education, assessments and target setting.

- Governors must also ensure that the school has a character in line with its ethos and mission, particularly in voluntary-aided schools. To do this, they must determine the aims of the school as well as the conduct, and appoint, promote, support and discipline staff (including headteachers and deputies) as appropriate. They also set the times of the school day and the governors in foundation and voluntary schools can set term dates as well.

- Governors must manage the school's budget in accordance with current education law.

When these roles are considered, it is essential that the governing body and the senior management team have a good working rela-

ABOUT

WORKING WITH YOUR GOVERNORS

Your governing body must meet at least once a term. Between meetings, the headteacher of your school will keep governors informed of curriculum matters and anything else that is relevant and there should always be a continuous dialogue between these two aspects of management. The agenda, minutes and related papers from governors meetings must be available for staff to read. Teacher governors are usually the ones to ensure that this is done.

- Get to know the teacher governors in your school. They are the conduits of information between teachers and governors although they are not the delegates of the teaching body. You may pass on your views to teacher governors but they don't necessarily have to be represented at meetings.
- Find out who the parent governors are at your school. This is particularly important if you teach their children.
- Attend the annual meeting between parents and governors at your school.
- If a governor visits you, find the time to talk about the issues that are facing you in your classroom.
- Try to think of the governors at your school as 'critical friends' as well as nurturers and supporters of your work. Allow (or ask!) them to be motivational and inspirational.
- Use governors as a valuable resource.
- When a vacancy arises for a teacher governor in your school, consider applying (although ideally not in your first year in the profession).
- Governing bodies must establish a complaints procedure and make it public to all it concerns. If you have a grievance with your governing body you should seek advice from your headteacher, Redress, your union and diocese (if you work in a church school). If you work in a community school you can also seek advice from your LEA. Governing bodies have a duty to deal with grievances fairly and promptly.

tionship. The strength of a governing body comes from the ability of its members to work as a team using the resources and skills at their disposal.

EXAMPLE: A teacher in her fourth year in the profession was staggered to realise the extent of the power that the chair of governors of her school had assumed, following the withholding of her salary. He denied access to minutes of meetings, offered no complaints procedure and blocked communication with other members of the governing body. This is an example of how damaging this power can be when misused by someone with personal agendas. This is by no means the norm, but has happened nonetheless. Always insist on your rights to correct procedure.

Key figures

In an ideal world, you would get on well with everyone. However, these people will be of particular use to you and all will support different aspects of your work:

- your headteacher
- those governors that may be attached to your department or class
- your induction tutor/mentor
- your line managers
- secretaries and bursars
- library staff
- cleaners and caretaker – don't underestimate how valuable these may be when it comes to staging displays for they will know where unusual resources and props may be found
- technicians and reprographic staff.

GETTING ON WITH YOUR COLLEAGUES

It can be easy to forget what impact other people are making in order to ease your day when you are busy and rushed off your feet. However, it is important to recognise the efforts of others. It is also vital that you get to know the pressures that other people are under – you are not the only busy person. Positive comments about what other people have done for you will never go amiss. Perhaps a small gift for the secretary who prepared your worksheet at the last minute or the bursar who dealt with your muddle of monies for the school trip will nurture your relationships. You could also get to know your cleaners' working times and ask if there is anything you and your classes can do to help them.

The school and the community

The school in which you teach is not isolated. It forms part of the complex structure of society in which many institutions are co-dependent. Schools are crucial in the preparation of the community's young for adult life, and the many institutions and companies that will either employ them, or educate them when they leave your school, seem to be playing an increasing part in the education these children receive. For this reason, NQTs should look to the community in which they are working for ways of involving the many agencies that can add to the quality of education they offer.

UTILISING CONNECTIONS

Your school may already have well-established links with schools and businesses in the community. Ask your induction tutor/mentor or headteacher for details of such links so that you may benefit from them. There is much to be gained here, such as:

- the possible sharing of resources between schools
- co-operation on major projects such as school plays, concerts and sometimes even residential trips
- input from specialists who may not be on the school's staff
- support for the needs of the school – many businesses are happy to supply equipment if it means good publicity
- opportunities for work experience for pupils, and for them to gain greater economic awareness
- the chance for teachers to update their knowledge of the world outside education, and what will be required of their pupils.

ABOUT

UTILISING CONNECTIONS

If your school does have well-established links with other schools and businesses, aim to make use of them where possible. Think of ways in which you can supplement your lessons therefore adding an extra dimension as well as easing your own pressures. Always explain to your classes the relevance of any visitors and try to devise follow-up work that will record the event in some way.

Links with other schools

This is where you can really benefit from sharing resources and ideas with colleagues from outside your own school. The value of developing strong working relationships with other schools cannot be overestimated. On a professional level, such links will ensure that your teaching and resources enjoy regular injections of added inspiration and, on a personal level, they put you in a better position for retaining your perspective.

Ways of creating links with other schools

Use INSET courses to strike up friendships with your counterparts in other schools. With your headteacher's consent, liaise with another school over a particular project by way of experiment. If it works, the road is open for future collaboration.

Ask any LEA advisors you meet if they can put you in touch with suitable colleagues in local schools. Advisors are in the position of knowing a wide selection of schools and the strengths and weaknesses of individual teachers. They also have an overall view of the work in progress in their subject area across a range of schools.

Links with businesses and public services

There is so much scope for combining education and the world of employment. It may take a little time to set up useful links, but you could find that it's time well spent. The choice of possible visitors is vast from police, the church, the medical profession and civil servants to all levels of business, retail and charity personnel. There is, therefore, bound to be someone who could add a dimension to a scheme of work in some way. It is also worth considering that it is generally lessons that outsiders have attended that pupils remember.

Ways of creating links with businesses and public services

- Ask your headteacher about links that currently exist, and get permission to create your own as appropriate.
- Read the local press, flick through the 'Yellow Pages' and listen to local commercial radio to gain ideas and information on businesses and public services in your area.
- Find out if there are any parents and governors at your school who might be useful to you. You could also involve any family and friends who may be able to contribute to a lesson.
- When contacting appropriate businesses, find out if there is an education officer. These people will be in the best position to arrange what you require.

INVOLVING OUTSIDERS

It seems today that it's not only teachers who are pushed for time. Many of the people you need to contact when creating and utilising links with outsiders will be giving up time in order to help you out. Follow these points to help ensure everything goes smoothly:

- Think about what aspects of the curriculum you teach could benefit from outside input before contacting anyone. You will probably need to explain your ideas to your head of department and headteacher, so make sure they are relevant to the curriculum and make sure you have identified clear learning intentions that would not be possible without the input of the outsider.

- Decide what level of input you would like – information and free items such as posters etc., someone to visit the school or a chance to take your class out into the community.

- Follow your school's guidelines on visitors. It is extremely important that anyone you involve is suitable for the task and under no circumstances should you leave your visitor alone with pupils.

- Try to greet him/her personally and make your visitor feel at ease. The last time he/she visited a school could have been as a pupil.

- Be respectful of your visitor's time. Tell him/her exactly when they are needed.

- Arrange for your visitor to be offered at least a drink.

- Always involve the class in thanking outsiders, whether visitors or contributors, for their input. This will make them more likely to help again in the future.

- Be aware of any biases that may be presented. These can then be discussed with your class as appropriate.

- Share your contacts with colleagues. You may want to invite other classes to listen to outside speakers.

Public relations

There are few professions so much in the public domain as teaching. It sometimes seems that the only qualification needed to pass judgement on the state of education today is attendance at school yourself! For this reason it is particularly important to appreciate that the extra roles related to teaching that you may not have been informed about include marketing and public relations for your school.

Before you open your classroom up to visitors, consider these points:

- Cast an eye over the appearance of pupils before they meet outsiders. Deal with any obvious grime and untidiness discreetly.
- Take a look at your own appearance. Is your clothing appropriate for your day and reflective of your professional status?
- Think about how your class will greet a visitor.
- Make sure your classroom is tidy and that wall displays look neat and up to date.
- Your headteacher may want to meet any visitors personally. Arrange beforehand the best time to do this so you don't have to drag your guest around the school on a hunt for him or her.
- Spend time creating a congenial atmosphere in the class before visitors arrive. Deal with questions such as, 'What's this got to do with anything?' in good time.
- Encourage your pupils to interact freely with visitors and talk about the processes they have used in their work related to the visit.
- Plan questions in advance with your pupils that they may want to ask the guest. Prompt individuals if necessary.
- Take any opportunities to demonstrate good achievement and progress.
- Involve the local media (and national educational press if appropriate). Favourable reporting will undoubtedly impress the governors.

ACTION: Make a list of any local businesses or services that may be able to support your teaching. Keep a keen eye on any organisation that is in the local news or that seems to be raising their public profile. Perhaps these are the ones to approach when you want to involve outsiders.

Education Action Zones

Education Action Zones (EAZs) aim to provide an opportunity for parents, businesses, LEAs and others in the community to work with schools (usually in clusters) to develop new approaches to improving learning and education in the area. These approaches must be eminently suitable for the locality and aim to help alleviate the deprivation that is experienced by the community. The idea of zones recognises the fact that education alone cannot tackle the problems faced by the zone's community and they give business and the voluntary sector the opportunities to contribute to improvements. It is planned that they will run for three years, although this could be extended to five.

EAZs can cover up to 20 primary and secondary schools, and receive additional funding to help enable it to reach the targets for learning that it has set itself. A forum of businesses, parents, schools, the LEA and community organisations run each zone, led by a Project Director.

It is hoped that EAZs will help by:

- *increasing achievement, for example by improving pupils' results in literacy, numeracy and GCSE examinations*
- *increasing opportunities for pupils*
- *increasing the number of pupils entering further education*
- *improving pupil attendance*
- *reducing exclusions from schools*
- *providing a broader programme of out-of-school activities*
- *improving the co-ordination of services to the community*
- *reducing youth crime.*[2]

The first 25 EAZs are:

- Barnsley
- Basildon
- Birmingham
  (Aston and Nechells)
- Birmingham
  (Kitts Green and Shard End)
- Blackburn with Darwen
- Brighton
- Croydon
- Halifax
- Herefordshire
- Kingston-upon-Hull
- North East Lincolnshire
- Lambeth
- Leicester City
- Middlesborough
- Newcastle-upon-Tyne
- Newham
- Norfolk
- Nottingham
- Plymouth
- Salford and Trafford
- Sheffield
- North Somerset
- Southwark
- South Tyneside
- Wigan

ABOUT

TEACHING IN AN EDUCATION ACTION ZONE

If you decide to work in an action zone, or if your school becomes part of a zone during your employment there, contact your union for current information on the implications for teachers. EAZs are still at the experimental stage and, even though they may prove to be very successful, you will need to know if the expectations made of you will be different from those made of teachers outside EAZs. It may be that teaching in a zone puts you at the forefront of change in education, making your experience extremely valuable in the eyes of other schools. Your OFSTED experiences should not be different if you teach in an EAZ.

Staffroom politics and etiquette

'The best teachers are positive teachers.' Robert Grice.

Is the staffroom a place of peaceful sanctuary or of frightening fiends waiting to devour the fresh NQT? Whatever the presumptions about teachers being nurturers, educators and balanced all-rounders, staffrooms across the country may appear to contradict this. NQTs can be forgiven for believing that some teachers gracing the nation's schools really do live in the cupboards and are suffering from a severe dose of teaching dis-ease! The symptoms of this 'dis-ease' manifest in myriad ways resulting in a plethora of colourful characters.

Before you mutter, 'There but for the grace of God...' it is important to consider how you can ensure solid working relationships with *all* your colleagues. You may have to bite your tongue a few times as yet another old timer mutters, 'Career Entry Profile – didn't have anything so flash in my day' or 'Why on earth did you choose a career in teaching?' Don't forget that the time spent in staffrooms can be all too short an opportunity to divest yourself of the frustrations of the day. These have to be stored until you have an adult audience and this is the same for all teachers, regardless of their age or experience.

STAFFROOM CHARACTERS

In order to gain understanding of the dynamics of the staffroom it is necessary to look at some of the characters you are likely to meet. Always be aware that you are joining an institution that probably has an extended history, and long-serving staff at the school will have distinct habits and traditions.

Don't be put off by what seem to be incorrigible moaners. Try to observe your fellow teachers rather than be drawn into another indi-

COFFEE MUGS

Only when you have taught a full morning, dealt with the miscreants you have had cause to keep behind and made the four-minute dash down to the staffroom can you appreciate the importance of a clean coffee mug. Many a teacher has been known to cry at the sight of an empty mug rack, or worse still, someone else using their mug! To guard against this, take at least two mugs into your new school, one of which could bear your name. If all teachers did this there would always be plenty to go round.

vidual's perspective. It is sometimes possible for a dominant staff member to dictate the whole tone of the staffroom, which is not at all constructive.

Find your place in the staffroom by following these tips.

- Don't be daunted by other teachers' approaches to their jobs. Some will be bursting with enthusiasm while others will be counting the days to the next holiday. Try to retain your own perspective.

- Don't judge your fellow teachers too harshly. Everyone has reasons for the way they are and a little understanding can go a long way.

- Remove yourself from any situation or conversation that makes you feel uncomfortable. Teachers always have a plethora of excuses they can employ to excuse themselves, e.g. an arrangement to see a pupil, photocopying to do or books that urgently need marking. If you don't like the atmosphere, take a walk outside in the fresh air for a few minutes.

- Be yourself. The staffroom is your place to rest and recuperate in time for the next lesson.

- Be discreet when others confide in you. Staffrooms can become hotbeds of gossip, but this serves no purpose other than to distress the victim. Also, take care over discussing confidential matters within earshot of colleagues.

- Try not to use the staffroom as an extension of your working space. Not only is it hard to concentrate in a room full of chattering people, but your 'mess' could annoy your colleagues. Clear your lunch things away too – you won't be popular with the cleaners if you leave it all to them.

ABOUT

STAFFROOM SEATING ARRANGEMENTS

It would be great to report that the days of military style occupation of certain items of furniture located in optimum positions of the room are over! Sadly, they are not. However, you are unlikely to be told of the Law of Seating Arrangements in your school until you commit the ultimate offence. Observe your colleagues for a few days before attaching yourself to a particular area in the staffroom. After a few weeks you will appreciate your caution as you realise how hard it is to move from one group's area to another. Above all, respect the elderly, long-serving member of staff in the corner however much you covet his/her seat!

The alternative power structure

The staffroom is the place where the real power structure of your school can be revealed. It is worth observing the reaction of certain members of staff to new ideals and innovations and seeing how influential they are on the mood of the staffroom. Understanding the dynamics of the staffroom in this way will help you to resist the flow of current staff thinking and make your own informed decisions over particular issues.

STAFFROOM ROMANCE

When you fall in love, and with whom, is rarely the concern of others unless you work in a school. If the thought of having the entire school community as chaperones doesn't faze you, then go ahead, but do bear these points in mind:

- Be discreet about your blossoming romance. Pupils will catch on very quickly about what is going on and any public displays of affection will undoubtedly fuel the rumours.
- Be aware of the wishes of your headteacher – he/she may want you to show particular discretion especially if you start arriving at school in the same car!
- Have answers ready for the presumptuous pupils who ask you direct questions about your relationship.
- Be aware of the immense pressures that working with a partner can bring.
- Think about what impact an end to the relationship might have on your work together.

STAFFROOM BULLYING

It is not just in the playground where members of the school community can experience bullying. Sadly, the concept of bullying seems inextricably linked with educational establishments and while all respectable institutions will have a policy on how to deal with child victims and perpetrators it can take a long time for staffroom bullying to be identified and dealt with.

Research suggests that teachers form the largest occupational group to suffer from workplace stress – it appears that schools can be hostile places for some teachers. For NQTs, being forewarned is being forearmed. Bullying and stress are closely linked and negative stress invariably leads to illness. Bullying amongst staff presents great complications, not least because there is no consensus of approach over how it should be dealt with. However, your school should have devised a specific policy, rather than squeezing it under the heading of 'harassment'.

PERSONALITY CLASHES

Personality clashes are almost inevitable, especially in large schools with huge numbers of staff. It could be that the person you are having difficulties with is someone that other teachers find hard to relate to as well. Some surreptitious observation may help you here.

Never write off a relationship as being beyond hope. It may be stretching your abilities to be compassionate, but there is always a thread of empathy that can be built on. You don't always have to agree with the opinions of others, but you can try to understand why they hold their opinions and why they behave as they do. You may find that those with whom you initially clashed become your closest allies.

Identifying what bullying is

It is important to establish a definition of bullying as opposed to a personality clash or difference of opinion. True bullying can involve:

- insidious, relentless criticism
- fault-finding
- humiliation
- excessive work expectations
- abuse of discipline and competence procedures
- inappropriate forms of communication (e.g. shouting, ordering or 'death by a thousand memos')
- inexcusable blocks to promotion and training
- withholding of recognition for performance
- manipulation
- lack of compassion in difficult circumstances.

ADULT BULLIES

An adult bully aims to exert power negatively and consistently over another person with the purpose of inciting fear and causing professional and emotional damage. The bully is inherently destructive, but his/her actions could result from feelings of inadequacy, which have been deflected on to another person, who may be accused of the very flaws the bully detects in him or herself.

How bullying can affect you

Victims of bullying often have to cope with a multitude of symptoms. Most victims of staffroom bullying find themselves dealing with:

- reactive depression
- hyper-vigilance
- shattered confidence
- anxiety
- fatigue
- stress
- digestive disorders
- menstrual disorders.

This is perfectly normal under the circumstances, and can be short-lived as long as the cause of the bullying is dealt with. Victims of bullying can also anguish over the question, 'Why me?' The answer is often the same as why a child is bullied – peers may perceive them as being too popular, too accomplished, incorruptible or highlighting incompetence through competence.

EXAMPLE: As soon as she realised that one member of staff was responding to her negatively, NQT, Nessa, started to develop a selection of symptoms, most worrying of which was uncharacteristic introversion. She started to question every action she took, which had a negative effect on her work. It became a downward spiral with every criticism leading to a worsening of her performance and so attracting further criticism.

Strong management or bullying?

'Never pay attention to what critics say... A statue has never been set up in honour of a critic!' Jean Sibelius.

There is a clear difference between strong management and bullying. All managers have the facilities to correct the behaviour or work performance of an employee, but this must be done in accordance with proper procedure. A sign of good management is how nurtured and encouraged you feel after a 'pep talk'. If you are left feeling despondent or humiliated, it is likely that bullying tactics have been employed. Good managers will observe aspects of your work performance that might need correcting and advise you in good time. In fact, they are obliged to do so. Your side of the bargain is to take on board what has been said and act on improving the areas that need attention.

However, there are tell-tale signs of bully-tolerant institutions. High absenteeism and turnover of staff seem to indicate staffroom distress. This in turn reduces the morale of the staff and a sub-culture of disrespect towards the management quickly develops.

Workplace bullying is illegal on several grounds. The responsibility for its prevention lies firmly with your employers.

Dealing with bullies

If you feel you are experiencing bullying at work, there are many things you can do to minimise its ill effects. Try following this action plan:

- Talk to a trusted friend about your experiences. A second opinion can really help to give you a sense of perspective about the situation and will help you to decide whether to take action.

- Re-read your job description, the Standards for Qualified Teacher Status, the Induction Standards and any information on the responsibilities of teachers, including the *Burgundy Book* available for inspection from the school office. This will re-affirm what tasks you should and should not be performing in your job. It is also worth reading the latest version of the 'Governors' Guide to the Law', which will inform you of procedures relevant to your situation.

- Attend an assertiveness course, or read about it. Your professionalism may be under question and you will need to be able to deal with it calmly and rationally. Confidential professional counselling would also be a good idea at this stage and may be on offer from your LEA. Again, retaining perspective is crucial to the way in which you approach your bully. Try to avoid allowing the situation to permeate every aspect of your life.

- Seek advice from your union and Redress – The Bullied Teachers' Support Network. Bullying destroys good teaching and you don't want to be facing accusations of incompetence in addition to the bullying. Most unions have their own documents on dealing with bullying which are available to members and non-members. Read the literature from all of them (you may have to pay for booklets from the unions you do not belong to).

- Ask for a copy of your school's policy on workplace bullying.

- Read about workplace bullying. There are some excellent books available (see Appendix 8) and these will serve to reassure you that this problem is widespread – you are not alone.

- Gather support for your cause by speaking to carefully selected colleagues. Divulge a little of what is happening to you and you may find that other members of staff come forward as sufferers too.

REDRESS

Redress is an organisation set up to offer advice to teachers who feel they may be suffering from workplace bullying. It offers many forms of support and aims for fast effective intervention in order to bring an end to the bullying.

The success of Redress can be attributed to many factors. With the consent of the sufferer, Redress may make public their situation before it escalates, or inform the governors or senior management of a school about what is happening. The organisation realises that the umbrella of confidentiality can sometimes hide a multitude of sins, including professional misconduct and seeks to stop this from happening. Redress also uses the services of lawyers who are expert in both employment and education law. Do, however, contact Redress sooner rather than later.

- Document all communication you have with your bully – even relatively informal contacts. This is not being unnecessarily paranoid, but will serve you well at a later stage if you need to refer to previous conversations. Aim to ease any possible stress and anxiety.

- Refute all unfair claims that have been made against you – in writing if necessary – and keep records of anything you say or write.

- Monitor changes in your work performance due to bullying. This might include getting behind on marking and preparation, or feeling inhibited in your teaching. Keep copies of any appraisals and OFSTED reports you may have and read all the positive comments when your confidence is low.

- Visit your GP, even if your health doesn't appear to be suffering. It is sensible to have formally recorded what is happening to you and whom you consider to be responsible. Your GP will be able to offer constructive stress-busting advice and will be a source of support should you need to take time off school. If your GP recommends sick leave, follow his/her advice. Time taken now could prevent a health crisis. You should record any ill health resulting from bullying in your school's accident/incident book.

- Never be encouraged to 'slide out gracefully' or leave the profession if that is not what you want to do.

Seeking help

It is an unfortunate character trait of many competent professionals, such as teachers, not to ask for help when they could benefit from it. In the case of workplace bullying, the more advice you can get from different agencies and individuals the better.

Possible sources of help from within your school

- Anyone who is not your bully could be the source of valuable support, from the caretaker to the headteacher, so be open to the advice you are given. More specifically, try these sources:
- your induction tutor/mentor
- other NQTs
- your union rep
- the person with responsibilities for staff welfare (usually a deputy headteacher)
- a governor who is attached to your class or department.

ABOUT

ACTING PROMPTLY

As soon as you think you may be victim to bully tactics, seek help. Acting promptly can help to circumvent more serious situations such as a disciplinary or incompetence claim being made against you. Gloomy as it may sound, the longer you leave it to act, the harder the situation will be to resolve. There is a wealth of support for victims of bullying – you don't have to suffer alone. Just don't sit on any experiences of bullying you may have had without talking to someone.

Possible sources of help from outside the school

- your union
- Redress
- your LEA education personnel department
- books on dealing with bullying
- your GP or other health care practitioner
- family and friends.

Unions

Without wanting to sound alarmist, the importance of membership of a professional association or union cannot be over-stressed for new teachers. You may have joined a union while you were still training, but if you haven't, join one now. Don't leave it to chance that you will not be involved in any number of the many disputes that arise between teachers, employers, parents and pupils.

THE BENEFITS OF MEMBERSHIP

Unions perform many functions for their members, but for NQTs, these are the most useful:

- they give advice over work-related matters
- they represent members at many levels of discussions with employers
- they provide welfare benefits, personal legal help and financial services and
- they offer confidential crisis support.

On a more general level, your membership will enable unions to continue their work towards improving pay and working conditions for teachers everywhere in the country and give you national representation.

Questions to ask before joining a union

Think carefully before you decide what union to join. Unions are usually under the impression that, once a new member has joined, they can count on that membership for life, so they always covet NQTs. The assumption is that NQTs have their whole career ahead of them – a career during which they will perhaps encourage others to join the same union they did.

The services offered by teaching unions vary little from union to union. The difference lies in the way these services are delivered, the extent of the support offered and the amount of time it takes to receive *appropriate* help.

Resist the wooing, and obtain answers to these questions before making your decision:

- If I am involved in a disciplinary matter, will you supply a *legally qualified* representative to defend me? (Some unions don't consult a solicitor – who may or may not be an education law specialist – until after dismissal, preferring regional representatives to deal with hearings.)
- Will you ensure that any case in which I am involved will be passed on to a suitably qualified person at an appropriate stage? (You don't want representatives to struggle at a local level if someone higher up the union ladder will be able to settle the dispute sooner.)
- What responsibility do you take for the advice you give me? (If union advice causes you to lose a case, or significantly disadvantages you, will you have recourse to redress?)
- If I choose not to follow your advice or want a second opinion, will you still represent me? (You don't want your case to be dropped with this excuse.)

Being aware of these issues will ensure that you can glean maximum advantage from the fees you will pay throughout the course of your career.

UNION MEMBERSHIP

Although the 'beer and sandwiches' days of the government/unions relationship are certainly over, there are many issues today which unions can use to gain ground lost previously. A good way to contribute to change in teachers' pay and conditions is to be part of a union from your first day of teaching. However, choose wisely and question thoroughly.

Regardless of which union you join, do take out your own professional insurance as extra protection. It is inexpensive, and can usually be added to your car or house contents insurance. Make sure the policy allows you to choose your own legal representative and covers you for at least £50,000 legal expenses.

> *EXAMPLE: David needed union representation after suffering a breach of contract. The case went to court but when, nine days before the hearing, David still had no legal representation from the union, he arranged his own. His union dropped the case on the grounds that he had gone against union advice. The personal cost to David was £35,000. This is an exceptional case – many teachers are happy with the level of support they receive from their union – but it does illustrate how important it is to arrange your own professional insurance.*

Parent–teacher associations

Most schools run a parent–teacher association (PTA), which usually has responsibilities for raising funds for the school to be spent on items not allowed for in the school's budget. It may be a registered charity and/or affiliated to the National Confederation of Parent Teacher Associations.

THEIR VALUE TO THE SCHOOL

Given that PTAs raise money – that all too rare resource – they are generally of great value to the school that they serve. If it were not for the PTA in some schools, it would be impossible to provide equipment such as mini-buses, videos and sports and computer equipment or to pay for end-of-term celebrations such as a Christmas meal for staff and pupils.

In addition to the funds that PTAs can raise, they also offer the opportunity for parents to become more directly involved in the work of the school, without taking on the responsibilities of governorship. A well-functioning PTA draws from the parent, teacher and pupil community of a school and therefore can consider itself, in many ways, at the hub of school life.

The pros and cons of membership

As an NQT you will have the opportunity to become involved in your school's PTA at some level. Before deciding how much commitment you would like to make to the PTA, you should consider these points.

PTA MEMBERSHIP

Pros	Cons
Gives you the opportunity to influence the decisions of the PTA, for example the way funds are spent.	Some schools see PTA membership as a burden and 'nominate' the newest member of staff to join.
Gives you the chance to contribute to constructive ways of improving the teaching and learning environment in your school.	Being a member will commit you to evening meetings at times when you may rather be preparing, marking or relaxing.
You can become known to a significantly involved group of parents in a relatively relaxed atmosphere.	You may end up being committed to turning up early on Saturday mornings to prepare for car boot and jumble sales.
Gives you contacts for use in your lessons. Many parents are able to make valid contributions to the curriculum.	If membership becomes a 'duty' your enjoyment will be seriously affected.

1   The Equal Opportunities Commission and OFSTED (1996). *The Gender Divide*. The Stationery Office, London.
2   *Meet the Challenge* (1999). Standards and Effectiveness Unit, Department of Education and Employment.

CHAPTER 3

Working through your induction year

I THINK COMING IN THROUGH THE WINDOW WITH STUN GRENADES IS A LITTLE OTT FOR YOUR FIRST LESSON WITH A ROWDY CLASS.

The Career Entry Profile

The Career Entry Profile (along with the notes of guidance) should accompany all NQTs with Qualified Teacher Status (QTS) to their first job. Designed by the Teacher Training Agency, it is a framework for target setting and action planning so as to enable your school to deliver to you the necessary support in a structured manner based on your strengths and development needs.

It consists of three sections, the first two of which (sections A and B) are to be completed by you and your ITT provider between May and June of your final year of training. The last part (section C) is to be completed in agreement with your new school once you are in post (ideally in September).

The three sections are as follows:

A This section forms a summary of your initial teacher training. When completing it, do include any distinguishing features such as additional qualifications (perhaps a First Aid certificate) or opportunities for learning beyond those usually encountered while training (for example, a visit to a school overseas).

B This section summarises your strengths and priorities (up to four main areas for each) for development during the induction period, based on your training experiences and in relation to the standards for the award of Qualified Teacher Status (see Appendix 1). It is essential that these are 'genuinely individualised' so that they can become an effective part of your induction.

C This is the planning part of the profile and the core of the statutory induction arrangements, to be completed by you and your induction tutor/mentor once in post. You will need to take into account the priorities for development identified in section B as well as the induction standards and any specific needs that have immediately arisen out of your new circumstances. It is intended that this section will be reviewed regularly and revised and updated if necessary in order to keep the focus sharp. Section C will record:

- Your *agreed* targets; agreement is the essential part of this process
- the actions that need to be taken and by whom
- the success criteria
- the resources needed to achieve success (which can only be achieved if resource allocation is *realistic*, so be honest about what you think you will need to reach a target)
- the dates by which these targets should ideally be met
- the dates by when your progress should be reviewed.

THE PURPOSES OF THE CAREER ENTRY PROFILE

There are two main purposes of the Career Entry Profile:

- to provide information about your strengths and development needs
- to prioritise your needs for further professional development and target areas for support, thus playing a central role in your induction into the profession.

It is a way of linking your skills directly to the standards for the award of Qualified Teacher Status and the Induction Standards and recognising the transition from training to working in post. What it is not,

---

however, is a reference, nor a definitive record of all your achievements and progress. You will still need to keep your own records of work completed with classes, and of particularly successful lessons for the purposes of future appraisals, inspections and personal gratification!

Used to its best advantage, the Career Entry Profile will enable schools to deploy NQTs in the most appropriate way, according to their skills and strengths. It is a part of a process, but is not an end in itself.

Who is responsible for the Career Entry Profile?

There are three main people with responsibilities for your Career Entry Profile under the statutory induction arrangements:

- your headteacher, who will have to ensure that all the monitoring, support and assessment that you receive takes your Career Entry Profile into account
- your induction tutor/mentor, who will help to set up a suitable programme of monitoring, support and review that should be firmly based in your action plan as set out in your Career Entry Profile
- you yourself will be responsible, as you will be expected to work with your headteacher and induction tutor/mentor in target setting and generally be 'fully engaged' in your induction period.

What the Career Entry Profile does for you

The Career Entry Profile does actually allow you to take control of your career – providing it is treated as intended by your training institution and your school. You can identify aspects of your skills-base that need improvement. Don't think of these aspects as weaknesses, rather as areas you would like to develop further. When you start your first teaching job you are not expected to be an expert at everything – far from it. Most experienced teachers agree that it took them at least three years before they felt they had a strong understanding of what it meant to be a teacher, and even then, they continue to learn. In order, moreover, to be in the position of taking up a teaching post, you have satisfied high standards of competence.

Think of the Career Entry Profile as a way of helping to bridge the inevitable gap between training and working in post. The fact that there probably is a gap between training and working should not be considered as a shortcoming of your ITT provider – whatever the standard of your training, there will always be a period of transition at this time.

Maximising the use of the Career Entry Profile

- Use it as evidence of progress. It can then serve as an excellent foundation for appraisal.
- Adapt it as necessary to take account of progress made in early days and the context of your school. Don't consider it to be set in stone. Voice your needs if they change as a result of your first few weeks of teaching and talk about the possibility of accommodating them in your profile. What knowledge would make it easier for you to perform your job? Think of short-, medium- and long-term goals.
- Use it to support your induction programme at your new school – it should help you to receive the support you *need* rather than the help your school wants to give.
- Allow it to strengthen your bargaining position when it comes to further training – in the past in some schools, new teachers have been at the bottom of the INSET pile and missed out on valuable professional development. There should be a file of forthcoming INSET courses in your school. If not, ask the advisor with responsibilities for NQTs about what is coming up.
- Think of the *processes* by which you will achieve desired *outcomes*. Both process and outcome are relevant to your development. What do you want? How will you get it?
- Use it to establish sound reflective practices – vital for life-long learning.

Induction

'Be aware of your own achievements.' Dan Millman.

Not only is it vital that you receive induction into working at your new school, but you will also need inducting into the profession as a whole. In order to ensure that NQTs across the country receive equitable induction (as far as possible), a statutory induction period has recently been introduced in England, which will combine support, monitoring and assessment of your performance as an NQT.

The induction you receive in your first year in the profession can really influence your attitude to, and opinion of, the teaching profession. For some, it is the main factor in whether they remain in teaching and it certainly forms the foundation of your further professional development.

For this reason, it is essential that you become familiar with the induction arrangements for NQTs. Get a copy of circular 5/99 (The Induction Period for Newly Qualified Teachers) from the DfEE (telephone the order line on 0845 602 2260) for the finer details and copies of the forms that will be used for your assessment. The main points of this circular have been summarised below, but the most important aspect of the statutory induction period is that if you are ultimately unsuccessful, you cannot work as a teacher in a state school – there are no second chances.

THE STATUTORY INDUCTION ARRANGEMENTS

- All teachers who gain Qualified Teacher Status after 7 May 1999 in England must complete a statutory induction period satisfactorily. Failure to do so will result in ineligibility for employment as a teacher in a maintained school (or non-maintained special school).

- The induction period to be served is the equivalent of one school year (three, four or five terms, depending on the system in place in your school), pro-rata for part-time teachers.

- You must complete at least a term for that period to count towards your induction. This is particularly important to NQTs working as supply teachers in their first year. The headteacher will be able to tell you if your time at his/her school can count towards your induction period.
- You will be given a reduced timetable, which will be 90% of the normal timetable for teachers at your school (this applies pro-rata to part-time and supply NQTs).
- You will have at least three formal assessment meetings, e.g. at the end of each term in a three-term year.
- Your headteacher must write to the appropriate body (usually your LEA) within ten working days of the completion of your induction period with his/her recommendation on whether you should pass or fail the year.
- Within three working days of the decision being made, the appropriate body must write to inform you as to whether you have passed or failed your induction period.
- Your induction period will be extended if you miss more than an aggregate total of 30 school days. It will be extended by the number of working days you have missed.
- If you have to take maternity leave during your induction year, you may extend your induction period if you choose to do so.
- If you have not completed your induction period within five years, you may apply to your appropriate body for an extension. This may or may not be granted.
- If you are deemed to have failed your induction year, you may appeal against the decision within 20 working days of receiving notification.
- Failure to complete successfully the induction period will mean that you will not ever be eligible to teach in a maintained school (or non-maintained special school).

Who is responsible for your induction period?
Responsibility for your induction period is shared between you, your headteacher, your induction tutor/mentor, the 'appropriate body' and the governing body.

The NQT's responsibilities

- You must make your Career Entry Profile available to your headteacher and induction tutor/mentor and use it as a basis for your induction period.
- You should be actively involved in the planning of your induction period.
- You must raise any concerns you have through the appropriate channels as soon as they arise. Failure to do so could mean that your chances of successfully completing your induction period are severely limited.

ABOUT

RAISING CONCERNS

If you have any concerns about the way that your induction period is progressing, it is essential that you discuss these sooner rather than later. Your school must have an internal procedure set up for NQTs to raise concerns and it is best to use this first. If this route does not bring a satisfactory result, contact the named person at the appropriate body with responsibility for dealing with NQTs' concerns. This person should be someone who does not also have responsibilities for supporting and monitoring NQTs and making decisions about passing or failing the induction period. It would also be sensible to get advice from your union at this stage too. Document all concerns you have for your own reference. Include details of why you are concerned, who else is involved, what you have done to help the situation and what you consider may alleviate your concerns. Also keep a record of what your induction tutor/mentor and headteacher do to solve any problems you raise. Do not leave anything to drift in the hope that things will resolve themselves. It is not over-dramatic to say that your future in the teaching profession could be at stake.

The headteacher's responsibilities

- Your headteacher (along with the appropriate body) has overall responsibility for ensuring that the induction you receive is suitable and individualised.

- S/he will have to keep in close contact with the appropriate body regarding all aspects of your support, monitoring and assessment.

- S/he must liaise with other headteachers if you are completing your induction period in more than one school.

- Your headteacher will recommend whether you should pass or fail your induction period.

The induction tutor/mentor's responsibilities

- Your induction tutor/mentor is, in effect, your line manager as far as your induction goes and s/he must be fully aware of his/her duties.

- S/he must devise a suitable programme of induction for you that is individualised and will allow for fair and thorough assessment of your abilities as a teacher as well as suitable support and monitoring on a day-to-day basis.

- S/he must formally assess you at regular intervals and make fair and rigorous judgements about you.

- S/he must make recommendations to your headteacher on the outcome of your induction period.

The appropriate body's responsibilities

- With your headteacher, the appropriate body is responsible for your training and supervision during your induction period.

- It is responsible for quality assurance of induction arrangements and may give guidance and assistance to schools and individuals.

- It must ensure that your headteacher and governing body are aware of what they should be doing and are doing it.

- It must make the final decision on whether you are deemed to have completed the induction period satisfactorily based on your headteacher's recommendations.

- It must inform the secretary of state on its decision.
- It must give the NQT at risk of failing additional support, and assure itself that the induction being offered is of the highest quality.

The governing body's responsibilities

- The governing body must be fully aware of the implications of employing an NQT and ensure that the key personnel involved in the induction of NQTs are in a position to perform their duties to the highest standards.

WHAT THE INDUCTION PERIOD MEANS FOR THE NQT

There are many distinct advantages for NQTs undergoing statutory induction, providing all concerned are aware of their responsibilities and are keen to maximise the benefits of the situation. For this reason, it is worth knowing these points:

- All concerned in your induction period must be conscious of its developmental purpose.
- You should be fully involved and actively participate in self-monitoring and assessment against the standards for QTS and the Induction Standards (see Appendices 1 and 2).

ABOUT

THE INDUCTION STANDARDS

These are designed to build on the standards for the award of QTS in that they require you to show that you can perform all standards independently (as opposed to being under supervision when training). They also aid the focusing process so that professional development is valued and useful. The crux of your role here is to move towards performing all standards consistently.

- You should be informed from the start of your responsibilities for your professional development.
- The induction you receive should be equitable to induction received by NQTs in different schools, as the statutory arrangements and the monitoring procedures (OFSTED will be looking the quality of the induction NQTs receive when schools and LEAs are inspected) encourage national standards.
- Your induction should be individualised and well targeted rather than vaguely supportive.
- You won't simply be expected to meet the induction standards, but to build on the standards for QTS consistently and draw together your other skills and achievements as well.
- If your induction tutor/mentor is also your headteacher (be extremely wary of this set up, although in some very small schools this may be unavoidable), a third party should also be involved at formal assessment meetings.
- Your teaching post should be one that does not require you to teach outside your age range and subject specialism, that means you teach the same classes regularly, that doesn't involve extra responsibilities (without preparation and support) and that does not present severe discipline challenges.
- Your timetable should be reduced and this must allow for targeted induction rather than extra preparation time. The timetable reductions should be evenly distributed throughout your induction period.
- If your school is unable to provide induction of a high enough standard, your headteacher is responsible for arranging experience for you in another school. Be sure to talk to your induction tutor/mentor and named person at the appropriate body if you suspect this should be happening.
- Although you cannot complete your induction period in a sixth form college, you can gain experience in one as part of your induction.
- You will be observed at least once in any six to eight week period and certainly within your first four weeks (and ideally in your first week). After these observations you should be given the opportunity to discuss the lesson and the conclusions your observer has reached.

- Assessment observations must be focused and a written record must be kept including details of any action needed as a result of the observations. Induction objectives can then be revised.
- You must have a professional review of progress at least once every half term in a typical three-term year and these reviews should be informed by evidence drawn from all aspects of your work. Again, a written record should be kept, including any steps needed for further development.

ABOUT

ASSESSMENT MEETINGS

The best way to view assessment meetings is as markers of your progress throughout your induction period. It is important that you feel free to discuss all your concerns, achievements and needs for further professional development. You should have at least three formal assessment meetings (i.e. one at the end of each term in a three-term year) with informal assessment meetings in between. At no point should you be surprised by any conclusion that has been reached on your work as, if everyone involved is performing their duties as they should, opinion on your progress should be made known to you throughout your induction period and not saved for formal assessment times.

- The first formal meeting will look at how consistently you are meeting the standards for QTS and beginning to meet the Induction Standards based on evidence from meetings and observations as well as your self-assessments, evaluations and lesson plans etc.
- The second formal meeting will look at how well you are meeting the Induction Standards.
- The third formal meeting is the final assessment of whether you are to be successful or not. If you are thought to have successfully completed your induction period, the meeting can also be used to discuss your development needs for the next academic year. For this reason it is worth thinking about what these may be in advance.

You should receive copies of every written report on you.

- Your induction period must include the opportunity to observe experienced colleagues and teachers in 'beacon schools' (schools where good practice has been identified). Each observation must have a focus.

ABOUT

MAKING UNSATISFACTORY PROGRESS

It is expected that the vast majority of NQTs will be successful in completing their induction period, especially as concerns on both sides can be raised very early on. You should be informed of any chance that you may not be successful as soon as concerns arise and the summative assessment forms from your formal assessment meetings must record that you risk failing the induction period. Individual weaknesses must be identified and a structured plan of action put in place. You must also be told exactly why you are thought to be at risk of failing and a third party (i.e. your headteacher) must observe your teaching. The appropriate body will be informed that you are considered to be at risk of failing the induction period and your headteacher should write to you about the improvements that you need to make in order to be successful. You must also be told formally of the consequences of not making the necessary improvements.

If, at any stage of this process, you are unhappy with your treatment, talk to the named person at the appropriate body (usually this will be your LEA) as soon as possible. Also seek advice from your union.

In the event of being informed that you have failed your induction period, you must be told the exact details of your right to appeal. If you decide to appeal, you may not be dismissed, but your teaching duties will be restricted before the appeal is heard. If you decide not to appeal, you will be dismissed within ten working days of announcing your decision. Do not attempt to take yourself through the appeal process. Always seek union advice.

- There must be the opportunity to be a part of the general staff training that is on offer at your school. This includes being given information on all whole-school policies and training from outside your school (important for achieving a broad perspective on the profession) and having the chance to spend time with your school's Special Educational Needs Co-ordinator (SENCO).

THE APPEAL PROCEDURE

1 This section has been taken from the circular 5/99 'The Induction Period for Newly Qualified Teachers' (annex D) and sets out the arrangements for appeals against decisions to extend or fail the induction period. Eventually, the General Teaching Council (GTC) will take over the role of the Appeal Body, but until then, the Secretary of State is responsible for appeals. The decision of the Appeal Body is final.

Making an appeal

2 If an NQT fails induction, or has the induction period extended by the Appropriate Body, that body must tell the NQT of the right to appeal, who to appeal to, and the time limit for appeal.

3 The NQT (the appellant) must send notice of appeal to the Secretary of State (or when they take over that function, the GTC) within 20 days beginning with the date the appellant received notice of the Appropriate Body's decision. The Appeal Body will have discretion to extend this time limit where not to extend the time limit would result in substantial injustice to the NQT.

4 The NQT can appeal to the Appeal Body by sending a notice of appeal, which can be a letter. NQTs can present their appeal in whatever way they see fit. The notice of appeal must include all of the following information:

(a) the name and address of the appellant

(b) the name and address of the school at which he was employed at the end of his induction period

(c) the name and address of his employer, if any, at the date of the appeal

(d) the grounds of appeal

(e)   the name, address and profession of anyone representing the NQT in this matter, and an indication of whether the Appeal Body should send appeal documents to the representative rather than to the NQT

(f)   whether the teacher requests an oral hearing or not

(g)   if the appeal is going to miss the deadline, the NQT may give any justifications for the delay, and the Appeal Body must consider them.

The NQT must sign the appeal for it to be valid.

5   The NQT should send the following additional material with the appeal:

(a)   a copy of the document from the Appropriate Body notifying the NQT of its decision

(b)   a copy of any document from the Appropriate Body outlining its reasons for coming to this decision

(c)   a copy of every other document on which the NQT relies for the appeal.

6   Appellants can amend or withdraw their grounds of appeal or any part of their appeal material and they can also submit new material in support of the appeal. They can do these things without permission up to the date they receive notice of the appeal hearing date (or notice of the outcome of the appeal if it is decided without a hearing). After the hearing date has been arranged the appellant needs the permission of the Appeal Body to amend or withdraw his or her appeal or submit further material.

7   Once an appeal is withdrawn it cannot be reinstated.

8   The correspondence for an appeal is handled by the 'proper officer'. Within three working days of receiving the notice of appeal, that officer will:

(a)   send an acknowledgement to the appellant

(b)   send copies of the notice of appeal and accompanying documents to the Appropriate Body

(c)   send a copy to the head teacher who made the end of induction recommendation and any current employer, if not the LEA.

The proper officer will also copy any later amendments or additions or notices of withdrawal to the Appropriate Body.

9   The Appeal Body will be able to request additional material from the appellant if it thinks the appeal could be more fairly decided. If the appellant decides to provide such material in response to a request he should do so within 10 working days of the date of the request. The Appropriate Body will be informed that a notice has been sent, and sent copies of any material supplied by the appellant.

10 The Appropriate Body has 20 working days from receiving the notice of appeal to reply. If the Appropriate Body decides at any time that it does not want to uphold the disputed decision, it should inform the Appeal Body, who will allow the Appeal. The reply must contain:

(a) the name and address of the Appropriate Body

(b) whether it seeks to uphold the disputed decision

(c) where it seeks to uphold the decision:

(i)   its answer to each of the NQT's grounds of appeal

(ii) whether it requests an oral hearing

(iii) the name, address, and profession of anyone representing the Appropriate Body, and whether documents should be sent to them instead.

11 The Appropriate Body should also send any document on which it wishes to rely to oppose the appeal, and, if the NQT has not supplied it, a copy of the written statement giving its reasons for the decision.

12 The Appropriate Body can submit further documents and amend or withdraw its reply. The rules are as described in paragraph 6 above.

13 The proper officer must send a copy of the reply from the Appropriate Body to the appellant within three working days.

14 The Appeal Body can make a decision without a hearing if the Appropriate Body has not replied in time; if it does so it may only allow the appeal. Where the Appeal Body considers an oral hearing is not necessary and neither party has requested one, the Appeal Body can also decide the appeal without a hearing.

In other circumstances there must be a hearing. The Appeal Body must notify the parties of any such decision within 20 working days from the day after the expiry of the time limit for the Appropriate Body's reply.

Decision by oral hearing

15 The Appeal Body must fix a date for a hearing within 20 working days from the expiry of the time limit for the Appropriate Body's reply by sending the appellant and the Appropriate Body notice of the time and place of the hearing. The notice of the hearing must be accompanied by guidance about the procedure at the hearing, a warning about the consequence of not attending, and information about the right to submit written representations if they do not attend. The hearing will be at least 15 working days from the date of the notice.

16 Both the NQT and the Appropriate Body have to reply at least 10 working days before the hearing, to say if they will attend or be represented, what, if any, witnesses they wish to call, and if they are not proposing to attend or be represented at the hearing to provide any further written representations they wish to make. Any written representations submitted will be copied to the other party.

17 The procedure at the hearing will be decided by the Appeal Body, but will be subject to the rules of natural justice, with full and open disclosure of documents. Both sides will be able to call witnesses, though it will be up to the parties to arrange for their witnesses to appear. Hearings will be in public although the Appeal Body has the power to decide that a hearing or some part of it should be in private.

Cost of appeals

18 The appellant and the respondent will have to bear their own costs. There will be no requirement to bear the costs of the other party in the event of a decision against one party.

The appeal panel

19 While the Appeal Body is the Secretary of State, appeal committees will be convened to offer formal advice on individual cases. The members are expected to be teachers, Initial Teacher Training providers, and local education authorities, who will be expected to be familiar with the induction process and standards. They will be given training in their responsibilities. There will be an odd number on the appeal panel, so that if votes are necessary, the decision of the majority will prevail.

20 When the GTC takes on the role of Appeal Body, they will consider the detail of their procedures.

Considering the importance of your induction period in determining your future in the profession and the detail and finality of the appeal process, it would be worth keeping a file in which you collect all documentation relating to your induction period and records of conversations about any concerns you may have. This may seem over-cautious given that the vast majority of NQTs are expected to pass their induction period, but in the event of having to make an appeal, will greatly ease your task. Do not attempt to go through the appeal process without seeking extensive advice from your Appropriate Body and your union at least.

MENTORING

The quality of the mentoring you receive is central to the likelihood of passing or failing your induction period and being aware of this can help to ensure that you don't miss out.

Mentoring is still relatively new in the teaching profession and has been the subject of much research in recent years, perhaps reflecting the fact that the role involves far more than simply co-ordinating the support you receive. There has to be a real partnership between you and your induction tutor/mentor and a culture of effective, challenging support for your induction period to be of value. It would not be unrealistic for you to have high expectations of the mentoring process. At the very least you can expect:

● a carefully selected induction tutor/mentor with excellent interpersonal skills who knows the exact details of their role

- an induction tutor/mentor with sufficient time to devote to your induction period so that fair judgements can be made on your progress
- a relationship with your induction tutor/mentor that can develop over the time of your induction in response to your progress and changing needs, with support always remaining a constant.

Research from the USA suggests that the better the start you have in a profession, the greater are your chances of success. While mentoring and induction form only part of the picture, with conditions of service also playing a role in your levels of job satisfaction, it is important to be alert to the quality of mentoring you are being offered and the impact it can have on this consequential year.

Your relationship with your induction tutor/mentor

While you should expect great things of your induction tutor/mentor, there is an obligation on NQTs to work at this relationship to help ensure that your induction period is an extremely positive springboard into the profession allowing for your skills to be built on year after year.

If, for any reason, your relationship is not working effectively, make every effort to resolve this diplomatically within your school. If you are unsuccessful, the named person at your Appropriate Body will be able to help. Do keep records of your attempts to improve your situation. Usually, however, good communication skills will be sufficient in making your needs known.

What is known to be helpful

- The opportunity to visit your school and even take part in team-teaching as much as possible before taking up your post.
- Early observations, particularly in your first two weeks at the school.
- A relationship with your induction tutor/mentor that facilitates frank discussions. This should include having the opportunity to discuss your respective roles.

- Frequent informal support from your induction tutor/mentor as well as other colleagues, perhaps through a 'buddy' system (where you are allocated a particular person who does not have responsibilities for assessing you in whom you may confide). This way, each meeting need only cover a few issues.
- An induction tutor/mentor trained in listening skills.
- The opportunity to observe and then analyse with colleagues *why* a particular technique works.
- Support that covers curriculum issues as well as day-to-day job management.
- Encouragement off plateaux so that consolidation does not turn into stagnation.
- Co-ordinated approaches to mentoring rather than *ad hoc* arrangements.
- A school ethos of learning from mistakes.
- Asking for support before problems develop.

However, there are some potential pitfalls to be aware of:

- If your induction tutor/mentor is not supported in his/her work, time constraints may mean that your induction depends heavily on the goodwill of colleagues.
- Your school may have little or no experience of mentoring NQTs.
- Your mentor may be untrained.

If you suspect any of the above to be the case in your school, discuss your situation with your union and the named person at your Appropriate Body.

IN-SERVICE TRAINING (INSET)

This is met with mixed feelings in schools across the country. Some relish the opportunity to spend time with teachers from other schools, or work on projects and concepts for a longer period of uninterrupted time than is usually the case. Others would rather spend the time catching up with marking and preparation.

ENCOURAGING EFFECTIVE MENTORING

There are certainly things that NQTs can do to encourage effective mentoring during the induction period. Use these points as starters:

- get to know the Induction Standards and Standards for the Award of Qualified Teacher Status thoroughly
- attend all the induction sessions you are offered
- work hard at building a solid relationship with your induction tutor/mentor
- be aware of the time constraints your induction tutor/mentor may be facing, but donít let that put you off asking any questions or raising any concerns
- be receptive to new ideas that may be different from those you have encountered in the past
- express your needs related to your workload as early as possible – be honest about this as seemingly confident and capable NQTs can miss out on support
- put forward your ideas for your induction and think carefully about how challenging you want your targets to be
- get to know last year's NQTs and draw on them for additional support
- get to know the areas of expertise of your colleagues
- do regular evaluations of your work and acknowledge your progress
- when possible, give feedback on the quality of the mentoring you are receiving
- facilitate constructive discussions by displaying good listening skills, and asking for clarification on anything you don't understand or don't agree with
- aim to integrate what you learn from colleagues into your work on a daily basis.

Although INSET is only a small part of your overall induction, aim to cultivate a healthy attitude to it (regardless of the prevailing view of your staffroom) because there are undoubtedly benefits you can gather from attending.

The INSET offered to new teachers covers a wide variety of topics from the generic such as classroom management and assessment to the specific such as special educational needs at your school. It may be delivered by specialists from outside your school at a central location (such as a teachers' professional centre) or by colleagues in your school.

ABOUT

GETTING YOUR FAIR SHARE OF INSET

There is no set quota of in-service training for NQTs, but you can expect to be sent on a variety of courses throughout your induction period, simply because no school can provide all aspects of the training and support that NQTs need. Ask your induction tutor/mentor how many courses you will be sent on over your induction period and, when you get the opportunity, ask the advisor with responsibilities for NQTs the same question. If there is a discrepancy, raise this at your next meeting with your induction tutor/mentor.

Most LEAs provide each school with a folder of forthcoming INSET. Look through this to see if there are any suitable courses for you. If there are and you have not been informed of them, ask your induction tutor/mentor if it would be possible for you to attend. Unfortunately, money for INSET is limited so those in charge of the budget will have to make difficult decisions about who gets training.

Maximising the benefit of INSET

The best way to glean the most from any INSET you are offered is to make a conscious decision to gain from each session. Whether this is from the information that has been presented, teachers from other schools or inspiration for the formulation of an idea to incorporate in your teaching, there will always be something that you can leave the session with. Think about these points too:

- before attending any INSET, be it in your school or provided externally, think about what the course is about and what you hope to gain from it
- plan some questions to ask those giving the INSET
- use the tutors/advisors as a resource – find out their specialisms and get names and numbers if you think they may be useful in the future
- take the opportunity to meet NQTs from other schools and perhaps build up your own support network for the exchange of resources
- tell INSET providers if there are any areas you think NQTs would benefit from covering – you could inspire a new course.

Using the information given

You may well leave a session of in-service training with a bundle of handouts and an array of ideas floating around your mind. As most teachers then return home with the usual demands on their time (marking, preparation, family etc.) it is no surprise that the information collected may never make it into everyday use.

- Keep a record of any INSET you attend that includes what was covered and how you can incorporate what you learnt into your work.
- Review these records regularly throughout each term. Even if this only takes a few minutes, you may be inspired by something you read at just the right moment.
- Photocopy any handouts that may be useful for colleagues at your school.
- Talk about the impact of INSET you have attended at meetings with your induction tutor/mentor.

Your domain – the classroom

Whether you work in a classroom or an open-plan environment, the area in which you teach is *your* domain. The changes you make to this space can greatly affect the organisation and ambience of your lessons.

Before you go ahead and redecorate, do check with your line manager and induction tutor/mentor what house rules there are regarding classrooms and displays and always follow the guidelines given. For example, some schools insist on double mounting or triple mounting pupils' work before it is displayed, or will only allow work and posters to be put up within notice/display boards. Even within such restrictions, there will still be plenty of scope to make your mark.

CREATING THE ENVIRONMENT YOU WANT

If you are fortunate enough to have a room assigned to you, without having to share, you can start your interior design from scratch. While the amount of work you do in any holiday should be kept to an absolute minimum, preparation before the start of a term can help to give you an empty space in which to create the environment you want.

- Throw out any clutter from previous years as well as anything that does not serve a purpose.
- Aim to zone your room – you could have an area for you and your administration and areas for different aspects of the work that takes place within the room. For example, many teachers have set places for books to mark and books that have been marked, and separate display areas for written work and design work or the efforts of different year groups. This all helps to establish order and routines in your space.
- Brighten dingy corners with plants. You could involve pupils in their care.
- Think about creating a 'peaceful' corner. Look out for pictures of natural scenes and place them where you can see them when

addressing the class. If possible, swathe the background of this corner with paper or fabric in a shade of blue or green.

- If space permits, allow your class or tutor group to decorate a small area of your room.

- Be aware of the light in your classroom. Try not to let the room get too dark, as this will make for gloomy lessons and gloomy pupils.

- Keep the air in your room circulating; have a window open all the time. Anyone who has walked into a room after 35 sweaty adolescents have just vacated it will know exactly how important fresh air is – and infants can be just as fragrant!

- Watch the heating levels – too cold and your pupils will grumble, too hot and you'll all become sleepy.

- Keep your room tidy and safe on a day-to-day basis. Don't wait until the end of term for a tidying blitz because the chances are you won't want to be bothered then. Utilise storage drawers and cupboards and avoid using your own unique filing systems. Label *everything* so that anyone can use your room and understand your systems. This will also encourage others to keep your space tidy.

- You could try spraying your room with a well-diluted essential oil to help keep the air fresh. Get an empty spray bottle (available from most chemists and toiletries shops), half-fill it with water and add 8–10 drops of a pure essential oil of your choice. Shake the bottle well before spraying the room. Neroli is said to be stress reducing, juniper stimulating, lavender relaxing and lemon uplifting.

- Think about the use of colour in your room. You may not be able to do anything about the colour of the walls, but most teachers are free to choose what colour they use as a background to wall-mounted work. Reds and oranges are said to be stimulating while greens and blues are relaxing. Black can be a stunning base for mounted work. Be aware of the way colour affects your classes both in the classroom surroundings and in the clothes you wear – do you want unnecessarily to stimulate your pupils?

- Explore the possibilities of using music in your room. The use of appropriate sound can have a positive effect on learning situations and some teachers consider it as an additional resource, particularly for art and history (as well as music) lessons.

- Wipe your board clean as soon as you have finished with the work. This will help to keep lessons flowing smoothly, as you won't have to waste time with chores like this when you really want to be writing on it.
- Keep a stock of tissues and paper towels in your room. This will help in the event of spillages and will also prevent requests to go to the toilet for a tissue. If you teach the very young, you may want to consider keeping a stock of spare children's pants for those little disasters!

ABOUT

BEING AN ITINERANT TEACHER

You may be unfortunate in your first year in that you do not have your own classroom. However pushed your school is for space, you should at least be given a base from which to work. Although it may not be appropriate to start redecorating a colleague's classroom, you could ask for a display area of your own. Use the time without your own classroom to formulate ideas for classroom design. Observe the displays around the school and note the ones that seem to work and the ones that don't. Think about why this might be so.

How far can you go?

The changes that can be made depend entirely on the school in which you work. Some have very strict rules on the way classrooms are set out and decorated while others allow for individual teachers to impress their style on the environment around them. Teaching is an inherently creative occupation and this is a great area in which to set your ideas to work.

Rather than bedeck your room as soon as you arrive, have a look at other classrooms and talk to colleagues. It would be fairly unusual for an NQT's ideas on classroom décor to be totally squashed. Teachers spend a great deal of their working day in the classroom and it is important to think of that space as a metaphor for you. How far does it reflect your nature? It is usually possible to implement any sound ideas subtly – even surreptitiously!

Getting the most from your space

Work on the assumption that change and movement is more advantageous than stagnation. Make sure, though, that you can always see all the pupils, that they can see you and any materials you use, and that you can see the door if you have one.

- Try different seating arrangements. Horizontal rows, vertical rows, conference style, grouped tables – all are useful for different purposes and it may be appropriate to change the furniture around at regular intervals. You could ask pupils to create seating plans.
- Alter the position in the room from which you function.
- Change displays regularly, making sure they are clearly labelled.
- You don't have to do everything in one go – altering displays on a rotation basis is fine. Aim to change at least one aspect of your room once every half-term.
- Make sure that everything in your room is functioning as it should. This includes such things as power points, windows and blinds.

ACTION: Contact one museum, one publisher and one bookshop to ask for display materials for your classroom. You may be pleasantly surprised by the selection you receive.

Behaviour management

One of the areas of greatest concern for new teachers is behaviour management. The need for this is certainly not a recent development; pupils have been misbehaving since schools began and people have been devising methods of managing misbehaviour for just as long. Yet teachers appear to be experiencing a worsening in pupil behaviour. Whether this is real, or a symptom of reduced tolerance because of the other demands of teaching remains to be seen. Nevertheless, these views of teachers need to be addressed.

The following section draws on commonly accepted good practice and cannot be attributed to any one behaviour management method. The first thing to remember when thinking about behaviour management is that you are human. For all the rules you may devise with your classes and all your good intentions, there will be some days when they are harder to implement than others. This is natural, so don't give yourself a hard time. Also, it is not violence and serious confrontation that causes the most problems in schools, but the persistent interruptions of chatterers and comedians. This relatively low-level misbehaviour is what is most likely to stress new (and established) teachers. Being aware of this can help you protect yourself from the harm that such antagonisms cause.

When thinking about your own model for behaviour management (for that is, in effect, what will emerge – teachers may use a model as a base but the reality is that only you can develop systems that work with the dynamics between you and your classes), find out how much freedom you have in this area. If your school has set discipline procedures you will have to follow them but, to a certain extent, within your own room, you are free. It hardly needs to be said that *any* behaviour that contravenes the school's code on equal opportunities and discrimination needs to be dealt with promptly and severely. Sir William MacPherson's report on the Stephen Lawrence inquiry recommends that consideration be given to amending the National Curriculum with the aim of 'valuing diversity and preventing racism'. Clearly everyone involved in education can contribute, through behaviour management, to this end.

It does seem to be the case that classes behave best when teachers are working in a style most natural to them. If you like order and calm you are never going to be happy with the apparent 'chaos' of the teacher who likes to work less formally. Do also be aware of the fine line between order and anarchy. Good behaviour can be dependent to some extent on the goodwill and acceptance of pupils, which is why every minute spent on nurturing good relationships is time well invested.

Here are some more points to consider:

- Anger is often at the heart of a child's misbehaviour. Be aware of the many battles that the child may have already fought that day before he/she started messing around in your class. Don't greet their anger with your own. Remember what it was like being the age of the children you teach.
- Think about how you have behaved in lectures, seminars and meetings. Can you honestly say you have never talked when someone else is speaking, or looked bored, or yawned?
- Don't think of discipline as a means of control, but accept that everyone needs discipline for a variety of reasons, not least security and protection.
- Plan your ideas around the rewarding of success.
- Think about how children gain your attention in your lessons – is it through good or bad behaviour?
- Are there any changes you could make to the way you teach in order to minimise the need to correct behaviour?
- When implementing a behaviour management plan, never give up on your expectations. It may be a long (continuous) haul, but you cannot plant seeds today and pick flowers tomorrow.

Eight points to remember about managing behaviour:

- Don't speak too fast or too loudly and try not to blush; all these reactions can be interpreted as weakness.
- Give known troublemakers a responsibility that involves an element of trust. This is a good way to make your worst 'nightmare' your 'best friend'.
- Explain the stages of your displeasure. Never go from cold to hot, as you will only confuse the folk you are trying to nurture.
- Don't look as though you are expecting trouble, even when faced with the toughest of classes.
- Address your displeasure specifically, not to the whole class.
- Time your interventions carefully. Does every misdemeanour need correction?
- Frequently convey to your pupils how much you enjoy your job and what specific aspects you like.
- Don't take on the world single-handed. Get support from your induction tutor/mentor or head of department. These people should be involved in rewards and sanctions anyway.

Above all, never resort to saying, 'This couldn't work with my classes.' Something certainly will, so what aspects can you modify for your own use?

CLASSROOM RULES AND ROUTINES

The only reason to have classroom rules and routines is to make life easier and safer, so improving the quality of learning that takes place in your room. This book cannot provide a list of rules and routines for you to adopt because they must be specific to you, your pupils and the subject(s) you teach. However, you may like to think about devising rules around these areas:

- the way pupils speak to each other and to you
- pupils' attitudes to homework
- pupils' attitudes to time and the completion of work
- the way pupils sit and move around the room
- eating and drinking
- the handing in (and out) of work.

Many teachers like to devise rules with the help of pupils. This serves to emphasise the fact that behaviour management is a continuous dialogue between pupils and teachers with commitments on both sides. When you actually write the rules with your pupils, keep them positive. 'In this room we sit in silence when Mr Brown is talking to us' is infinitely better than, 'Don't chatter when Mr Brown is talking.' Certainly don't create rules that put ideas into pupils' minds. Just think about the consequences of 'Don't throw chewing gum at teachers.' Does such a rule actually need to be written?

Here are some hints for using rules:

- Make sure your rules reflect the ethos of the school.
- Don't relax your rules or expectations, however familiar you become with pupils; they will appreciate the stability and security your lessons give them.
- Think about ways of using peer mediation/pressure to ensure your rules are met.
- Build on respect for the right to learn and to teach and pupil accountability.
- Once you have devised your rules and routines, stick to them, use them, refer to them and discuss any changes with pupils.
- Don't just aim to be 'master of the ship'. You also want a happy crew.

Being slick

Behaviour management is not about fighting every battle. If you do, your lessons will become far too stilted and pupils will become desensitised to your rules. The key is to be slick and deft, brisk and business-like in your behaviour management from the very first second of a lesson.

- Start work promptly. If pupils are taking a while to settle, give them a task to do in limited time. Make this first task simple and straightforward.
- Identify the cause of a disruption. Is it due to boredom, peer pressure, inappropriately pitched work or concentration difficulties?

- Use these three steps with any child who seems to be unfocused:

    (i)   *Anticipate* bad behaviour. This is much easier when you know your pupils well.

    (ii) *Distract* with simple instructions for work.

    (iii) *Praise* as soon as you can.

ABOUT

DEALING WITH INTERRUPTIONS

The best way of dealing with interruptions is to pre-empt them. Explain, in your first lesson and every lesson that follows, that you will allow plenty of time for questions so interruptions aren't necessary. Respond to all interruptions firmly – they are a huge source of stress for teachers and there is no harm in telling pupils how infuriating it is to have someone talk when you are trying to explain something, not to mention the violation of the most fundamental classroom rule. Always give jobs to interrupters such as tidying the room at the end of the lesson or picking up litter and connect the sanction to the interrupting. If you are able to anticipate an interruption, block the offender by raising your voice slightly, which sends the signal that you will not be stopped from finishing.

- Don't get into a dialogue about behaviour while the lesson is going on; this is unfair on the rest of the class and wastes valuable time.
- Go to where pupils are sitting rather than the other way round. This prevents the need for crowd control around your desk or chair.
- Don't be afraid to scan the room and say, 'That's good Ben', 'I don't like that behaviour Angie', 'Nice work Mustapha', 'That's better Annie.' Quick-fire feedback can whip a class into shape with speed.

EXAMPLE: 'I was getting increasingly incensed by a year 9 boy who was clearly passing something around the room. Instead of responding calmly, I shouted, 'What are you doing?' I was really embarrassed when the boy said that he was passing a Christmas card for me round for the class to sign. I'd lost my temper when I could have dealt with it earlier and minimised the disruption to the lesson.' Second-year teacher, West Sussex.

ABOUT

LARGE CLASSES

With some classes numbering over 40, behaviour management becomes a real skill. If chatting out of turn is the main cause of disturbance, this is compounded by large classes.

Minimise the hassles of misbehaviour by thinking about the space that pupils have to work in. Are they piled on top of each other with left-handed and right-handed pupils locked in eternal elbow battle? Is there an EU-rucksack mountain blocking your right to roam? You could also think about ways in which you may need to modify your teaching. Does group work increase the decibel level to such an extent that it causes actual damage to the eardrums? Can you make eye contact with each pupil? Can they all hear you? Can you hear them?

Appeal for co-operation by developing a strong group identity and a sense of belonging. The 'Dunkirk Spirit' – we're in this together – can work well.

MOTIVATION

'The ultimate goal of the educational system is to shift to the individual the burden of pursuing his own education.' J. W. Gardener.

The development of natural internal motivators must be at the heart of all behaviour management (and is in some of the management models). This is an ongoing task for teachers that cannot ever be forgotten. Motivated pupils have no time to misbehave.

In order to motivate your class, you need to know what their general mood is. Are pupils buoyant, mad, angry, petulant, playful or tired and slothful? You can use the time while they are settling to assess this and it may be necessary to adapt your lesson plan. A series of very short tasks may be more suitable than a longer project. This doesn't mean rewriting your plan, but it may mean changing the way you deliver it.

If pupils appear to be angry, it can be worth sacrificing some of your lesson to establish what the problem may be. Spend some time talking about it and focusing on solutions before attempting to start your lesson. This is more likely to result in receptive students and you have shown yourself to be aware of the greater picture of their school experience.

Try some of these ideas to help motivate your classes:

- Give pupils the chance to plan part of a lesson. Ask them how they want to do something and allow them to create their own conditions (within your parameters of course). You could then ask them to grade the lesson.

- A step up from this is to allow for children to teach part of a lesson. This shares the 'power' and allows you to take a back seat (literally).

- Time tasks throughout the lesson. This is a great motivator and also teaches time management. Do be flexible though. You want to motivate not stress.

- Think of ways of teaching through the interests of your pupils. If a particular craze is sweeping your class, how can that be incorporated into your lessons?
- Shun labels. Some children (and whole classes) get inextricably attached to a label they may have been given in the past. For example, 'I'm thick Sir – got anything else for me to do?', 'We're the bottom set Miss.' You could reply by saying, 'You can't be. I don't teach thick kids/troublemakers/lazy tykes etc.', and move quickly on to a positive aspect of the group or child.

ABOUT

SPENDING YOUR OWN MONEY ON CLASSES

All teachers spend some of their own money on their classes at some stage, especially as little extras can allow you to make your mark on your classes. However, it is worth asking your head of department or induction tutor/mentor if you can claim back any expenses. Some PTAs raise money for just this purpose.

Creating the habit of work

If, lesson after lesson, you allow time at the beginning and end that does not have a constructive purpose, pupils will certainly learn one thing – that work is not the habit in your room. Your starting work cues need to be totally understood and respected and your expectations for good behaviour high. If you know that what you are teaching is useful, that you would want to learn it and that it has an immediate application for pupils you can easily create a sense of urgency to start work.

You could also think about how you could use the peace of silence in your lessons. It can give children a boost as it offers temporary respite from having to respond to the many stimuli around them.

Silence also creates a sense of common purpose – everyone is working under the same conditions.

Why not ask pupils if there is anything you can do to improve their work habits? You may be pleasantly surprised by the suggestions of even the most demotivated of classes.

ACTION: Think about an occasion when a lesson has gone really well with little or no misbehaviour. What characterised that lesson? Can you harness those factors for future use?

REWARDS

'There is no such whetstone, to sharpen a good wit and encourage a will to learning, as is praise.' Roger Ascham.

ABOUT

APPROPRIATE AND EQUITABLE REWARDS

There is nothing more annoying to staff trying to build up respect amongst pupils for a system of reward than a maverick teacher dishing out praise lavishly and indiscriminately. The danger here is the slippery slope to piling on the praise because a child hasn't done something (e.g. hit his/her neighbour) rather than has done something (e.g. listened attentively and contributed to the lesson when usually this is not the case). Those members of the class who do not require this 'encouragement' will see this as grossly unfair.

Do also be aware of the many stages of praise before you reach for the high-prestige rewards. For example, a positive comment written in a book, a memo sent to the form tutor etc. could be more appropriate than a merit.

This is where your ingenuity can really shine. The more original and inspiring your rewards, the more likely pupils are to want them. Use these general ideas as a basis for any reward structure that you may devise.

- Follow school policy. There may be an existing house points or merits scheme or perhaps letters can be sent home detailing achievement. This still leaves you free to introduce some of your own incentives in your lessons.
- Think about power differentials when you praise a child. For example, are you communicating with your heads at the same height? This can make all the difference.
- Can you celebrate achievement in public? Do remember though, that this may seem more like a punishment for some pupils!
- Do your pupils have any preferred activities as a reward, such as being allowed extra time on a computer, being able to play a game in class, or being given an edible treat? Discuss this with them, and remember that these activities may well change. What's popular this week may be out next.
- Your rewards should be worth the effort and certainly not too easily attained. You want them to be held in high esteem by pupils and for them to know that you will be consistent.

SANCTIONS

'It is better that ten guilty persons escape than one innocent suffer.' William Blackstone.

Schools vary tremendously in their attitudes to sanctions and it is essential that you absorb school policy. The table will provide additional support.

ACTION: Whenever you have to deal with indiscipline, ask yourself how many pupils it involves. This will help you see that the 'subversiveness' is not that extensive.

HINTS ON SANCTIONS

Do	Don't
Avoid sanctions that simply reiterate what the rules are. They *know* them, that's why they broke them! Aim to teach through sanctions preferably about emotional intelligence, awareness of others and citizenship.	React impulsively to a 'crime'. Think about an appropriate sanction – perhaps have some ready prepared. Instant reactions will not lead to consistency.
Be courteous to pupils when punishing them. Always offer a good example and explain exactly what you believe to be right and wrong in the situation.	Threaten punishment and not follow through precisely.
Be extremely wary of detaining a child other than in a formal school detention. Rarely is detention considered by pupils to be anything more serious than a nuisance.	Be alone with pupils when reprimanding them. Always ask for another member of staff to be present to witness what happens.
Listen to a child if he/she offers an explanation or an apology.	Refer to siblings. The child may have had a lifetime of listening to cries of how well behaved his/her brothers and sisters are.
Address problems and administer sanctions after the lesson. You will not gain the respect of the child through humiliating them in public.	Give collective punishments. Have you ever taught a class in which every child deserves exactly the same level of punishment?

Avoiding punishing yourself

'A smooth sea never made a skilful mariner.' Anon.

Think about these questions:

- Do you respond and punish automatically? Could you halve the amount of sanctions you deliver?
- Do you talk to pupils about their behaviour at a time that is convenient to *you*, when you have cooled off?

CONFISCATING PROPERTY

This is a potentially problematic area best avoided. If a pupil has an illegal item in his/her possession a member of the senior management team should be dealing with the situation and your role is to pass on any information you have as soon as possible. If you want to remove any other item from a child's possession make sure that you have given the opportunity for the child to put the item away, that the child knows exactly why it is being removed and when and who from (perhaps the pastoral head) the child can retrieve the item. Never seize something or force yourself into a corner by saying, 'Give me that now'. You could easily be met with refusal. If something (e.g. a note) is being passed around the room, don't destroy it yourself – ask a pupil to. Take the dustbin to the child to minimise disruption.

- Do you take misbehaviour as a personal insult? (It is extremely rare for this to be the case. There are always other factors affecting a person's behaviour and there is no harm in letting pupils know that you are not the cause of their anger on this occasion.)

If you have a really bad day, when you feel as though all you have done is respond to poor behaviour, use this recovery plan:

- Put the day in perspective. Was it the whole day that went wrong or just part of it?
- Identify *what* went wrong and *who* contributed.
- Resolve to talk to the pupils and/or staff who contributed to your bad day before you go home if possible.
- Write down two things that you can do to prevent the same circumstances occurring again.
- Ask yourself why you expect to have perfect lessons and great days every day. Does it really matter if you don't?

- Give yourself an evening off – no marking, no preparation. What is not done now can wait. Don't even take work home; you need the break.
- Treat yourself to whatever makes you feel good, e.g. nice food for dinner, some flowers, a novel or a bottle of wine, etc.
- Book something enjoyable for the near future. Cinema tickets, a night out or even just some time with a loved one.

CLASSROOM FOLKLORE

There is no particular order to this list; just look through it for inspiration. Teachers of a variety of age groups and subjects have implemented these ideas, so they can work.

- Give A level and year 11 classes a short break mid-lesson. This gives them a chance to chat briefly and can result in everyone feeling refreshed.
- Do simple stretching exercises with young children (year 6 and below) mid-session. This can help to prevent fidgeting especially in those who cannot sit still for long. When the children are standing, ask them to stretch up as high as they can from toes to finger tips, then flop over and slowly come up again. This can be invigorating for the teacher too.

EXAMPLE: One NQT was having problems controlling a class with a particular child interrupting persistently. After numerous warnings she offered a final, 'If you carry on I'll move you out of the class'. He continued protesting so she sent him to the head's office. Grudgingly he pulled his crutches out from under the desk and hobbled off. His original complaint was that he needed to stretch his legs!

- Be spontaneous. This worked well for the teacher of a year 10 boy who was being particularly disruptive. She was working with a child at the back of the room when there was a sudden outburst of laughter. The boy was trying on her jumper! She laughed spontaneously simply because he looked so ridiculous and after a while everyone got back to work without the need for the teacher to say anything. Her relationship with the boy was much improved after as she had shown that she was human and able to overlook some aspects of his behaviour.

- Ask a child who has misbehaved to help you through your lunch break. You could use the opportunity to get a job done, e.g. mounting work, as well as chat to the child about aspects of their behaviour. This helps to minimise the chances of either party seeking to dominate and can work with all age groups. Don't do this too often – working through a break is not a good habit.

ABOUT

BEHAVIOUR MANAGEMENT MODELS

There are many models for behaviour management, all with their own ideas on why children misbehave. Many of these draw from existing good practice and require whole school approaches for their effectiveness. However, you may like to find out more about the following. The book, *Building Classroom Discipline*, by C. M. Charles[1] would be a good place to start.

- **The Canter model** This is based on assertive discipline with teachers firmly insisting on good behaviour.
- **The Jones model** This aims to help students support their own self-control through effective body language, incentive systems and efficient individual help.
- **The Rogers approach** This is based on the conscious awareness of the steps of teacher action. Such steps include the tactical ignoring of behaviour, taking pupils aside and giving simple choices.

There are also the Kuonin, Neo-Skinnerian, Ginott, Glasser, Dreikurs, Gordon, Curwin and Mendler, Redl and Wattenberg models of behaviour management to name but a few, but don't feel obliged to absorb them all.

- Introduce a 'stop' law. If anyone does anything that adversely affects another, anyone can say, 'Stop'. This can create a very safe environment and if managed well, with clear consequences for violation of the law, empowers everyone in the room.
- Keep a marble jar. When someone in the class does something good, put a marble in the jar. When the jar is full, give the class a treat. Don't take marbles out of the jar if someone misbehaves. You don't want to punish the whole class.
- Give out a token (e.g. a plastic disc or a raffle ticket etc.) for good behaviour. At the end of the day/week/term pupils can purchase treats with the tokens. For example, ten tokens might mean they can buy the choice of an end-of-term video, two tokens might pay for some sweets etc. Build up your own 'shop'.
- Offer the best worker the choice of what song you listen to when you pack away. You could play CDs through a PC, laptop with speakers or a portable CD player.

Using humour in the classroom

'The most wasted of all days is that on which one has not laughed.' Nicholas Chamfort.

The physical benefits of laughter are well documented and such that most teachers would do well to actively seek amusement on a daily basis. It is infectious, relaxing and an excellent reliever of tension, exercising hundreds of muscles in the face and neck.

You don't have to earn yourself the reputation of the one that tells terrible jokes all the time in order to employ a little humour in your lessons. There is no government circular stating that classrooms must be devoid of laughter and in fact, some teachers work laughter breaks into their lesson plans.

Don't worry about over-exciting children and not being able to bring them down again. They will soon get used to your routines and quirks and you will work out the best time to employ a little humour. If you fear an inappropriate response from your pupils at any time, leave the humour for another day. The key here is balance. Use too much

HUMOUR AT SCHOOL

You only have to glance through a newspaper and see all the cartoons and humour-based columns, or look through TV listings to see the amount of humour that surrounds us. There is nothing wrong with injecting some lightheartedness into school life. Some schools have humour boards in staff rooms so that staff can read it for light relief. Perhaps establish one in your school, or dedicate a small area of your room to appropriate humour (perhaps a cupboard door).

humour and you risk appearing to need adulation and affection from your pupils. Aim to throw in occasional high points of humour. But:

- be sure not to waste time
- be aware that any jokes or funny tales you tell will be repeated outside the lesson so keep them tasteful and inoffensive
- never employ humour at the expense of a pupil, however well you know them. This could easily be misunderstood.

Pupil–teacher confrontations

'Time cools, time clarifies; no mood can be maintained quite unaltered through the course of hours.' Thomas Mann.

Regardless of how well you establish routines and explain your expectations, there will inevitably be occasions when pupils cross the boundaries of acceptable behaviour. This then gives you cause to confront the miscreant. The nature of pupil/teacher confrontations is even something that OFSTED looks at during an inspection.

However you decide to approach these confrontations, you should aim to do it rationally and honestly. These solutions should perhaps be avoided:

- Some bright teenagers may understand sarcasm but generally it is lost and only serves to frustrate the teacher.
- Humiliating pupils is also unproductive and certainly not supportive of their welfare.
- Losing your temper is rarely beneficial especially if it happens in front of the whole class for the sake of one pupil.

Serious misdemeanours need to be dealt with immediately in accordance with the established policies in your school. The most effective method is to remove the offending pupil from the room and deal with the problem after a 'cooling off' period. Asking a trusted pupil to get a member of the senior management team to come to your class to collect the child is effective. This sends clear signals to the rest of the class that boundaries have been crossed and that teachers are united. It also ensures that you don't have to face the public humiliation of having your requests for a pupil to leave the room being ignored.

When you do face the child to resolve the situation, remember these points:

ABOUT

BEING ASSAULTED AT WORK

If a colleague, pupil or parent assaults you at school, you will need to record the incident with your headteacher (who may need to report it to the Health and Safety Commission). Also talk to your union and seek medical advice. Such a situation needs to be treated most seriously.

- Explain quietly, clearly and calmly (with 'soft words and hard arguments') what it is about their behaviour you cannot tolerate and why. Avoid ranting, 'How dare you … ' as this simply shows you have lost your cool and makes it very hard to bring the conversation to a constructive conclusion.

- Calmly insist on eye contact and general respect. A pupil should look at you when you talk to them and you may want to ensure that they don't slouch or overtly show that they simply aren't bothered. Pupils should always listen without interrupting.

- Don't exaggerate their behaviour. You can expect pupils to see that you are not unreasonable without the need to embellish.

- Avoid raising your voice during a one-to-one as this is always counterproductive:

    — There is no physical need.

    — You will alienate the pupil you are trying to make see reason.

    — You will raise your blood pressure unnecessarily.

    — You risk losing reason and saying something offensive – 'How can I get this into your (thick) head?'

    — You will earn a reputation for losing your temper.

    — You will disturb classes trying to work in the vicinity.

- Initially, don't spend a long time trying to sort out the problem. Once you have explained why you have had to reprimand him/her, dispense your punishment and leave it at that. However, you should arrange a mutually agreeable time when you can both discuss the child's behaviour and ways of enabling him/her to improve. This stage is vital in this process and allows you both to talk rationally while sufficiently distanced from the original misdemeanour. Your aim is to reach an understanding of each other's needs and a commitment to improving your relationship.

This whole process may take a long time. Some pupils may be resistant to your methods and it is important to persevere. You're not going to succeed with all pupils all the time, but calm determination can go a long way. Be consistent in your expectations and praise any subsequent improvement in behaviour. Never give up on a pupil.

'DIFFICULT' CHILDREN

Unless the child's crime is so heinous as to warrant exclusion, you are going to have to exist in the same institution with children who have behaved unacceptably towards you. Whatever methods you adopt to deal with the situation, keep this in mind. It is not enough to agree to disagree or to write a relationship off. Go for peaceful, constructive resolutions even if they take a term or year to achieve or if they result in you having to face your own role in the situation's demise (if you had one).

ABOUT

CONFRONTING CHILDREN

When you are confronting children with your disappointment and anger at their poor behaviour, always keep in the forefront of your mind what the best possible outcome would be. How do you want the situation resolved? Visualise your perfect scenario. There is no harm in telling the child the hopes you have for an improvement and involve them in creating some appropriate criteria by which you can both assess whether progress has been made. This approach can be taken with whole classes as well, and some teachers periodically set aside a part or whole lesson to discuss behaviour and attitude. It is extremely difficult for even the most deviant of pupils to completely ignore such reason from a teacher.

- When it looks as though a relationship with a child is beyond repair, you need, initially, to go for damage limitation.
- Think of examples when the child has worked well for you and tell the child what you have liked about them in the past.
- Seek advice from colleagues who teach the child, including the form tutor, or colleagues who have had success in dealing with 'difficult' children.

- Don't get into power games – you are the teacher and therefore always 'in charge'. However, that should be taken as read, so don't humiliate yourself by reiterating it in front of pupils.

- Avoid saying things like, 'When you're away the class works really well.' The child may already be battling with feelings of rejection to be misbehaving, so adding to these will do nothing for your relationship.

- Aim to reach an understanding of each other's needs and be prepared to concede something to the child.

Changing your perspective

It is very easy to make judgements of pupils that are extremely hard to remove or change. Sometimes it is appropriate to review your perspective of a child and situation.

- Do you really need to fight every battle? Perhaps some situations can be overlooked in order to preserve the overall ambience of a lesson. The fact that Johnny is doodling this week may be a huge improvement on his previous behaviour. You should have high expectations of all your pupils, but the reality of teaching means that you are sometimes going to have to ask yourself, 'Does it matter? Is it worth it?'

- Be prepared to question your own attitudes. Do you find that pupils' behaviour is much worse on days when you are tired or

ABOUT

YOUR PERSPECTIVE ON 'DIFFICULT' CHILDREN

When you feel you are spending disproportionate amounts of time on certain pupils it is easy to start viewing the whole class as being difficult. This is very rarely the case and it is important to retain a sense of perspective. You may find teaching a particular class difficult because of the actions of one or two pupils – don't let that taint your enjoyment of the group.

angry at some aspect of your life? Be aware of fluctuations in your levels of tolerance.

- Try to find out as much as possible about children that you consider being 'difficult'. There will be something you have in common and may be able to build on that as a basis for a better working relationship.

ATTENTION DEFICIT HYPERACTIVITY DISORDER

This condition, known as ADHD, is being diagnosed with increasing frequency in school-age children. It is believed that the condition is caused by a minor brain dysfunction affecting the part that deals with behaviour inhibition, perhaps due to an imbalance of neurotransmitters. The condition affects more boys than girls; the ratio is about 6:1. Stimulant medications can be used to try to correct imbalances.

Symptoms of ADHD include impulsiveness, overactivity, clumsiness, disorganisation and an inability to sustain attention. In the classroom this may manifest itself as fidgeting, being easily distracted, being forgetful, being disrespectful of authority, interrupting others, having difficulty listening, talking incessantly and being incapable of following instructions.

This can all be incredibly frustrating for a teacher (as well as for the pupil). You should have been told about any sufferers in your classes, and given management strategies for their particular learning difficulties, but there may be some others who are undiagnosed for various reasons. If you suspect that a child you teach may be suffering from ADHD, talk to your SEN co-ordinator.

Bear these general points in mind when teaching ADHD sufferers:

- Many children who have been diagnosed with ADHD suffer from poor self-esteem. They may be aware of their shortcomings, probably from years of criticism before their condition was diagnosed, but are somehow unable to remedy them. Use techniques to boost esteem as frequently as possible. *Any* behaviour that could warrant positive reinforcement should be praised.

- ADHD children may be very impatient and might use waiting time destructively. Try to avoid this situation by making sure they are occupied, even if this means dealing with them first within the class.
- Many ADHD children respond well to routines. Try to make your classroom routines consistent from the start, including the sufferer's seating arrangements, and explain any changes clearly and in good time wherever possible.

ABOUT

OTHER EDUCATIONAL AND MEDICAL NEEDS

There will be a wide variety of conditions and circumstances affecting children's learning in your classes. While it would be ideal if you could learn all about the conditions suffered by the children you teach, that is quite impractical. If you get a chance, read about Asperger's Syndrome, dyspraxia and autism, and lean on your SEN co-ordinator for ideas and guidance on educating children with extra needs.

Management strategies

When teaching ADHD pupils, these tips will be useful:

- Make sure the ADHD child sits as close to you as possible and away from distraction (e.g. windows and doors). Seat some positive role models nearby.
- When talking to the pupil maintain eye contact for as long as possible.
- Encourage the child to use tools to structure their day, for example, timetables, daybooks, diaries etc. These all help to create routines.
- Break any tasks down into timed sections. Aim to do this surreptitiously so that the ADHD child does not feel different. Avoid giving multiple commands and make sure the child has understood the instructions before beginning the task. You should

already have a culture of tolerance in your group for children who feel the need to clarify and question.

- Make sure that when you explain tasks the child is listening and not holding, touching or fiddling with anything.
- Calmly insist on consistent rules for politeness in the classroom. For example, no child should call out or interrupt another person. You may need to spend time teaching and re-teaching the ADHD child these rules.
- Work with your SEN department to modify work as necessary. You may agree that an ADHD child should have more time to complete certain tasks.
- Think about the way ICT can be used in your lessons as this can help to focus an ADHD child.
- Be aware of the amount of stimuli surrounding a sufferer. Is there anything you can do to reduce this?
- Be prepared to adjust your expectations of the ADHD child in terms of self-responsibility. There may be days when you have to explain tasks calmly several times and monitor each stage religiously. Perhaps these are the days when frequent rewards would provide the incentive for the child to carry on.

ABOUT

MEDICATION FOR ADHD

Medication for ADHD is still highly controversial. Some teachers fear that it is being used to calm disruptive children and there has been a steep rise in prescriptions for drugs used to control the condition and other similar ones.

Medication cannot cure ADHD but it can moderate its effects. However, this is usually only successful as part of a package of help – medication cannot teach and encourage, nurture and support, but may provide a backdrop against which help can be absorbed by the child.

- Stress and fatigue can affect the ADHD child more profoundly than other children. Be sensitive to their personal circumstances and try to avoid overload.
- As soon as behaviour starts to deteriorate use distraction strategies. Point out good work and behaviour and as far as possible ignore the child's challenges to your expectations. However, if other children are distracted then you will have to correct his or her behaviour. Aim to reward more frequently than you punish and, instead of focusing on the negative, express the positive, e.g. 'Sit still please' rather than 'Stop fidgeting.'
- Discuss the consequences of misbehaviour.
- Utilise the concept of breaks during lessons by giving the ADHD child a 'job' to do. This gives the child temporary respite from class work and also serves to boost self-esteem, as the child feels trusted.
- Encourage the child to reward him or herself. Teach them methods of positive self-talk. For example, when you praise good work ask the child what their opinion is. Try to draw out of them the aspects that they are particularly pleased with. The aim is to get the child to say, 'I'm pleased with my work' or 'I did that well' or 'This is good'.
- The therapeutic value of play has been shown to be great for ADHD children. Apparently the more play you have as a child the more rational and less impulsive you are as an adult. Avoid restricting an ADHD child's opportunities for play. This is most clearly illustrated by the stresses of teaching a class that has been prevented from playing after a wet break – they all seem to have ADHD then!

> EXAMPLE: 'For me personally, what helped was to be told exactly what to do stage by stage. If I was given something to do and told to go away and do it then I struggled, but if I was given a task at a time I could go away and complete that, then go back to the teacher for the next task. I found it very difficult working for myself. It helped when the teacher outlined specifically what I had to do but not when he or she made a big deal of it in front of the class because it just made me feel stupid and inferior.' Alex, 18, diagnosed ADHD.

CLASSROOM BODY LANGUAGE

There is no doubt that the non-verbal communications that we give convey messages more efficiently than the spoken word. For no profession is this more the case than teaching. When your greatest weapon in the battle for control is sheer force of character, your body language can serve as an excellent reinforcement.

There is an element of acting in all teaching and attention to body language and posture is a quick way into character. Exponents of the Alexander Technique know clearly the extent to which the way we use posture affects physical and mental health.

ACTION: Before focusing on your own body language, observe colleagues in action. How does their body language and posture change to deal with different situations? Now turn your attention to yourself. What posture do you adopt when talking to the whole class, talking to individuals, reprimanding, praising, and joking? Do you stand defensively (abdomen and chin pointing outwards) or protectively (shoulders rounded and pelvis tipped back)?

In order to achieve 'free' posture, whereby your body is able to function efficiently, you need to pay attention to your body's extremities – your head and your feet.

- Imagine your head is filled with helium, eager to float upwards. Notice the immediate lengthening effect on your spine, while your shoulders fall naturally into place.
- Now focus on your feet, making sure that when you stand they take your weight evenly, and when you sit, both feet are placed comfortably on the ground (crossing your legs does nothing for circulation).

By remembering these simple ideas, your basic posture will not only be physically correct, but will also have a positive effect on your mental state.

Subtleties for the classroom

Consciously using body language in the classroom can be an excellent way of correcting or recognising behaviour without speaking or interrupting the flow of your lesson. Do try to be aware of habits that may be annoying to pupils as these can totally dominate their concentration. Think back to your own school days – did you ever do something like count the number of times a teacher said a certain phrase or touched his beard?

BODY LANGUAGE

Do	Don't
Smile. Forget the old fashioned notion that no teacher should smile before Christmas! You're a human not a robot and showing that to pupils can only strengthen their respect for you.	Point at pupils. Always use names, even when trying to correct behaviour. Pointing can be perceived as far too aggressive for the classroom.
Use eye contact. Make a direct link with a pupil when you talk to them to encourage him/her to feel that they have your undivided attention.	Frown. It can be easy to hide behind a permanent frown, which forces you to tense your facial muscles. Reserve frowns to indicate displeasure at a specific individual or incident.
Look at the class when you talk. Some teachers don't bother to look up from what they are doing to issue further instructions to a class, or continue to speak when facing the board and writing.	Cry. As an expression of emotion, crying is fine, but you will save yourself unnecessary embarrassment if you can hold back the tears until there are no pupils around. However honest it may be to cry in front of children, there will be some who will only remember the loss of control.
Use hand and arm gestures to illustrate points. This will help to guard against stagnation in the delivery of your lessons.	Clench your jaw or fists. Pupils will spot the rising tension before you do and may play on your stress.

BODY LANGUAGE (continued)

Do	Don't
Use professional touch. For example, a hand on a pupil's shoulder can give reassurance or positive reinforcement.	Habitually touch parts of your head or face. This can be associated with insecurity.
Observe the body language of pupils for signs of boredom. This will help you pace your lessons.	Invade a pupil's personal space. Allow them some territory. This is perhaps more important for older pupils.
Actively give the impression of listening. This conveys a sense of the importance you are attaching to what is being said.	Adopt a 'hands on hips' posture. This is negative (and tedious).
Lean or walk towards a child who is talking. Again, this is a way to engage directly in what is being said.	Move around the room in a manic fashion. Gently paced movements will help to set the tone of lessons.
Use encouraging gestures to help a child to continue talking if they are stumbling when answering a question.	Make unnecessary sound to get attention, such as banging on desks etc. The noise is unsettling in itself, not to mention what it does to your own stress levels.

WHAT TO WEAR

Gone are the days when teachers paraded in gowns, although some schools do still use them for assemblies and similar occasions. This, in one way, is a pity; at least the problem of what to wear would not be so profound for some teachers!

You will need to find out what the dress code is for your school by asking colleagues if you are not formally told. It is pretty unusual for suits to be compulsory now – most schools allow teachers to be smartly comfortable.

- Respect the dress standards your school is trying to achieve.
- Don't use clothing as a way of expressing discontent.
- Think about the image you portray through your clothing.
- Aim to blend in with staff rather than stand out dramatically. Perhaps confine flamboyance to the weekends.
- Wear stimulating reds and oranges with caution and go easy with accessories.
- Aim to throw out any shoes or clothes that are beyond repair. This may be difficult considering the immense financial pressures NQTs are under, but there's no doubt that your self-image is reflected in your outer appearance.
- Build up a wardrobe of clothes that 'work'. A few good quality, co-ordinating items will be most useful.
- Think about whether you need to dress for occasions such as meeting parents or visitors. Perhaps dressing up a little may boost your confidence.

Whatever guidelines you have to follow when working out what to wear to school, do remember that it is still possible to convey individuality within the tightest of restrictions and extremism is rarely constructive.

What makes lessons effective?

Thousands of lessons are taught across the country every day, the effectiveness of which varies tremendously. Effective teaching is not something that can be taught, understood and regurgitated consistently; the effectiveness of your lessons is bound to fluctuate, but one thing is certain – if you have the skills to respond to the dynamics of the moment, the overall value of your lessons will be great.

During an effective lesson, the experienced teacher performs with a degree of intuitiveness. They make decisions about the pace and content of a lesson with ease and there is almost subconscious use of established routines to ensure that the lesson flows smoothly and effortlessly.

As an NQT, don't place such expectations on yourself. Allow time to develop your own skills of effectiveness and don't expect everything to work all the time. Use your experiences to propel you towards the goal of effectiveness through regular evaluation and analysis of your lessons.

When OFSTED visits your school, inspectors will be looking at questions of effectiveness, particularly regarding your planning, use of time and resources within a lesson as well as the overall pace, flow and rhythm of a lesson.

ABOUT

EFFECTIVENESS

What does 'effective' mean? If you consider effectiveness to mean having 100% of pupils on task 100% of the time, then no lesson that has ever been (or will ever be) taught can be thought to be effective! However, if learning has taken place you can consider the lesson to have been effective on some level. Even the teacher who abandons a planned lesson to respond to the behavioural needs of a class sets standards for future lessons and so facilitates effectiveness. The perfectly effective lesson is something that good teachers continue to strive for throughout their careers.

USEFUL HABITS
Get into the habit of sticking to certain routines that keep your lessons moving and minimise the opportunity for misbehaviour. The emphasis is on pace and rhythm.

ACTION: Think about what it would be like to experience one of your lessons. Would you feel safe enough to take part and offer your ideas, and feel stretched but not rushed, at peace in your environment? 'Be' one of your pupils for a moment. What image of you as the teacher do you see? Are you stimulated, inspired and motivated by what is being said? Is the presentation filled with vitality? Do you understand the purpose of the work you are given?

Before the lesson

Once in the flow of the first term, effective lessons presuppose good relationships with the pupils, adept group management and slick organisation of resources. These are all aspects to work on from day one until retirement!

- Make sure your planning is sound. Know what you want to teach and how. Do you know how the group is organised? Is it streamed, set or banded? Is the group 'mixed-ability'?

- Don't aim to plan too far ahead especially if you are teaching a topic that is unfamiliar. You can't be an expert in everything.

- Check any equipment you plan to use to make sure it works properly. Do all you can to avoid pupils having to share resources.

- Prepare your room as much as possible, including the board. Be creative with your board space, be it black, white or a murky shade of green! If you are lucky enough to have a rolling board you can design board work in advance and roll the prepared section away until you need it. This means you don't have to turn your back on pupils, and pupils don't have to look at a board displaying irrelevant information, which may be confusing for some. Think of board routines you can teach your class. Perhaps put directions in boxes and questions in bubbles. Once you have created your own formula, stick with it. Use the board as a way of presenting the lesson – a valuable resource.

- Whenever possible, be waiting for your class to arrive, even if that means missing a few minutes of your break. You can, perhaps, ask pupils to line up quietly (or in silence) outside if space permits, before they enter your room. Reiterate your need for pupils to enter quietly and calmly.

ABOUT

MIXED-ABILITY CLASSES

The notion of streamed classes as an alternative to mixed-ability classes is a little nonsensical. All groups are of mixed abilities and for this reason you will need to take into consideration the ability of each child in every class you teach.

Most schools have some mixed-ability classes but not necessarily mixed-ability teaching. A skill all teachers need is in finding the optimum level of differentiation needed – too much and you launch yourself into a planning nightmare while too little means that it's unlikely that you will stretch any child.

True mixed-ability teaching involves enabling children to work independently. Make sure you always have supplementary materials for the faster and slower learners and be aware that pupils' abilities will appear to change depending on how inspired they are by the topic. Under-achievement is to be avoided at all costs and at all levels of ability. Watch out for pupils who:

- occasionally offer flashes of brilliance in their work
- may seem permanently distracted
- lack confidence in the classroom
- over-criticise their own efforts
- apply creativity and originality to problem solving
- ask probing questions
- show you extra work they have done in their own time.

Gently raise your expectations of such pupils, praising and nurturing at every stage.

- Welcome pupils with confidence. The first two or three minutes of a lesson are crucial.
- Allow some time for pupils to unpack and settle and again insist on silence before beginning the lesson. Give a clear signal when the lesson is to begin. Be consistent so that pupils learn your cues.

ABOUT

OVERHEAD PROJECTORS

If you have an overhead projector and screen in your classroom, you can create acetates with overlays that can be used again and again, as long as you use permanent pens or computer-print them. Remember to use a large font size though. This is particularly useful for cover lessons and last-minute planning.

During the lesson

- Introduce each lesson. Think of them as works of art worthy of an introduction. You are, after all, composer and conductor.
- Link each lesson to the previous lesson through the use of questions and answers. It is essential that pupils see how the work they do is related. Aim to build on existing knowledge.
- Think about when you want to hand out books, paper and materials – before your introduction or after? Try to hand books out yourself and comment on the quality of the work of either individuals or of the class as a whole. Avoid broad generalisations.
- Don't let latecomers disrupt the lesson. Deal with them at an appropriate time during the lesson or at the end.
- State the lesson's subject, context and purpose. Pupils should always know what will be expected of them, how and why. What is the key competency they will be learning?
- Use examples that children can directly relate to. Clarify points throughout. Find the simple starting point and develop it.

- Keep the lesson bubbling. Be enthusiastic about what you are teaching.
- Encourage enthusiasm for related learning, for example through visits to the library, museums, further reading, visits from experts and the use of ICT (including video, radio, TV etc.). Make lessons interesting and dynamic through the use of themes. Guide each child's discovery.

ABOUT

USING TAPES AND VIDEOS

Contrary to popular belief, showing a class a video or playing a tape actually involves a great deal of work. You will have to ensure that all the necessary equipment is available (in some schools this means booking it in advance) and is working properly. You also need to be able to justify its connection with the work in progress. Above all, never play a tape or video without either giving pupils a list of points to listen out for. or stopping it in pertinent places to discuss what has happened. Be aware of any biases you may be presenting to children. Think about what alterations you need to make to seating and lighting and do as much of this yourself as possible to cut down on opportunities for indiscipline.

- Be flexible and adaptable. Abandon your lesson plan if necessary.
- Vary the timed activities you give children. Keep individual abilities constantly in your mind and draw on the practical, intellectual, oral and written. Can pupils keep track of their progress and take part in target setting? Are they surprised by the activities or can they predict them?
- Allow only minor digressions before pulling the group back to the topic. Minimise blocks to learning.

EXPLAINING

'The mediocre teacher tells. The good teacher explains. The superior teacher demonstrates. The great teacher inspires.' William Arthur Ward.

Whatever you teach, the basis of all lessons will be explanations. The universal law here is pace, although it is surprisingly difficult to assess this objectively. Think about the speed at which you talk. Are you too fast or too slow? Too loud or too quiet? Do you vary the tone, volume and speed of your speech?

- Start with the real basics – you can't begin too simply. From this point, you can always build on the complexity.
- Make good use of key terms and phrases in appropriate language. Use a natural, logical progression of concepts and repeat, repeat, repeat.
- Ask pupils to demonstrate their understanding of your explanation.
- Remember to vary the way you deliver explanations to accommodate the ways different children learn (e.g. verbal definitions, hands-on experience etc.).

- Think of ways you can draw key concepts from pupils. Are you appealing to their curiosity and encouraging them to respond creatively? Anecdotal input from teachers can have a profound effect on the learning environment that is created.
- Allow plenty of time to set homework and check that all pupils know exactly what they have to do. You could ask specific questions such as, 'Annie, when is the homework due in?', 'William, where will you find the information you need?', 'Emma, what page are the questions on?' etc.
- Allow time to clear away before recapping and reflecting on the lesson.
- Dismiss the class clearly, perhaps a few at a time. Don't allow them to simply wander out.

> EXAMPLE: As a student, Amanda, a secondary teacher in Greenwich, had to teach a class after the sudden death of a pupil had been announced. She had to abandon the lesson she had planned and simply respond to the children's reactions.

After the lesson

'Only the mediocre are always at their best.' Jean Giraudoux.

- Insist on an orderly exit from your room, or to another area of your teaching space.
- Clean your board for the next lesson.
- Be available to talk to pupils between lessons. Even a chat in the corridor can keep a pupil's enthusiasm bubbling.
- Evaluate the lesson and resources you used – even if only mentally.
- Be realistic about what you first think to be a disastrous lesson. Was it really? What can you change for the future? Don't expect to sparkle all the time and don't dwell on mistakes. There isn't an advanced skills teacher in the country that doesn't make mistakes – and learn from them.
- Praise yourself!

PERSONAL EVALUATION

For a lesson to be effective, you do need to plan, deliver and evaluate it. Your training probably saw you furiously writing out an evaluation for every lesson you delivered, as well as every resource you created. If it didn't, start evaluating *now*.

Keeping up good habits

It would be ridiculous to expect new teachers to fill in a proforma after every lesson documenting how it went, what resources were used, what worked and what failed, whether pupils were challenged and how you could improve things in the future. However, if you don't spend time reflecting on the lessons you deliver and your teaching, you are unlikely to be able to give effective lessons in which your skills as a teacher continue to develop.

ABOUT

QUESTIONING

'I was gratified to be able to answer promptly. I said, "I don't know".' Mark Twain.

- Aim questions at particular pupils and don't lean on the reliable few. Adapt questions to individuals.
- Asking questions to the whole class can prove to be a discipline debacle as some patiently put hands up and others yell out the first thought that comes to mind.
- Word questions carefully – you may be asking for a witty or glib answer.
- Aim to draw knowledge rather than a one-syllable grunt. Get pupils to analyse and synthesise in their answering. Higher order questions will do this. Avoid lower order questions such as basic comprehension as it is possible to answer these without any knowledge at all.
- Allow sufficient time for the pupil to think of an answer.
- Encourage through non-verbal cues.
- Select something positive about a wrong answer.
- Ask the same question to different pupils for variety in response.
- Repeat answers for the benefit of the class – they may not all have heard.
- Encourage pupils to ask you questions and be honest if you don't know the answer. Do, however, make a note to find the answer to tell the child the next time you see them.

Even if only for a few minutes you consider the lessons you have taught during a day, you will get into the habit of being a reflective practitioner, ever open to learning and improving. If you can get into the habit of jotting your thoughts down, all the better. Even a small resource evaluation notebook will enable you to keep track of improvements you can make and successes you've had. It can make great reading on a bad day!

Ask yourself:

- Did pupils achieve my learning intentions?
- Has learning actually taken place?
- Did pupils participate?
- Can I assess what pupils have achieved? (Think qualitative and quantitative assessment.)
- Did I enjoy the lesson?

You could even ask your pupils at the end of a lesson what they learned. Did they enjoy the lesson? Would they like to do it again?

EXAMPLE: For Sam, the evaluation process was much more natural once he was in his first job. It became an automatic mental assessment of what was achieved and learnt; a running commentary.

A group of West Sussex teachers developed the checklist opposite for use in lesson evaluation. It is based on Alastair Smith's 'Accelerated Learning Cycle' and is used effectively in Worthing High School[2] among others. It can easily be adapted for use with classes of all ages.

It would also be worth incorporating Section B, Part (k) of the 'National Standards for Qualified Teacher Status' in any personal evaluations you do.

CHECKLIST FOR LESSON EVALUATION

Did I:
- introduce the lesson? YES/NO
- put the lesson in context? YES/NO
- make sure the pupils listened in silence? YES/NO
- introduce the key words to be used? YES/NO

Did I:
- maintain the pace of the lesson? YES/NO
- maintain high expectations? YES/NO
- differentiate the tasks appropriately? YES/NO
- regularly interact with the pupils? YES/NO

Were the pupils:
- on task? YES/NO
- actively engaged in their learning? YES/NO
- aware of when they could talk or when they should remain silent? YES/NO

Did I:
- respond to the previous homework? YES/NO
- set homework? YES/NO
- make sure that the homework task was clearly understood? YES/NO
- make sure that all pupils entered the task into their organisers? YES/NO
- set a deadline for completion? YES/NO
- provide differentiated opportunities? YES/NO

Finally, did I:
- re-state the learning intentions? YES/NO
- summarise what had been achieved? YES/NO
- explain the intentions for the next lesson? YES/NO
- ensure that pupils were focused and listening in silence? YES/NO

OBSERVATIONS

An excellent way of helping you to improve the effectiveness of your lessons is to observe colleagues from all areas of the school's curriculum in action. This can give you good ideas to utilise yourself and bad ideas to avoid at all costs.

Before you observe a colleague, discuss why you want to watch them teach. Keep in mind that it can be intimidating to have a new teacher fresh from training in your class. Make sure they are in full agreement that you should be there. This process can help to create some strong, trusting relationships. Ask in advance if they mind you taking notes or moving around the room at appropriate times.

Learning from colleagues
- How did the teacher gain the attention of the pupils?
- How was the lesson introduced?
- What motivated the pupils?
- How were resources used?
- How did the teacher employ questions?
- How was the lesson paced?
- Did the teacher respond to the needs of the pupils with flexibility?
- What links were made to previous and future lessons?
- Was there an air of enthusiasm from both teacher and class?
- What would you have done differently? Why?

Aim to have a specific focus for your observations.

Getting personal

There are bound to be occasions when discussions with pupils move away from the curriculum. Being prepared for such situations will save unnecessary embarrassment and protect you from possible future criticism.

YOUR PERSONAL ISSUES

Regardless of the age of your pupils, you will almost certainly face from them some degree of interest in your personal life. While keeping yourself a complete mystery is neither necessary nor desirable – it is good for pupils to have some insight into the lives of their teachers – the skill is in achieving professional balance.

How much should you tell?

This is entirely for you to decide. The main thing is to be aware of your motives for revealing aspects of your life to pupils. Is it:

- because they frequently ask you?
- because you really do see some of them as friends?
- because you feel it may excuse your mood/behaviour?
- because it is relevant to a particular lesson?

You will know when you have established a good relationship with your pupils and when you have crossed the invisible boundaries of professional discretion.

Some points to remember:

- It can sometimes be appropriate to talk to a pupil about an aspect of your personal life to reassure him/her. For example, if a pupil is suffering from a broken heart, there can be no harm in empathising and telling an anecdote about your experiences. This illustrates your understanding of issues facing your pupils.
- Never reveal something to a pupil that should then be considered a secret. This places unfair expectations on the child and crosses professional boundaries.
- Be prepared for distorted repetitions of your revelations.
- Keep certain aspects of yourself back from the full knowledge of your class. It's not desirable for them to know all about your partner/children/hobbies/home/family/aspirations/dreams and, in any case, they probably won't be interested.
- Divert attention away from yourself by focusing on pupils. If you feel uncomfortable under questioning from pupils, establish early on that you would prefer it if they did not ask personal questions.

In many ways it is a compliment to your abilities to relate if pupils want to know more about you. However, flattering as this intrigue may be, inappropriate 'chumminess' can be damaging to your career and your more astute pupils will interpret it as insecurity and sense weakness.

PUPILS' PERSONAL ISSUES

This is something you will face time and again throughout your teaching career, from dealing with a child who has wet him/herself, to helping a child through the grieving process.

How much should you ask?

It can be easy to work out which pupils are carrying burdens above those of childhood and adolescence. There may be changes in behaviour and character that need addressing or dramatic changes in work performance. Even improvements can be cause for concern as they can be indicative of a child who is escaping from a situation by throwing him/herself into work.

- It is important to tread extremely carefully when talking to a child you feel may be suffering a personal difficulty. Your school may have guidelines to follow, but if not, talk to the child's pastoral head before doing anything. They may know the family, or know how to approach the problem.
- Discuss the child with colleagues to establish whether others have noticed a change.
- Always get guidance from pastoral heads and tutors before asking to speak to the child's parents or carers.
- If you decide to approach the child directly, having spoken to colleagues, do so in a relatively light-hearted (but not flippant) way. Ask, in passing, if there is anything wrong. Avoid saying, 'I've noticed you haven't been yourself recently', as this may place the child under undue pressure to discuss private matters. Pave the way for the child to come and talk to you if they want to. You could say, 'You know where I am if you want anything, don't you?' Then keep a close, surreptitious eye on the child for a week or so before trying again if things have clearly not improved.

Helping versus interfering

Your memory will tell you that many childhood and teenage issues often resolve themselves with time. Once you have established with pupils that they can talk to you, or a colleague of the opposite sex, whenever they need to, further questioning could well be construed as interfering. Unless you suspect some form of abuse or neglect, in which case you *must* speak to the named person dealing with all child protection issues, take a back seat and observe for a while, so as to preserve the relationship you have already created with the child.

ABOUT

PUPILS GETTING PERSONAL

Contrary to the opinions of some educationalists, intimate relationships (or even discussions) between teachers and their pupils should *always* be avoided. They represent a gross misuse of a teacher's professional status.

However, there may be situations when a pupil involves you in an issue of a personal nature – perhaps they declare their undying love for you. It goes without saying that you must respect and accept what the pupil says, but don't attempt to deal with the situation alone. Protect yourself by referring the issue to the child's pastoral head or tutor and make sure when you speak to the pupil, you do so either when there are others present in the room (preferably a colleague) or in a public place where others may be passing through.

Tutoring

The system of tutoring delivered through tutor groups or houses is one way in which a school cares for its pupils.

Pastoral care should never be confused with discipline – in fact the two are quite separate. When you discipline a child you are reacting to their behaviour. Effective pastoral care is pro-active and responsive and cannot really be confined to the tutor group; especially in the primary sector, the roles of individuals as teachers and tutors are inseparable.

Chris Watkins, of the Institute of Education, defines tutoring as being 'that aspect of teaching which helps the learner develop personal, social and learning strategies and choices to make the most of themselves and get the most from the school and from later life'.

Most people can think of times when they have not felt nurtured. Maybe this was at school or college, perhaps being ignored in a shop or failing to have needs met in a relationship. Those times usually result in de-motivation, despondency, demoralisation, frustration and even anger. Using those memories to empathise with the tutees in your care makes it easier to understand the importance of meeting all the needs of pupils to ensure that they believe in their personal value to the school community.

Ideally, you will not be given a new form in your first year of teaching as problems can arise when both teacher and class are new. You may be a co-tutor in your NQT year but will almost certainly be a tutor in your own right in your second year. However, you are not expected to sink or swim. There will be a pastoral team for you to call on and even pastoral heads may bring in experts to deal with certain situations, e.g. bereavement counsellors or drugs-awareness experts.

This section is based on the assumption that Personal, Social and Health Education (PSHE) is provided for elsewhere in your school's curriculum. Tutoring is a feature of the 'Standards for the Award of Qualified Teacher Status' and the quality of tutoring offered by your school will be looked at during an OFSTED inspection.

YOUR ROLE AS A TUTOR

As a tutor, you are in an extremely powerful position. You can make (and break) a child's experience of school life through your care for, and interpretation of, the issues important to your tutees. Make sure you have been given all the relevant documentation regarding your job as a tutor. You could also get ideas from colleagues and select what you feel would suit your group. Seek help if there is any issue that you do not feel happy dealing with alone. There will be other members of staff to refer to for advice, for example the pastoral head, your mentor or the SENCO.

It is wise to take all opportunities to get to know the families of your tutees. In particular, be aware of those who do not live in nuclear families, and who the home caregivers are.

> *EXAMPLE: One NQT taught a boy who only had one leg, but it took him a year to realise this! Since then he has read all the information on his tutees carefully.*

Aspects of your role as a tutor

A tutor is at the very least all of these:

- inspirer/morale-booster
- listener
- counsellor
- communicator
- problem-solver
- administrator
- nurturer
- enabler
- monitor of academic progress
- monitor of social development
- manager of behaviour
- praise-giver
- motivator
- team-builder
- confidante.

Inspirer and morale-booster

There will be times when you will have to try to inject some enthusiasm into a demoralised group. Perhaps they are suffering under the pressure of exams, or have been reprimanded all morning for the poor behaviour of certain members of the group. Your role would be to draw the group together and boost morale sufficiently for the group to continue the day. Try to create a sense of enthusiasm for learning.

Listener

Listening is an important aspect of tutoring, and knowing how to listen is an essential skill. A pupil may simply want to express what they are feeling without the intervention of a problem-solver, or may want you to act in their defence. Your job is to know the difference, and that will only become evident through listening. Allow pupils to describe their emotions.

Counsellor

There will be many occasions when pupils need the skill and understanding of a counsellor. As an NQT you may not be qualified in counselling, but will certainly use some counselling skills. You can always refer to a professional for problems that you are not happy dealing with, such as a bereaved child.

Communicator

Not only will you have to relay messages from other members of staff, but you will also have to communicate your own requirements to your group. The way in which this is achieved will have an impact upon the tone of your group.

Problem-solver

Tutors often have to inject a sense of reality into fraught and emotional circumstances. Your job here is to find solutions to the problems that your tutees present that are acceptable to all involved. However, there may be times when you will have to be honest and say, 'I'm sorry, but I don't know the answer to that.' There's never any shame in this, as long as you find out the necessary answers – this could even be done as a group.

Administrator

Not only do you have a legal requirement to keep attendance records of your group, but you will also have to deal with all the administration related to your group, e.g. letters from parents explaining absence from school and other school business.

Nurturer

Being a nurturer involves boosting the self-esteem of all the pupils in your care – even the ones you simply cannot get on with. A tutor can help minimise what can be the cruelty of school life for a child by boosting their self-esteem. Those with high self-esteem can retain perspective under pressure and self-esteem is most likely to be nurtured when children are dealt with consistently. You will need to give tutees proof that they are gaining in competence and that you are genuinely interested in them.

Enabler

The role of enabler is closely linked to your nurturing roles and involves creating the circumstance in which your tutees can gain maximum benefit from their school life. You will enable them to succeed. You can also ensure that your tutees have the maximum opportunity to make informed decisions. However, be sure to educate rather than advise. Don't inflict your opinions – allow them to create their own against a backdrop of sound information. This links in with the current trend for schools to be pro-active as opposed to reactive when it comes to pastoral care.

Monitor of academic progress

As a tutor you are in the optimum position to track the academic progress of your pupils including monitoring the time they spend on homework etc. When it comes to reports and assessments your input is essential. In some schools parents are invited to speak to form tutors as well as subject teachers at parents' evenings.

Above all, you want to encourage your tutees to become reflective practitioners and observe for themselves what is at the heart of all their schoolwork – what common threads are there? Why are they doing what they are doing? You could ask them to talk about what they have learned and the processes they used to achieve a learning outcome. Create the environment in which it is safe for pupils to praise each other.

Monitor of social development

The time spent in tutor periods is likely to be when social development (or lack of it) is most apparent. The tutor's job is to monitor this to ensure that all pupils are given the opportunity to grow socially. Most children at some stage face difficult questions of identity such as 'Who am I?' or 'What am I?' They will have to develop self-knowledge, self-growth and the capacity to adapt to situations and go with the flow, not to mention rational autonomy and the understanding of the impact of the self upon others.

Pupils also have to develop the ability to be flexible and responsive to their environment, especially as they move through the school system and have to interact with increasing numbers of teachers and styles.

Manager of behaviour

There may be occasions when colleagues complain to you about the behaviour of a member of your group. While the colleague may have dealt with the misbehaviour, they may also look to you as a tutor to reinforce the standards that are expected. You will also have to keep

ABOUT

REPRIMANDING INDIVIDUALS

If you do have to reprimand an individual, it is imperative that the pupil understands why. What was their role? How did they personally contribute to the situation? Ask the child to explain exactly what happened and be open to the possibility of a misinterpretation of events, without expressing doubt at a colleague's understanding of what happened. Throughout your dealings with the child, think of ways of enabling him/her rather than pushing them into a corner. How can the child be guided to a solution? Encourage tutees to be honest about their feelings even if it does mean listening to, 'I hate Mr Boyd', so that you can seek to find ways of turning these negative emotions into positive ones. Whatever the outcome, it must allow for good working relationships to be re-established.

The best way around this sort of situation is to prepare for it in advance. Many teachers run 'What would you do if …?' sessions, which give pupils many ideas to draw on as and when the situation arises. This will enable tutees to express grievances constructively and deal with the outcome sensibly.

an eye on the general level of behaviour in your group and praise or reprimand as appropriate.

Praise-giver

An unfortunate fact of school life is that you are more likely to hear about the misdemeanours of your group than their successes. You should aim to praise the group as a whole and individuals as frequently as possible. Remember how good it feels to be on the receiving end of positive feedback. Help colleagues in this role by reporting to them the good behaviour of their groups.

Motivator

Whether it is coping with the mid-term blues or dealing with a defeat in the inter-form football contest, there are bound to be occasions when you will have to lighten the tone of your group and motivate your tutees.

Team-builder

The only way to create a class that is happy to work together co-operatively is to spend time team building. As a tutor, you are at the centre of your team. Talk together, encourage unity and emphasise group successes. For example, 'Mrs Evans said you worked very co-operatively in Art today – that's great to hear. What did you do?'

Confidante

There are likely to be situations when tutees confide in you. However, you do have legal obligations to look after the welfare of the children in your care. This may entail passing information on to other agencies if necessary, therefore you must never promise to keep secrets. A teacher cannot be bound by a pupil's request for total confidentiality.

Setting the tone of your group

Your personality will be the main factor controlling the tone of your tutor group. You can set your own rules and limits for your tutees, although involving older pupils in this can work extremely well.

DETECTING SIGNS OF ABUSE

Tutors are obliged, as part of their role as teachers in safeguarding children's welfare, to observe tutees for signs of neglect and abuse. Be aware of changes in behaviour such as increased aggression, withdrawal or over-dependence, as well as physical signs such as bruising etc.

Always follow your school's guidelines on dealing with suspected abuse. Never try to tackle this complex area alone.

Consider some of these points:

- If you are punctual, your pupils are more likely to be.
- Make the administration side of your tutoring duties slick and efficient. A stock of class lists will be extremely useful for keeping track of money collected etc.
- Place importance on preparation for the school day. Urge pupils to be fully equipped.
- Create routines and stick with them, for example, silence when the register is being taken, any notices to be read out immediately after the register has been taken etc.
- Encourage tidiness and pride in your room.
- Constantly reiterate the purpose of your role – you are there for your tutees.
- Encourage togetherness and celebrate differences.
- Strive for balance and fairness.

Maximising the opportunities of tutoring

Whatever the extent of your role as a tutor and the lessons you have to deliver, there are always methods of maximising the opportunities that tutoring presents:

- Use any spare time in tutor periods to chat to your class, whatever their age group. Treat it as 'circle time' – you can glean so much about your tutees, the way they work and what motivates them in this way. Just make sure that those who want to speak have the opportunity and that such chats are not dominated by the few.
- Create the opportunities for tutees to talk to you when they want to. Approachability is an important characteristic for a good tutor to have.
- Remember the finer details of your tutees' lives. Draw attention to birthdays (you could even give a card or small present) and celebrate the achievements of pupils in your group, as a group.
- Pay attention to your obligations to provide equality of opportunity for your pupils.
- Discuss the strengths and weaknesses of the group and devise strategies for improvement.
- Encourage a climate of openness.
- Never forget the role of the tutor in boosting self-esteem. You will probably find that this becomes a two-way process!

ABOUT

SYMPATHY

It is important not to mix sympathy and empathy. Too much sympathy can lead to draining emotional involvement and away from problem solving. It is usually best to keep the focus on finding solutions so that pupils don't fall into the habit of seeking sympathy from you for its own sake. Hearing the expression of sorrow or sympathy can become a prop for certain character types and there will come a day when you are no longer able to fulfil the sympathetic role. That leaves the pupil in a vulnerable position, no longer trusting of the relationship you have. Your role here is as a non-judgemental enabler.

GIVING PUPILS BAD NEWS

There may be occasions in your career when you have to break bad news to pupils. This can stretch the skills of the most experienced teachers. If you do need to break some bad news to a pupil, bear these points in mind:

- Arrange it that a colleague is with you when you break the bad news. This is particularly important, as the pupil will need some form of comfort.

- Try to detach yourself from what has happened and focus on the immediate needs of the pupil. You may need to arrange for the pupil to be taken somewhere.

- Make sure you know all the facts and try to answer the pupil's questions as honestly and tenderly as possible. Have tissues and a drink ready (but not open to see).

- Allow the child to express their emotional reaction as freely as possible.

- Think about how much you need to tell other pupils. Seek advice from your headteacher on what should be said and when.

- Keep track of pupils who may need follow-up care after a personal trauma.

- Be prepared for tutorial periods, as you would be for a lesson. Leave your subject behind and get to know your tutees as individuals. You should aim to have learning intentions for tutor periods as well as lessons.

- Liaise well with the co-ordinator of tutor groups in your year and also with the person in charge of personal and social education. If someone else is planning activities for you to do with your group, let them know if there was anything that worked particularly well, or anything that was a complete disaster.

- Know the line of pastoral authority in your school. You may need to seek help urgently to deal with a situation and should know exactly who to turn to.
- Ask your tutees what they would like to do or discuss. You could set some time aside each week or month to focus on their choices.

TUTORING FOLKLORE

'Remember that a man's name is to him the sweetest and most important sound in the English Language.' Dale Carnegie.

There is no doubt that sound tutoring is a skill that may come naturally to some teachers and not others. A great deal of your success in tutoring will come as a result of trial and error and it isn't possible to present a winning formula for this complicated task. However, you will pick up hints and tips from colleagues and books, which can inspire you into loving this aspect of teaching.

Ideas that have worked for others

Use these as inspiration, but don't feel under pressure to try them all!

- Take photographs of your tutees to put up on the wall. Pupils could add to the gallery photographs of sporting achievements or school trips etc.
- At the start of the school year, ask your group to write down their hopes and fears for the year/term. Store their ideas away and review them at the end of this period. This is a particularly good exercise to use to illustrate the personal development of your pupils over time.
- Keep a folder for each member of the group in which they can record the work done in tutorial periods.
- Some tutors keep their own records of their tutees in addition to the school records. These can be useful in monitoring progress over the year and for report writing. They also help for reference writing. These records should be considered confidential. You could also include references made to your group by other teachers.

- Encourage your pupils to help you to settle in to your new school (providing they aren't new as well). Ask them about the school and its history etc. Try not to get drawn into discussions about other members of staff – this is inevitable, but remain professional.
- Create a list of discussion topics that pupils can choose from for specific purposes. These could include just about anything from smoking, citizenship or rites of passage to animals, music or body language. Involve pupils in this process.
- Organise cards and/or presents from the group for your cleaner – certainly at Christmas time, but also at the end of each term would be nice. This encourages pupils to be more responsible for their actions as they become aware of the thanking process and why this needs to be done.
- Some tutors like to split their tutor groups into smaller 'care' groups. These groups can be responsible for making the room tidy at the end of each day, or doing any 'housework' tasks that need to be done. This encourages pride in the group's immediate surroundings, while ensuring the work is done on a rotation basis.
- End-of-term parties are relatively easy to organise yet will mark important transitions for you and your group. You would have to check this out with the powers that be in your school, but it may be possible to organise some food and drinks as well, perhaps with small contributions from your pupils. Be sensitive towards anyone who does not celebrate Christmas and Easter – it can be better to simply celebrate the end of the term or year.
- Ask pupils to write a 'this is me' letter to include details like where they live, who lives with them, likes and dislikes, hopes, fears and aspirations etc.
- Gain as much experience as possible. Observe other tutors in action and talk about ways of adding to your tutoring skills.
- Give pupils an inspirational quote as thought for the day/week.
- Encourage ongoing tournaments perhaps with cards, a computer game or scrabble etc.
- Work as a group to solve problems. For example, if the group is not responding to a particular teacher, work together to devise ways of remedying the situation.

ABOUT

CHILD BULLYING

This is a hugely important aspect of school life – too great to deal with here in detail. Research indicates that over 50% of pupils experience bullying at school at some stage and the 'Standards for the Award of Qualified Teacher Status' state that teachers should, 'understand their professional responsibilities in relation to school policies and practices, including those concerned with pastoral and personal safety matters, including bullying.' Make sure that you read your school's policy on dealing with child bullying and any advice that is issued by your LEA. Talk to teachers who have tackled bullying in the past about techniques that have proved successful. It is also worth reading some of the excellent books on bullying (see Appendix 8) and discussing the issue regularly with your tutor group. You could devise a role-play or encourage your class to talk openly about bullying they have witnessed. Taking time to look at language, how it is used and how it can be misinterpreted also leads to a greater understanding of bullying situations. Try to encourage pupils to view the bullying from both sides, therefore developing skills of empathy with all involved.

- You could give pupils something to think about while you call the register. For example, something they learned that day, something that would improve their achievement, someone they would like to thank, the best thing they did that morning, someone they need to apologise to etc. Do, however, make sure you allow time for a quick feedback.
- Always explain to your tutees why you are doing something. If you can't do that, the process or procedure doesn't need doing.
- Reassure colleagues that you will deal with their complaints of any member of your group. Both teachers and pupils have to believe that teachers are united.

- Some tutors write to their tutees' parents at the start of the year to introduce themselves. This is also a good opportunity to express your hopes for the group and explain the best way for parents and carers to contact you. Not only does this put you in control of the demands made of you, but also it establishes, from the start, lines of communication. Do get clearance from the pastoral heads first, before going ahead and sending letters home – there are still some schools out there that believe a teacher must reach at least the age of 45 before having direct contact with the outside world!
- Observe your group while they are being taught by another teacher.
- Consider how you might use peer-tutoring. This is becoming increasingly popular both overseas and in the UK.

Homework strategies

Your school should have a clear homework policy outlining how much homework should be given to each class, and how frequently it should be given. At best, this will be written into schemes of work, making the setting of homework relatively painless for new teachers. At worst, common practice in your school will be to yell out the homework at the backs of departing pupils as they rapidly disappear into the corridor!

The notion of homework suffers from the hugely differing interpretations of what constitutes good practice. The line from the DfEE is that homework is not an 'optional extra', but is an 'essential' part of a child's work.

If you do have an element of freedom in the way you set homework it is worth regularly affirming to pupils and parents your commitment to setting meaningful homework. This tends to create a positive homework ethos that you can build on.

When OFSTED inspectors visit your school they will look at how homework is used as an effective part of your lessons. While the actual work you set is important, you also need to consider such issues as how you will collect in the work. Do you have a space on a table for pupils to deposit books, do you ask a pupil to collect them or will you walk round the class, marking off in your register when you collect a book? Establish firm routines with your classes so that

ABOUT

SETTING APPROPRIATE HOMEWORK

Ask yourself these questions when you are planning and setting homework:

- Does it have a place in my scheme of work?
- Can pupils make use of libraries and study centres?
- Is it fair in length and context?
- Have I differentiated?
- Does the task discriminate in any way?
- Does the homework vary in length and nature?
- Does the class have access to the relevant information?
- Can the homework lead to pupil achievement?
- Am I encouraging motivation in pupils?
- Can pupils derive from the work set what I want them to?
- Do pupils know what my learning intentions and assessment criteria are?
- Can my pupils value the work set?
- Am I forging links between school and home?
- Can I ascertain whether the homework has been completed?
- Do pupils know I will follow homework up?
- Is my focus on quality (as it should be) or quantity?

everyone knows your arrangements (which, incidentally, should be mutually helpful).

The OFSTED study, *Homework: Learning from Practice*,[3] identifies the various dimensions of homework and these are listed in the table 'Aspects of Homework'.

Throughout any topic you should aim to set a variety of homework tasks, without relying on any one dimension.

GETTING WHAT YOU WANT FROM A TASK

Homework that is hastily set is unlikely to produce the results you want. If you have placed the task within a scheme of work and your pupils know the context of what they have been asked to do, the chances of getting what you want from a particular task are much greater. Basically, the only way to get what you want is to know what you want.

- Have homework tasks pre-prepared on sheets of paper or written on the board.

- Allow plenty of time at the end of a lesson to explain the homework. You need to make sure that pupils have written down the details of the task, when it is due in and how it should be completed.

- Never explain the task while pupils are copying into their books. Wait until they have all finished reading and writing and then explain.

- Ask pupils to explain to you what their task is.

- Make sure every child has the resources to complete the task. Ask your SEN department to help differentiate the work you want to set.

Utilising the homework notion

The best way to ensure that your classes actually complete the homework tasks you set is regularly to reiterate the value of independent study at home. You could also explain to your classes a few general tasks that they could do as homework in the event of your absence. Make sure you keep a stock of such tasks and that pupils

ASPECTS OF HOMEWORK

(from *Homework: Learning from Practice*)

Completion	*versus*	**Preparation**
Finishing off class work, 'catching up', following up what has been done in class		Reading around new unit/text, research for project, learning new terms
Reinforcement	*versus*	**Research**
Practice exercises, learning, revising		Information retrieval, from school or home sources
Written work	*versus*	**Other modes**
Essays, notes, compositions, exercises, diagrams		Reading, oral inquiry, practical work, drawing, painting
Time-limited	*versus*	**Open-ended**
For example, an exercise timed to last 20 minutes – a set of ten spellings		For example, a 'research task', TV review or practical design
Direct parent involvement	*versus*	**Pupil independence encouraged**
For example, parent reading with/to child		For example, year 6 pupils, preparing for secondary school, parental encouragement only
School resources only	*versus*	**Non-school resources important**
Homework can be completed with text book or other school-supplied materials only		Pupils encouraged/expected to use materials from libraries, homes and family members' experience
'Over-night' task	*versus*	**Longer-term task**
Short-term task to be completed in one homework session		Homework used to contribute to progress of ongoing topic

know the circumstances in which they should complete them. They could even have them written down in the back of their exercise books or homework diaries and you could nominate someone from the class to inform the cover teacher which task should be done. Although it is harder to place such tasks in the context of current work, this does give pupils an element of choice and responsibility over their work. Tell other members of staff about your system. They will know what to expect if they have to cover your classes and may even want to adopt your idea.

Homework is another opportunity to do some positive PR for your school. View the tasks you set through the eyes of parents. Are they varied and relevant? Are the books that go home in good condition? Can parents easily discern the purpose of a task?

ABOUT

SETTING 'WEAK' HOMEWORK

There are bound to be occasions when you have to think on the hoof as far as homework is concerned. Obviously this is not going to be a problem if it only occurs once or twice, but if classes get the impression that homework is not a priority for you, it certainly won't be for them. Try and ensure that the tasks you set will be useful in furthering or consolidating knowledge.

Avoid giving homework tasks connected to your subject or class work as a punishment. You run the risk of putting the child off your subject forever. Punitive tasks should be complete in their own right.

Be reasonable in your homework expectations. Just like you, your pupils have lives outside school.

EXCUSES

Throughout the course of your career you will hear some of the most amazing excuses for non-completion of homework. Make your homework tasks excuse-proof by following these ideas:

- Be consistent with your sanctions for homework not completed. Giving the benefit of the doubt once is just about permissible but certainly no more. It would be a good idea to discuss with the pupil what the problems may be.
- Explain tasks carefully and slowly and offer your class the opportunity to talk to you about the task at a later stage if necessary.
- Create routines for the setting and collection of homework for each class. Have homework days.
- Make the reason for the homework clear. If pupils know the relevance of what they have to do they are more likely to do it.
- Where appropriate, explain to pupils the assessment criteria you will use.
- Think of how tutors can help you create good attitudes towards homework in pupils.

You will need to discuss with persistent offenders exactly what the problems may be. Explain what your expectations are and what the shortfall is. It may be appropriate to adapt homework tasks or to work with the child after school for a while.

One teacher posted this to the uk.education.staffroom newsgroup:

'My all time favourite reply to the question, "Where is your homework?" is: "My book is covered with banana but it's being wiped today." Top that!'

MARKING STRATEGIES

The whole point of homework is that pupils work independently at home, or at least outside school hours. An unfortunate by-product of this arrangement is the amount of marking that this can generate for teachers.

Once you have decided whether your marking of a piece of work will be summative, formative or diagnostic, there are a number of strategies you can employ to cope with the burden:

- Create tasks that can be self-marked or peer-marked in class.
- Set some non-written homework.
- Pace your homework setting so that you don't have hundreds of projects to mark at the same time. It can take a while to get into the rhythm of a term but homework is one area of teaching you can control.

ABOUT

GATHERING GOOD IDEAS

Keep a record of all the homework tasks you have set for each scheme of work. These will probably be suitable for future use and you can adapt them on the basis of previous evaluations on their effectiveness. You could even ask pupils what homework tasks they have enjoyed and have found inspiring.

- Plan homework setting to complement your energy levels. There's little point in arranging piles of marking when you know you are coming down with a cold.
- Think about how you can create tasks requiring short answers. Some subjects lend themselves to this more easily than others. However, you should not rely on short-answer questions too heavily, in any subject.

- Have your marking criteria and the task set in front of you as you work through the books, for quick reference.
- Set a time limit for marking a set of work and stick to it. Minimise distractions and *focus*. Perhaps introduce an element of surprise by using different coloured inks – do you always want to use red?
- Find out if there are any possibilities of help with marking from your department or year colleagues.

Penelope Weston's book, *Homework: Learning from Practice,* summarises indicators of good practice in homework in both primary schools and secondary schools. These are reproduced in the list below and overleaf.

INDICATORS OF GOOD PRACTICE

Primary schools

Giving a lead
- Homework policy is led and co-ordinated by a senior manager.
- Staff and parents are actively involved in all aspects of the programme.

Developing and disseminating policy
- There is a written policy, developed consensually with staff and parents; the consultation process has taken time and reflected the local and school context.
- A range of approaches is used to continue to convey the ideas in the policy, including guidelines for pupils and parents, workshops and newsletters.

Managing time
- Homework allocations are clearly set out, probably in the form of a weekly and termly schedule setting out what work is due and when, and indicating an estimated time for tasks.
- Homework is structured to help pupils (with parental support) to develop regular study patterns they can manage.

Motivating pupils

- Pupils are encouraged to complete their work by regular feedback, praise and rewards for effort.
- Requirements are made clear to parents, and their support is enlisted so that homework is completed.
- Sanctions for non-completion are clear, but seldom need to be enforced.
- Failure to do homework is investigated before sanctions are applied.

Providing resources

- The school supports teachers by providing commercial resources or time and materials to prepare resources.
- Opportunities are taken to offer pupils additional resources where possible, e.g. access to computers or library books.

Reviewing performance

- Learning goals are defined for homework and teachers evaluate whether the tasks set are meeting these goals.
- There are systematic procedures for monitoring how programme requirements are being fulfilled by staff and pupils, and how the programme meets their needs.
- The policy itself is regularly and fully reviewed against school development goals.

Secondary schools

Giving a lead

- Homework policy is led and co-ordinated by a senior manager.
- Other managers share the responsibility of planning and review.

Developing and disseminating policy

- There is a written whole-school policy, with common criteria for department policies.
- A range of approaches is used to continue to convey the ideas in the policy, including guidelines for staff, pupils and parents.

Managing time

- Homework allocations are clearly set out, probably in a homework timetable which is clear to parents and pupils and adhered to by staff.
- Deadlines for completing tasks are explicit and manageable.
- Homework is structured to help pupils to develop regular study patterns they can manage.

Motivating pupils

- Pupils are encouraged to complete their work by regular feedback, praise and rewards for effort.
- Requirements are made clear to parents, and their support is enlisted so that homework is completed.
- Sanctions for non-completion are clear and consistent, but seldom need to be enforced.
- Failure to do homework is investigated before sanctions are applied.

Providing resources

- The school enables staff to buy or prepare appropriate resources.
- Opportunities are taken to offer pupils additional resources where possible, e.g. access to computers or the resource centre.

Reviewing performance

- Learning goals are defined for homework and teachers evaluate whether the tasks set are meeting these goals.
- There are systematic procedures for monitoring how programme requirements are being fulfilled by staff and pupils, and how the programme meets their needs.
- The policy itself is regularly and fully reviewed against school development goals.

First aid in the classroom – pleasure or pain?

'Accidents will occur in the best-regulated families.' Charles Dickens.

Without being too dramatic, your ability to administer first aid can mean the difference between life and death. Quick action to help a child suffering a health crisis will greatly ease his/her distress and the physical trauma suffered.

Individual schools and LEAs will have developed their own procedures regarding first aid and the administering of medicines so make sure you have been appropriately informed (you should never be *directed* to give a child medicine). While responsibility for first aid will rest with the qualified first-aiders and 'appointed persons' in your school (know who they are and where they can be found at any time), knowing what to do in certain circumstances will add to your confidence in the classroom. As a teacher you are not obliged to give first aid, but you are expected to do your best for the welfare of a child according to the DfEE document, 'Guidance on First Aid for Schools'.

- Do find out as soon as possible if you are indemnified in the event of any claim of negligence made against you. Your employer (LEA for county schools and governing body for voluntary-aided schools) will be able to confirm this in writing for you. Also find out if assisting with any form of medical procedure comes under the scope of your employment.

- You may consider obtaining a first aid qualification yourself – courses are run by the British Red Cross, St John Ambulance and sometimes by LEAs. Becoming a first-aider should be undertaken on a strictly voluntary basis. Under no circumstances should you ever be persuaded or 'encouraged' to take this on.

- If you do decide to volunteer to undertake first aid training, your employer should provide it.

- According to the *Dorling Kindersley First Aid Manual*,[4] an important rule of first aid is 'First do no harm'. Bear this is mind when looking after a child, and be aware of your limitations. If for example the sight of blood really does cause you to pass out, you need to get someone else to deal with the situation immediately so there aren't two casualties in the classroom. A copy of the *Dorling Kindersley First Aid Manual* will probably be available in every school – if not, treat yourself to a copy to keep in your classroom.

- It goes without saying that you *must* protect yourself at all times. If you have to deal with a child's body fluids in any way, *always* wear protective gloves. It's a good idea to keep a pair handy, but remember to throw them away and replace them after use.

- If there is a medical emergency while you are teaching, consider the rest of the class. There may be pupils who are shocked or affected in some way and it could be necessary to clear the room of everyone except the casualty. A teacher in a neighbouring classroom should be able to help you out here. This will also help to protect the dignity of the casualty.

- Remember to follow your school's regulations on reporting accidents and incidents.

- You may feel perfectly calm and able to cope while you are dealing with a situation, but be prepared for a possible reaction afterwards. You may need to nurture yourself a little after the event.

TYPICAL CHILDHOOD AILMENTS

There are a number of medical situations you could encounter in your classroom. The following advice is designed to give basic information and is not a replacement for qualified medical advice, which you should seek at the earliest opportunity. Send a child to the school office with a request for immediate first aid assistance, so that you don't have to leave the casualty.

Accident injuries

Depending on what subject and age range you teach you could encounter varying degrees of injuries from accidents that have happened in your classroom. The first thing to remember is that accidents do happen. There is usually little reason to blame yourself for an accident that has happened to a child in your care, as long as you are aware of basic accident prevention.

Bleeding

With gloved hands, apply pressure to the wound. Take great care if an object is embedded in it – you may only be able to raise the wound so that it is above the child's heart. Wait for help to arrive – a first-aider should do any bandaging or call for an ambulance if necessary.

Broken bones

While you are waiting for help, simply protect the injury site from further damage. Don't forget to reassure the child, who could be in great pain. You could talk the child through a visualisation of a peaceful scene to prevent panic setting in. Only move the child with the help of a qualified first-aider.

Eye injuries

Personal experience will probably tell you how excruciatingly painful an eye injury can be. Immediate medical assistance is required for anything more serious than simply dust or grit in the eye – use your discretion. You may need to comfort the child who should be sitting still. The child will probably be protecting the site of the injury with his or her hand – this is fine as long as they do not apply pressure.

Head injuries

If the child is bleeding, apply the same advice as given above. It is possible that the child may be suffering concussion, the symptoms of which may not become evident immediately. For this reason, a doctor must see a child who has suffered a head injury as soon as possible. Confusion, vomiting, sleepiness and uncharacteristic aggression are all signs of concussion.

Anaphylactic shock

Anaphylactic shock is a severe allergic reaction to a particular substance. This could typically be a bee sting, nuts or drugs, or anything that the particular individual happens to be allergic to. The onset of symptoms, such as increasing difficulty breathing, tends to be rapid and they require immediate medical attention. Sit the child some-

ACCIDENT PREVENTION

Some areas of a school are potentially more hazardous than others, such as science rooms, technology rooms and workshops. However, all classrooms present potential risks, so taking these steps could reduce the possibility of an accident taking place in your room:

- Take a look round your classroom regularly throughout the day to make sure there are no obvious hazards such as chairs out of place or broken furniture.
- Make sure the windows in your room are all safe, that the catches work and there is no cracked or broken glass. If necessary, make the window area a pupil-free zone.
- Check your room for leaks. One teacher had to spend a lesson that was being observed by an OFSTED inspector finding suitable receptacles for rainwater that was dripping through the ceiling on to her guest.
- Check the furniture in your room regularly for damage, cracks and splinters. Ask your classes to inform you of broken items.
- Make sure any necessary repairs are carried out promptly. You may have to remind the powers that be about what needs doing.
- Be strict about the way pupils enter and leave your room. Bundles can quickly become dangerous. Also be firm about the way pupils move around the classroom.
- Make sure pupils' bags are safely stowed away during lessons. Many a teacher has tripped on stray bag straps as they move around the room to work with children.
- Be strict about food consumption in your room. Children who are trying to surreptitiously chew gum or suck sweets are more likely to choke.
- Check that any leads and wiring in your room are safe. If you are not sure, ask a colleague to check for you.

where quiet and try to stop them from panicking while you wait for help. The child may carry adrenaline (if known to have an allergy) which can be administered either by the child or a suitably qualified adult. Don't be fazed by the speed with which the child's condition may deteriorate. This is usual under the circumstances and can be corrected if the right medical assistance is given in good time.

Asthma

Children known to be asthmatics should know what to do in the event of an attack. Many will have their own inhalers which they can administer themselves. It is essential to call for immediate assistance and while you wait encourage the child to sit upright as this eases breathing. Do not put your arm around their shoulders but offer verbal reassurance instead. The child may naturally place his or her arms up on a table; this is a natural reflex that also aids breathing. Try to encourage the child to breathe in through their nose and out slowly through their mouth. This helps to prevent hyperventilation.

Choking

This is a difficult situation to deal with unless you are a fully qualified first-aider. The only safe thing for you to do is to look for any obvious obstruction in the child's mouth that could easily be hooked out with a finger. Medical assistance is urgently required.

Diabetes

Many people suffer sudden drops in blood sugar and will recognise the urgency for food that this causes. In normal circumstances, blood sugar can be regulated by eating something sweet but in diabetics, treatment can be more complicated, and the fluctuations in blood sugar more dramatic. The child may also suffer from sweating, shaking and loss of concentration. Your role, having called for assistance, should be to support the child's needs. Allow them to eat immediately, regardless of any rules about food in the classroom.

Epilepsy

You should have been informed of any children in your classes known to suffer from epilepsy, but remember a child's first fit may occur in your classroom. There are different classifications of fits, some more severe than others. Minor fits may simply involve temporary losses of concentration, in which case you may need to repeat instructions to a sufferer or offer some reassurance. However, in the case of a serious fit, after calling for assistance, you need to ensure that the area around the child is cleared of any potentially dangerous objects. Lay the child on their side and watch for any changes in their colour or choking. Try to protect the child's head but do not restrict their movement in any way. Talk reassuringly to the child throughout the whole fit as this is thought to ease anxiety. It may be essential to clear the other children from the room, as a fit can be frightening to witness and embarrassing for the sufferer on recovery as it is common to be incontinent during a fit.

Fainting

Children can faint for a variety of reasons. For some, simply standing for an extended period of time will be enough to bring on a faint. There is usually little warning of an impending faint and the first you may know is when a child hits the deck! If this is the case, place something soft under their head, raise their feet above the level of their heart and talk reassuringly as they come round. They may be confused or disorientated. After a faint a child should be encouraged to drink water, eat something and rest until they feel fully recovered. Medical assistance should be sought, as fainting can be a symptom requiring further investigation. If a child reports feeling faint, place their head between their knees and talk reassuringly until the feeling has passed.

Nosebleeds

These are relatively common in children as receiving a hit on the nose or blowing and picking the nose can bring them on. Often nose bleeds are slight and do not require any intervention. However, if the bleeding shows no sign of abating, place the child's head in a forward position and pinch the fleshy part of the nose (not the bridge). Take every precaution to protect yourself.

Period pains

Period pain can be severe in some adolescent girls and it can be mistaken for other ailments such as appendicitis. A girl suffering from excessive period pain should be encouraged to seek medical assistance as it could be indicative of an underlying condition. This situation needs to be treated with sensitivity particularly because the girl may not want to reveal why she feels unwell. For this reason it would be sensible to enable the girl to spend some time away from the class, perhaps doing some work in an office or sick room. A qualified first-aider may decide to send the child home where painkillers can be administered.

Vomiting

Hopefully the child will have given you plenty of warning of feeling sick, but this is not always the case. If a child vomits in your classroom you need to arrange for it to be cleaned up as soon as possible. Usually the caretaker has this enviable task! If possible, cordon off the area. In the meantime do your best to clean the child's face and reassure him or her that all is well. A first-aider will probably suggest that the child goes home. In any case, arrange for the child to have a glass of water if they feel they could manage this and to change their clothes if they are soiled.

1   Charles, C. M. (1995). *Building Classroom Discipline*. Longman.
2   Worthing High School is an 'Investors-in-People' school.
3   Weston, P. (1999). *Homework: Learning from Practice*. The Stationery Office, London.
4   *Dorling Kindersley First Aid Manual* (7th edition) (1999). Dorling Kindersley, London.

CHAPTER 4

Managing the job

Coping with meetings

Part of the bureaucratic burden of teaching is attending numerous meetings. In fact, the end of your teaching day is only half the story for most teachers, not least NQTs.

You may be asked to attend any or all of the following:

- full staff meetings
- induction tutor/mentor and advisor meetings
- year or department meetings
- union meetings/briefings
- planning meetings
- SEN meetings
- ICT meetings
- PTA meetings
- special events meetings.

You will also have informal meetings about your day-to-day planning and progress. For some this could amount to many meetings each week, requiring preparation and follow-up.

The DfEE Circular, 2/98, 'Reducing the Bureaucratic Burden on Teachers', sets out guidance for schools to follow in an attempt to reduce the non-teaching commitments of staff members. The circular states that:

Well-run meetings are essential to the internal management and communications of a school. Schools need to have flexibility to determine the pattern and number of meetings. Those are matters for sensible professional judgement. But schools do need to establish a pattern of meetings which is fully justified.

All schools should regularly review the number and quality of their meetings, and should assess their existing practice against the following considerations:

- *only hold meetings when they are justified and cancel unnecessary ones*
- *circulate agendas and papers in good time*
- *set time limits and stick to them*
- *ensure meetings are effectively chaired*
- *always set a clear purpose for a meeting*
- *encourage and take account of all points of view while guiding the meeting to definite conclusions*
- *communicate the conclusions to all with an interest*
- *ensure effective action is taken as a result.*

As schools differ so greatly in their organisation and administration, NQTs can have very different experiences of meetings. In order to maximise their use consider these points:

- If you are unable to discern the relevance of a meeting, ask its organiser if you need to attend. If you can't contribute to, or learn from a meeting, there is little point in attending.
- Make sure you know the purpose of the meeting.

- Send your apologies if you are unable to attend.
- Be particularly aware of any items on the agenda that directly relate to you or your classes.
- Ask for clarification on any aspect of the meeting that you don't understand, although the chair should have ensured that there was no possibility for confusion. If you allow jargon to whiz over your head, the crux of the discussion could pass you by.
- Plan in advance any input you would like to have. Perhaps you could prepare some questions to ask or comments to refer to. Be clear and succinct in your speech and make sure you stick to the point. Try not to feel intimidated and don't be put off asking questions; it's only by questioning that progress through dogma can be made.
- If you feel the chair is being manipulative or dominating, keep your tone of voice consistent and maintain eye contact with calm assertion.

ORGANISING THE INFORMATION YOU NEED

Attending meetings invariably means gathering a small forest's worth of paper. Avoid information overload by:

- assessing what is relevant to you while you are in the meeting
- using highlighter pens to colour code what needs immediate action, what can wait and what can be thrown away
- sticking to a rigid filing system. For each piece of paper that comes into your possession, you have only three options; file immediately for future reference, act on it immediately or destroy it (you could consider scanning important documents into a computer to cut down on storage space – this also allows you to 'manage' documents more efficiently)
- creating a 'recycle bin' for documents you cannot bring yourself to file or destroy – make sure you empty this bin regularly.

If a meeting results in you having a task to perform, make sure you have been given the means by which to achieve it, i.e. time and resources. Any deadlines must be realistic.

Minutes

You should be given the minutes a few days after the meeting. Once you have read them, mention anything you disagree with to the person who produced them. Be especially vigilant if you are quoted. If you feel that an important matter has been omitted from the minutes, raise this as soon as possible. If necessary, you can have it recorded that you disagree with the minutes when they are discussed at the next meeting.

If you would like to have something included on the next agenda, ask the chair of the meeting. You may not be successful, but your request should at least be heard and discussed.

Time management

'If it weren't for the last minute, nothing would get done.' Anon.

Few professions rely on effective time management and awareness quite as much as teaching. As an NQT, it would be helpful to think of effective time management as a way of enabling you to live a full life outside your work – a life that allows for relaxation and rest as well as hobbies and relationships. It is not a way of creating time to do more work or of managing crises.

ACTION: Think about your relationship with time. Do you have enough time to complete the tasks you want to complete, or are you always running against the clock? Are you in control, or does time control you?

In order to develop time management skills, you need to become *aware* of time. Teachers often suffer from time 'poverty' – too much to do in the time available. Added to this is the fact that, as an NQT, you are less likely to be in a position to delegate your tasks and, often, jobs will be delegated to you.

PACING YOURSELF

Working in such a structured environment, it is important for teachers to pace themselves, not only on a daily basis, but on a termly and yearly basis as well. Just as each day has its own rhythm, so does each term and year. Therefore, your targets for a day, term and year need to be realistic and take into account rhythms and fluctuations. If you tend to collapse after pressured times with exhaustion or some other ailment, you are clearly not pacing yourself.

- First look at the calendar for the whole year and write down anything that applies to you. For example, parents' evenings, reports etc. This will give you an initial picture of the busy times of the year.
- Then look at the term – where do your biggest commitments fall? Do you have extra departmental or curriculum work, for example writing exams or schemes of work to do? This will give you the basic shape of the term. Pinpoint the very busy times when other aspects of your job like marking and preparation will have to be minimised. Aim to ease your workload at these times. Lean on pre-prepared work and take opportunities for pupils to self-assess.
- Next, look at the rhythms of your week. Do you have any nightmarish days? Where are your opportunities to catch up on administration and marking?
- Throughout each day, get to know the times when you work most efficiently. If you suffer from a 4 pm low, don't attempt to work. The aim is to maximise productivity at productive times. It is simply a waste of time to attempt to work at the same pace all through the day. It is better to rest, or turn your attentions to other things rather than work unproductively.

Once you have established the rhythm of your days, aim to give yourself treats at low points of the day, term and year. Perhaps plan a weekend away mid-term or spend some time indulging your interests. Planning is an essential part of this process as anticipation and excitement are part of the enjoyment.

- When you are working slowly, don't punish yourself. Recognise it as a part of your natural rhythms and energy levels.
- Taking on piles of work will not add to your feelings of self-worth and esteem, but will add to your stress and anxiety levels.
- When you feel yourself working at a pace that is uncomfortable, slow down, regardless of any deadlines.
- Learn to know when to stop working on a project. There will be an optimum time to let it go.

Prioritising

Rather than attempting to work through each task as it comes to you, manage the time you have by prioritising. This means allowing yourself the time to *think* before launching into work. For every job ask yourself, does this *need* to be done? If the answer is yes, assess its importance as being:

- high
- moderate
- low.

Another question to ask is, 'Will this make life easier?' For example, spending time sorting through a pile of papers may be beneficial if it means you are now more organised. It is worth accepting at the start of your career that reaching the end of your list is highly unlikely!

> *EXAMPLE: One deputy head had learnt not to do anything his headteacher asked for only once. If something really needed doing, he would ask two or three times. An easy way to prioritise!*

It is best to go through the prioritising process as soon as you can so that jobs don't pile up. Once you have done this, you have created a 'to do' list that takes account of any deadlines and can be worked through systematically. If you find yourself getting behind, either knock something off your list, or seek help. This is sensible and, at times, vital. Aim to empty your pigeonhole daily and respond to memos or phone calls as soon as possible.

Prioritising should not just be done in relation to work. Sometimes you will have to put your private life above work if you are to remain an effective teacher. In his book, *Time Shifting*,[1] Stephan Rechtschaffen writes about the 'trickle down' approach to time. He explains that, generally, we place our work first, followed by our primary relationship/family, then our everyday chores, then social life and finally ourselves – if there is any time left. We tend to neglect the bottom of the list upwards, so if you find you're neglecting your social life, alarm bells should be sounding. If you find it hard to devote time to your primary relationships, your work really is dominating beyond reason.

MANAGING YOUR PREPARATION AND PLANNING

Preparation and planning, in combination with the resulting marking, make huge demands on your time.

- Take as much help as possible. If your department has a successful scheme of work for a topic, use it. If a textbook covers a topic well, use it rather than create your own worksheets. Only produce a scheme of work yourself when you have time. You may even be given some (extra) non-contact hours for the purpose.

- Don't feel inadequate if you are only one step ahead of the class – it doesn't matter. However, if you can get a little ahead of yourself, you will relieve some of the pressure to plan every night.

- When you are planning for one lesson, see if there are ways of planning for two, three or four lessons at the same time. Block planning in this way helps to relieve pressure.

- Don't spend time filling in lesson plans unless this is your way of record keeping. For most teachers, keeping track of plans in a teacher's organiser (usually given out free at the start of the autumn term) is sufficient, as there is space to record the contents of the lesson as well as any homework set.

- Talk to colleagues and your induction tutor/mentor about your preparation and marking. Are you overdoing it? Do they know any shortcuts you could be taking? Do you know when to stop?

- If, through your experience this year, you can see ways of saving time next time you plan and teach the topic, write them down.
- Keep good records of all your planning and preparation for the next time you cover the topic.

Working at optimum levels

'Some people can stay longer in one hour than others can in one week.' William Dean Howells.

Beware the law of diminishing returns. You will have an optimum level at which you can work effectively. Go beyond that level and you risk wasting your time and wearing yourself out. If your working hours are so long that you have to force yourself out of bed in the mornings, ask yourself what it is that you hope to teach your pupils? If you feel depressed about your work, it is likely that you are not working at an optimal level and it is essential that you reduce the hours you work before you burn out.

Working fewer hours does not mean that you get less done; just that the time you spend working is probably more productive. When you decide to work, focus on what you are doing. Minimise all distractions; better to do that for one hour and complete your task than spend three hours unfocused and still not finish what you have to do.

- Establish what it is you like to do and aim to spend time on that. For example, if you enjoy designing worksheets, create that job for yourself. Perhaps others in your department will tackle some of the tasks you don't relish.
- Take opportunities throughout the day to get work done. Your class may be needed for sport or music practice etc.
- Delegate as much as possible. If your school has reprographics staff, let them perform that aspect of your job. Fully utilise non-teaching assistants.
- Time your tasks, but be realistic with your deadlines. Giving yourself a specific time limit to complete a task is far more likely to result in success.

ENCOURAGING YOURSELF TO WORK AT YOUR OPTIMUM LEVEL

If you suspect you are not working at a pace that is good for you, think about these questions:

Do I avoid beginning tasks because it all seems like too much?

Do I allow myself time to plan what needs to be done?

Do I spend time on tasks that are not essential?

Do I allow myself to be interrupted by colleagues and pupils?

Do I help others to achieve tasks at the expense of my own work?

Do I view deadlines as constructive encouragement or a source of unparalleled stress?

Do I struggle with tasks that could or should be done by someone else?

Do I underestimate how long something will take me?

If you answered yes to some or all of these questions, take the opportunity to discuss time management and awareness with your induction tutor/mentor at your next meeting. It may be a gradual process, but time management does get easier as your confidence and experience grows. Don't, however, give yourself a hard time!

- Try to avoid feeling pressurised into working at the perceived pace of others around you.
- Do you have time-wasting habits or inefficiencies? Try to develop a conscious awareness when you work and assess how efficient you are.
- Take regular breaks from intense work like exam marking.
- Buddhists practise 'mindfulness'. This means being aware of the present moment, of what you are doing and how you are doing it. This is quite the opposite of doing A while thinking of B and C. Practising mindfulness tends to have the effect of apparently expanding time.

BALANCING WORK WITH YOUR HOME LIFE

'The intellect of man is forced to choose
Perfection of the life, or of the work.' W. B. Yeats.

'Personal relations are the important thing for ever and ever, and
not this outer life of telegrams and anger.' E. M. Forster.

Balancing work and home life is an extremely difficult skill, and one which many teachers never quite master. This is mostly due to the extent to which school work encroaches on the evening. The irony is that evidence seems to suggest that teachers who can maintain a work/home balance tend to be more effective in the classroom, not to mention more enthusiastic about their job. Teachers most profoundly affected tend to be those who live alone as there is no one to say, 'Stop working now, it's 11.30. Why don't you relax for a while?' or 'Can I help you with anything?'

The key word is flexibility. It would be ideal if you were more than a day ahead of yourself, as this would enable you to take an evening off at short notice. However, the teacher who can avoid working at home at all is rarer than a heat wave at Christmas.

That said, there are going to be times when you will have to focus more intently on work after school – perhaps just before an inspection, or at report time – and therefore need flexibility from those you live with.

- Always be aware that you need to maintain good relationships outside work. If you find yourself cancelling arrangements, ask yourself why. Are you over-committed to your work?
- Allocate some time for nothing and everything – whatever you most feel like doing. Keep spontaneity alive in your life.
- Make sure that at least 75% of your holidays are work free. If you do have to do some work, do it at the start of the break so you can then enjoy uninterrupted free time.

- Instead of thinking about how much time you spend working, calculate how much time that you spend *not* working.

Keeping your identity

It can be easy to work yourself into the belief that you are a teacher and *only* a teacher. Use time management and awareness to free up space when you can nurture hitherto neglected needs.

- Are there hobbies you would like to pursue but don't because of work?
- Have any aspects of your character changed since you started work?
- Are you forgetting birthdays and other events you would normally remember or paying more attention to the finer details of schoolwork rather than the finer details of your life?
- If you had to stop teaching, where would that leave you? At a total loss as to what to do?
- Do you have more or less fun in your life since you began teaching?

Help yourself maintain balance by the following:

- Spend time on indulging yourself. Whether you enjoy sport, going to the theatre or cinema, going out with friends or pursuing your favourite hobby, ring-fence time when you can do these things without feeling guilty.
- Have at least one evening a week totally devoted to relaxation.
- Allocate time to keep in touch with friends and family. Make phone calls, write letters or send e-mail – take an interest in the lives of those around you.
- Spend some time each day simply focusing on you. Some people meditate, others go for a walk, listen to music or take a long bubble bath. Whatever works for you, do it! Those you live with will soon learn that this time is sacrosanct to you, and that to allow you uninterrupted space makes you easier to live with.
- If necessary, take a sick day for the benefit of your mental health if nothing else. You would not be the first (nor the last) teacher to take a day for catching up and resting.

Stress busting

'Instead of seeing the rug being pulled from under us, we can learn to dance on a shifting carpet.' Thomas Crum.

The degree of stress experienced by members of the same profession varies tremendously from individual to individual, but it is fair to say that workplace stress does appear to be on the increase. Stress is not to be ignored. Its effects are far-reaching and can lead to life-threatening conditions.

The *New Oxford Dictionary of English* defines stress as, 'a state of mental or emotional strain or tension resulting from adverse or very demanding circumstances'. There is nothing intrinsically wrong with being stressed; it is virtually impossible to avoid at times and can lead to the necessary stimulation required to complete a task. It is when stress continues beyond the event for which you were preparing or the interview etc. that you should start to take evasive action before mental, physical and emotional symptoms occur and the stress becomes negative.

RECOGNISING THE SYMPTOMS OF NEGATIVE STRESS

Negative stress can be hard to identify despite the fact that it can cause your body to present a wide variety of behavioural, physical and emotional symptoms. If you think you may be suffering from negative stress, consider these questions:

- What do others say about you? How are you described?
- How do you interact with others? Are you patient and attentive or snappy and distracted?
- Are you less confident that you used to be? Shyer and more introspective?
- Is your mood stable and balanced or do you find yourself swinging from contentment to distress in one go?
- Is decision making more difficult than it used to be and concentration a thing of the past?

- Are your thoughts generally positive or negative? Do you have any thoughts of impending doom?
- Do you rely on stimulants more than usual? Has the occasional drink become a daily necessity?
- Has work taken over where leisure once reigned? Once you have completed your work do you have the energy for a full social life?
- What are your energy levels like? Do you experience the highs and lows of adrenaline 'dependence'?

Recognising the symptoms of negative stress requires self-observance and honesty. Denial of stress-related problems compounds the situation and prolongs recovery time.

THE CAUSES OF STRESS IN TEACHING

It is impossible to identify the exact causes of stress in teaching especially when you consider that one person's stress is another's motivation. However, these factors do seem to have some responsibility for negative stress amongst teachers:

- **Time** Feeling unable to perform the required tasks in the time available.
- **Control** Not being in control of the number of tasks that have to be completed. External pressure.
- **Information** Having to keep up with a rapid pace of change and feeling ill-informed about the latest situation. Ever increasing expectations.
- **Workload** Having to complete work at home in order to keep up to date. Sometimes unrealistic expectations and possible inequality in work distribution. Also the tremendously diverse nature of the job.
- **Indiscipline** Having to control unruly pupils and deal with constant interruptions on a daily basis.
- **Deadlines** Facing many deadlines each day as work must be prepared and books marked for each class or part of the day.
- **Personality overload** Depending on what age group you teach, you could interact with over one hundred different personalities each day.

- **Fear** About accountability, inspections, job insecurity etc.
- **Resource limitations** Having to prepare resources to supplement material in the school and for differentiation purposes. The poor condition of some classrooms.
- **Aggression** The potential threat from pupils and parents as well as possible bullying from staff members.

ACTION: Think about areas of possible stress in your job. Are you able to identify clear factors that contribute to the pressures you face? Do any of these seem to be intractable? Talk about the stresses you have identified with your induction tutor/mentor and read on for further advice. What action can you take to reduce your stress?

STRESS-BUSTING SKILLS

Begging your doctor for tranquillisers to calm your mind and ease your day is probably not a good idea without adopting some stress-busting techniques. However, stress is now thought to be a contributory factor in many diseases and it is well worth talking to a doctor or other health-care provider about any stress you feel.

Managing through a crisis

Whether you are experiencing the sudden symptoms of feeling overwhelmed or worse, a panic attack, take these steps:

- Stop. There isn't *anything* that cannot be dropped, even if you are in the middle of a lesson. Someone will be free to take over from you.
- Focus on your breathing. Count slowly as you breathe in through your nose and out through your mouth until a sense of calm gradually pervades your body and mind. The more you practise this when you are already calm the easier it will be to do in a crisis.
- Look at ways of immediately reducing your workload. Go home if necessary.

THE PHYSICAL SYMPTOMS OF STRESS

A number of changes take place in the body when it is working under stress.

- The blood supply to muscles is increased.
- The adrenal glands produce more adrenaline.
- Pupils become dilated.
- The heart rate increases.
- Blood pressure can rise.
- The sweat glands produce more sweat.
- Breathing becomes more rapid.
- The menstrual cycle can become disturbed.
- The digestive system can become upset.
- The immune system becomes less effective.
- Skin problems can develop.

It is important to consult your GP or other health-care provider if you find yourself suffering from any of the above sooner rather than later. It is easier to correct minor health disturbances than major ones.

- Talk to someone about your feelings before leaving school. Take support from senior colleagues and any stress counsellors your school or LEA may have. Don't worry about admitting your anxiety to a senior member of staff. They would be lying if they said they hadn't suffered in the same way at some point in their career!
- Release the stress of the day when you get home. Cry, shout, exercise or go for a walk – whatever works for you.
- Commit yourself to undertaking some of the maintenance tips that follow. For example, book a massage. Now!
- Compose an affirmation that you can use the next day.

- Visit your doctor or other health-care provider if you feel that stress is piling up. It may be best for you and the school to take some time out.

Managing day to day

'Focus 90% of your time on solutions and only 10% of your time on problems.' Anthony J. D'Angelo.

- Develop a flexible attitude to your work. Detachment can sometimes be necessary as the path of least resistance affords some freedom from stress.
- Adopt the 80% philosophy. Drop your need for perfection; you can still get an 'A' grade with 80%!
- Have at least one evening and one full day at the weekend off. Even if you are tempted to work, don't.
- Don't expect yourself to be on task 100% of the time. Day dreaming is good for you!

ABOUT

USING AFFIRMATIONS

An affirmation is an often-repeated phrase, which focuses on something positive. They are an excellent way of managing negativity, but there are some important points to remember when constructing them.

- Always use positive statements. Say, 'My work is enjoyable and manageable' rather than, 'I am not stressed about my work'.
- Use present rather than future statements. 'I am calm and relaxed' is better than, 'I will be calm and relaxed'.
- Visualise your ideal scenario while you use affirmations. Believe that you can create the situations you want to create.
- Repeat your affirmations often throughout the day.

- Be aware of times when you can still your mind throughout the day even if it is during assembly or in the toilet!
- Stay in the present. Avoid thinking about what you have to do in the future and what you've done in the past. Give all your attention to the task in hand – divided attention leads to tension.
- Set realistic goals for yourself.
- Prepare your room for the next day the night before.
- Take any opportunities to share the burden of your work. For example, a classroom assistant may offer to put up a wall display or the SEN department may want to develop some differentiated work for a statemented child.
- Identify the *value* of the tasks you have to perform. If you cannot discern the value of a task, speak to your induction tutor/mentor; perhaps it needn't be performed in the future.
- Break each project down into manageable chunks.
- Aim to inject more humour into your life. Laughter is a tremendous stress releaser.

Maintenance tips

The long-term management of stress requires you (and those you work with) to be ever vigilant. Ignoring stress in schools is costly and short-sighted.

- In his book, *Calm at Work*,[2] Paul Wilson writes that *deciding* to become calm is the first step in being calm. Analyse how much your attitude is responsible for the degree of stress you experience.
- Work with colleagues to encourage stress-reducing practices that can be adopted. Even the development of a forum for the discussion of stress would be helpful.
- Once you are in the habit of dealing with stress on a daily basis, you can resolve to learn from the experience rather than let stress accumulate unaddressed.
- Keep an ongoing list of what triggers stress in you. This will probably need to be updated regularly as your proficiencies develop.

- Keep a running list of everything that calms and relaxes you. Perhaps a book, a person or a place, anything that makes you feel good. You could even include photographs of yourself when you were relaxed and happy. Refer to the list whenever the ill effects of stress start to develop.
- Maintain a positive attitude about the work that you do. If talking to certain people results in you feeling down, avoid them.
- Pursue a hobby – something you have always wanted to do. If it increases physical activity, even better. Outside interests often serve to balance your working life.
- If massage, reflexology or some other relaxing experience works for you, book a session regularly.

MORALE BOOSTING

There can be few things more depressing than a staffroom full of teachers constantly bemoaning the state of their working conditions. Listening to all that does nothing for your morale and the way you view your career.

One way round such a situation is actively to aim to raise the morale of colleagues, providing, of course, that you have the energy! Although listening to the grievances of others is an important way to help, there comes a point when the negative cries of colleagues need to be balanced by some positive responses.

'Lifting' colleagues

'We don't see things as they are, we see them as we are.' Anais Nin.

The idea behind lifting colleagues is that everyone should benefit.
- Remembering the birthday of a fellow teacher can do wonders for morale. Alternatively you could take a treat in for colleagues on your birthday. This will change the pattern of the usual break-time.
- You could set up a staff entertainments committee that could arrange staff social events such as cinema or theatre trips, sporting competitions or just a visit to the local pub.

- Make one day of the week (perhaps Friday) a treat day. Take it in turns to bring something in for the benefit of all the staff.
- Try to mark significant events such as the end of a half term or term, or the end of an inspection.
- Perhaps have an ongoing quiz, board game or competition to lighten the atmosphere in the staffroom.
- Show an interest in the home lives of colleagues.
- Be vigilant of others and offer to listen to anxieties.

Health and lifestyle

During the school year 1996/7, 15,610 teachers took early retirement. One-third of those were forced to retire on the grounds of ill health.[3] Some were in their twenties – shocking evidence that the job can take its toll.

Good health is not a foregone conclusion for any of us, yet so often we can find excuses not to undertake health-improving pursuits. However, a little effort can reap great rewards in terms of increasing vitality and enjoyment of life. Teachers have the responsibility to give themselves a chance. Sit on early warning signs of health problems and you're nurturing a certain crisis.

The advice given here is intended to provide ideas on how health and lifestyle might be improved. Your health-care practitioner should check out persistent health problems.

DIET AND EXERCISE

In order to operate, we have to feed and move our bodies. Without good food and exercise we cannot function at optimum levels. This has tremendous implications for work performance and stress levels, and consequently enjoyment of the job could be much diminished.

Eating for health

'It's not the horse that draws the cart, but the oats.' Russian proverb.

Erratic eating patterns and a deficient diet are increasingly being held responsible for many symptoms of ill health. There are several ways that teachers can use food to create health, providing these rules are followed:

- Always ensure you have at least 20 minutes in which to consume your lunch uninterrupted.
- Never eat while emotionally upset.

Despite the plethora of healthy eating books on the market, there are only two basic tenets of a good diet and health, which are easy to remember:

- Eat plenty of fresh, raw fruits and vegetables (at least five helpings a day)
- Avoid harmful substances such as sugar, caffeine, cocoa, alcohol, tobacco and recreational drugs.

While you can increase your intake of fruits and vegetables immediately, it is important to wean yourself off harmful substances. For example, if you consume caffeine in the form of tea, coffee or fizzy drinks, reduce your intake by one cup a day, every day, until you are no longer reliant on the boost it gave you. By reducing gradually, you should avoid the withdrawal symptoms associated with addiction.

Replace caffeinated drinks with fresh, diluted fruit juices, filtered tap water or fruit/herb teas. Once you have cleared your body of caffeine you will not want to go back to being dependent on it.

A varied diet is important, but not one that includes a variety of cakes, biscuits and chocolate! Go for unprocessed wholefoods as often as possible and avoid eating combinations of white flour, sugar and fat.

ACTION: Spend time at least one day a week preparing a really fantastic meal including plenty of fresh produce. Sit at a properly laid table, even if you are eating alone. Invite some friends to share your meal, but if they are teachers, avoid school-talk!

In his book, *The Vitamin Bible*,[4] Earl Mindell suggests that teachers should take supplements vitamin B-complex, vitamin C with bioflavanoids and good-quality multi-vitamin and mineral tablets, to help replenish the nutrients used up during the teaching day (refer to *The Vitamin Bible* for exact details). Always go for natural supplements, and buy them from your local health shop rather than supermarket. It is relatively easy to ensure an intake of at least five fruits and vegetables a day. Try these suggestions:

- Buy them! This may sound obvious, but if you are not in the habit of buying fresh fruit and vegetables, it will be easy to sail past the section in the supermarket.
- Drink pure (diluted) fruit juices. Make sure, however, they don't contain hidden sugars and other additives.
- Add fruit to breakfast cereals and main-course dishes.
- Prepare a fresh salad to eat with your evening meal.
- Add salad vegetables to sandwiches.
- Make a batch of homemade soup and freeze it in portions. Eat it as a starter or main course.

This is not about being a food fanatic, but it is about treating foods that drain energy and vitality with caution.

Moving for energy

Any form of exercise is to be encouraged, as it undoubtedly boosts immunity and helps to relieve symptoms of depression and stress, but it doesn't have to be a chore. There are many ways of incorporating more movement into your working day.

SNACKING AND HYPOGLYCAEMIA

When the brain is starved of glucose (which is carried in the blood) the body cannot function properly. Most people have experienced attacks of low blood sugar (or hypoglycaemia) and know how uncomfortable the associated feelings are such as sweating, shaking, feeling irritable and confused and suddenly, ravenously hungry. Usually these feelings can be relieved by eating, but if they aren't you must visit your health-care practitioner. The best way to balance blood sugar levels is to eat little and often. Fortunately the teaching day lends itself to snacking in this way, but it is important to snack on the right foods.

According to the Institute for Optimum Nutrition, the best snack is one that consists of a carbohydrate plus a first class protein (e.g. white meat, fish, dairy produce or tofu). This means eating, for example, a crispbread with cottage cheese, or raw vegetables with tuna paté. This combination of carbohydrate and protein produces the optimum rate of sugar release into the blood stream, which sustains even energy levels over time.

- Everyone needs fresh air. Take a lunchtime walk around the school field and do some deep breathing as you go.
- Jog up stairs whenever possible.
- Walk short journeys instead of relying on the car. This is not always easy as a teacher, with books, boxes and bags to carry, but certainly possible on occasion.
- Give yourself some time each day to move freely. You might like to do this in private! Allow your body to sway, dance, shake etc. Whatever it wants to do.
- Work into your diary a regular slot each week for an organised sporting activity, such as a class, or a game, of tennis or badminton with a friend. These exercise slots will soon become sacrosanct!

Stretching is a wonderful way to tone muscles, increase suppleness and allow oxygen to flow freely around the body. Get into the habit of doing some simple stretching exercises in the morning, and throughout the day as appropriate. See Appendix 8 for further reading.

DISEASE PREVENTION

People can have a very strange attitude towards illness and disease, or dis-ease. Preventing ill health takes a low priority, yet when illness does strike we think it has done so unexpectedly, and feel victims of bad luck. Illness is simply evidence that your body is fighting to re-balance itself. Your body is your last line of defence and before manifesting your symptoms, it will have been sending signals that all is not well. Physical or mental dis-ease is the loudest signal it can send so you owe it to yourself to listen.

A GP is usually the first port of call when illness strikes. Before you attend the surgery, you may have already taken time off work, and tried various over-the-counter remedies. However, if you take a preventative approach, you may be able to stop your symptoms from taking hold. Fortunately there are now many widely accepted complementary therapies such as homeopathy, acupuncture, massage and reflexology that work by boosting immunity and vitality through taking an holistic approach. A complementary practitioner will look at all aspects of your life in the process of healing.

For ease of reference, the following section has been divided into physical health and mental health, although it is important to consider both.

Physical health

The best way to prevent physical dis-ease is to boost your natural immunity to illness. When you consider the number of people a teacher interacts with every day and that each individual carries a different cocktail of germs, a healthy immune system is essential.

Frequent infections, colds, coughs, sore throats, allergies and even persistent tiredness are all signs of an immune system under pressure.

Become self-observant and listen to your body's needs. There are valid reasons for feeling tired; most cell repair takes place while we sleep. If we ignore tiredness, we are preventing this from taking place.

ABOUT

TAKING TIME OFF SICK

It can sometimes be easier as a teacher to struggle through feelings of ill health rather than take time off and organise work for missed classes. Added to that is the burden of knowing that a colleague will probably lose valuable non-contact time in order to cover for you while you are at home. Struggling on to avoid the guilt so often associated with taking time off will not be positive in the long run. Inconvenient as it may seem, take a day sooner rather than a month later.

If you do need to take time off, follow your school's procedures for this closely. You will need to keep your headteacher informed and, if possible, anticipate how much time off you will need so that cover arrangements can be made (this is not always possible, so don't worry if you cannot be specific). You will need to get a doctor's certificate explaining your absence if you are away for eight or more days. These certificates should be forwarded to your headteacher immediately and he/she is obliged to treat them as confidential documents. You will need to refer to local arrangements if you are sick during the holidays. Look in your contract, the *Burgundy Book* and talk to someone from your LEA's education personnel department and your union. *Always seek a second opinion on any instructions you are given from your school regarding sickness and holidays. You could inadvertently put your entitlement to holiday pay at stake.*

Other ways to boost your immune system include:

- Increase your intake of antioxidants which help to boost your immunity. Vitamin A strengthens cells that keep viruses at bay and vitamin C will fight any that do get through. Zinc helps immune cells to mature and selenium helps them identify invaders. Eat more apples, oranges, red, green and yellow vegetables, carrots, potatoes, grains, seeds, nuts and cereals.

- Take an immunity-boosting supplement such as echinacea, aloe vera, garlic or bee pollen. Your local health food stockist will help you identify which one is most suited to you.

- Keep your lungs healthy by exercising, singing or playing a wind instrument.

ABOUT

CHOOSING A COMPLEMENTARY PRACTITIONER

We should take as much care over choosing complementary therapists as we do over choosing a conventional doctor. Follow these guidelines to avoid the 'therapy merry-go-round':

- Read about the different therapies and make a list of the ones that sound interesting.

- Look for local practitioners in the 'Yellow Pages' or on notice boards in health shops and health centres, or by asking friends and family for personal recommendations. Make contact with your chosen practitioner before making an appointment to establish whether you think they can help you.

- Ensure that the practitioner you have chosen is fully qualified and a member of a recognised, professional body with specific codes of practice. Do they have insurance to cover their actions as a health-care practitioner?

- Many complementary therapies are now available on the NHS. If money is restricted, ask your GP if you can be referred.

Remember that you are in control of any form of health care.

FIGHTING COLDS

'Take rest; a field that has rested gives a beautiful crop'. Ovid.

The staffroom that doesn't have at least one teacher crouched in a chair desperately trying to muster the energy to teach through a severe cold simply doesn't exist!

At the first sign of congestion:

- Take high doses of vitamin C (one gram three times a day). Vitamins A and B complex will help too.
- Suck a zinc lozenge. Zinc is thought to reduce the time you are sick.
- Eat lightly and drink plenty of water as this washes out toxins.
- Use eucalyptus essential oil to clear sinuses.

Mental health

A key word in the maintenance of good mental health is *balance*. More specifically, balance between home commitments including family, personal needs such as social activities and self-pampering, leisure and rest, and the demands of work. Ironically, many new teachers find themselves in the 'Catch 22' situation of not having time to create balance, yet suffering because of the resulting imbalance!

A big step towards regaining balance is to recognise what aspects of your life you can be in charge of, and retaining that control. For example, your timetable commitments are part of your contract and you cannot arrive at school one day and say, 'I really need some time to prepare for the science afternoon so can someone else teach year 3 this morning?' However, you can arrange to give homework requiring minimal assessment during weeks when you know your workload will be especially heavy. Remember that you have *choices* and *control*. Put *your* needs first.

When pressures are mounting and the control is slipping away, be assertive in asking for support, and limiting the demands made on you. There is not a teacher in the profession who has not had to take stock at some stage, and this is much harder to do alone. Support can come from:

- other NQTs
- your induction tutor/mentor
- your head of year/school/department
- friends and family.

Ignoring signs of overload can lead to anxiety, depression and stress.

There are four particularly effective ways to improve mental health that even the most serene could usefully employ:

- Deal with your emotions. It might not be appropriate or constructive to shout at a class, however angry you feel, but that emotion must be discharged later on. Frustration and anger at pupils or colleagues can be vented on a pillow, or in a car parked in a secluded place (open the windows and yell it out). Do be sure to address the problem calmly when the initial anger has subsided. Seek counselling if it would help.

ABOUT

PANIC ATTACKS

These episodes which may involve shortness of breath, palpitations, sweating and a feeling of impending doom signify severe discontent and must be treated seriously. However, they are perfectly treatable and there are many techniques which can be employed to restore balance. Do visit your health-care practitioner if you suffer a panic attack.

- Utilise your in-built remedies. Crying is an excellent way to release emotion and research has shown that laughter can help to cure even the most serious of illnesses. Some staffrooms have a joke board, which encourages laughter and lifts tension, helping staff regain a positive perspective. Try watching comedy shows and films, or reading a few pages of a funny book each evening.

- Develop relaxation skills. Not only will all aspects of your life seem more manageable, but there will be noticeable improvements in your physical health too. When we are deeply relaxed our pulse and breathing rates slow down and blood pressure drops. However, few people are able to relax deeply without learning techniques from a book or a class. Information on local classes can be found in health centres, libraries and adult education programmes. You may prefer to learn yoga or t'ai chi, both of which incorporate movement with relaxation and meditation.

- Utilise the power of the mind to cultivate a positive attitude. There are always two ways to view any situation, positively and negatively; remember those choices. Affirmations can be very useful in helping to assert the positive and minimise the negative.

ACTION: When a problem or anxiety is getting out of hand, write it down as a heading. Underneath, write answers to these questions:

- *What is the core of this problem?*
- *What can I do about it?*
- *Can anyone help me out?*
- *What can they do about it?*
- *What are the best and worst scenarios?*

This should help you see that the problem is not insurmountable.

LOOKING AFTER YOURSELF

'Things turn out best for the people who make the best out of the way things turn out.' Art Linkletter.

Most teachers are extremely conscientious when it comes to nurturing those in their care, but don't extend that generosity to themselves. It cannot be expressed strongly enough how important self-nurturing is for NQTs. Do not take yourself for granted. Rather, engage in meaningful self-care.

Day-to-day maintenance

'Live and work but do not forget to play, to have fun in life and to really enjoy it.' Eileen Caddy.

Making improvements to your health and lifestyle is best done gradually. Dramatic changes will probably lead to a reversion to the old way. Try adopting one item at a time from the list of day-to-day maintenance and then reap the rewards.

- Take care over breathing. Rapid, shallow breathing can lead to varying degrees of hyperventilation, the symptoms of which can be dizziness, irritability, tension in the abdomen and excessive sighing. Spend a few moments several times a day doing simple breathing exercises, for example: breathe in to a count of four, hold for two, breathe out to a count of four and pause for two. Repeat five times. Not only is this calming, but energising too.

- Develop awareness of your 'slack' times and learn to anticipate them. Treat energy slumps with breathing exercises and appropriate snacks, and pace yourself.

- Pay attention to your posture. You should aim for a balance between tension and relaxation, with your back straight and shoulders down.

- Create good sleeping patterns rather than 'crashing out' patterns. If you don't wake feeling rested, aim to get more hours of sleep *before* midnight.

- Talk about work frustrations with colleagues. Start a support circle for this purpose if there is no forum for this sort of discussion at your school.

- Pursue a hobby – something you really enjoy, be it painting, ceramics, woodwork, sport, gardening or cookery. Just let your creativity flow.

- Get used to saying, 'I can't afford it!' Not the cruises and convertibles, but the multi-tasking and working without adequate breaks.

ACTION: Write down a list of five things that make you feel good. These can be anything at all – whatever comes to mind. Keep the list somewhere where you will see it every day and resolve to do something from the list as regularly as possible.

Above and beyond: extra commitments

From school plays, outings, clubs and gardens to PTAs, staff committees and looking after class pets, there is no end to the extra commitments you may be cajoled into making. It is also no coincidence that NQTs often get asked to do extra jobs; existing staff have been there and done that and now say, 'Sorry, I don't have time to take anything else on.'

KNOWING YOUR NATURAL LIMITS

The best line to take with extra commitments is to avoid them, if possible, in your first year unless you really want the experience that the commitment will provide, or unless it will add to your relaxation, e.g. acting in the school play if drama is a recreation for you. You will have enough on your plate working through your induction year without adding to the demands on your time. Taking extras on can result in you working at a pace above your optimum, which could result in a reduction in your effectiveness.

If you are not sure whether you can manage an extra commitment, agree to do it on the condition that you can review it after a few weeks. Provide yourself with a get-out and the extra work will not seem like such an added stress.

If you are asked to take on duties in your department or curriculum area, such as being an ICT co-ordinator or being responsible for SEN, talk to your induction tutor/mentor. There will probably be a clause in your contract giving your headteacher the ability to ask you to do what he/she deems reasonable, but it is not practical for you to take on such duties as an NQT.

CAN YOU SAY 'NO'?

Most teachers, when asked if they are assertive, will reply positively, simply because of the nature of their job. Yet, if they are asked the question, 'Do you ever feel put upon?' they will still give a positive answer. So how does this add up? Perhaps some teachers are not as assertive as they think they are! In order to express yourself assertively, you have to be able to view yourself and your work positively. If you don't, you can hardly justify why others should listen to your assertions.

There are three main reasons why some teachers find it difficult to say 'no' to additional tasks they don't want to take on:

- Managers lead them to believe they are obliged to complete the extra tasks.
- They are insecure in their performance and think that performing the extra tasks will improve their feelings of self-worth.
- They want to create the impression that they are ready for anything.

These reasons are more destructive than positive. There is no doubt that it is the assertive (as opposed to aggressive, dominating or weak) individual who gains the most respect in the workplace. See Appendix 8 for further reading .

BEING ASSERTIVE

An easy route to stress and anxiety is by committing to too many projects. This usually results in feelings of being overwhelmed and unable to cope.

- An important step in the development of assertiveness skills is to practise some positive self-recognition. If you allow yourself to acknowledge what you are good at you will boost your feelings of self-worth.
- Use affirmations daily, based on your skills. This will help to remove the need for positive strokes through taking on additional work.
- Accept any positive recognition that others give you.

When you are in the position of needing to express yourself assertively, use these ideas:

- Use 'I' statements to express yourself positively, e.g, 'I would be interested in playing the part of the beast in "Beauty and the Beast" but I feel it would adversely affect the way I manage my workload at the moment.'
- Don't put yourself down. Say, 'I don't feel that is appropriate for me at the moment', rather than 'I can't do that.'
- Think about how you are using your body when you are being assertive. Tone of voice, body language, eye contact etc. all make a difference to the way your words are received.
- If you are anticipating a situation when you fear you will be 'put upon', use creative visualisation to enable you to 'see' yourself behaving assertively. Focus on the best possible outcome for you.

Being assertive is not just about saying 'no'. It is also about making requests yourself. 'I need', 'I would like', 'Do you think I could have' are all statements that NQTs will need to use throughout their first year of teaching, and probably beyond.

DUTIES

You will probably be involved in the supervision of pupils at some stage in the school day, whether as a paid lunchtime duty (the supervision of pupils at lunchtime is not something you can be directed to do without receiving additional payment) or a break or end-of-day duty. Before doing your first such duty:

- Find out exactly what the procedure is. Ask questions such as:
  Where do you have to patrol?
  How long for?
  What happens if you are detained with your class?
  Who will you be on duty with?
  Will you have the same duties each week?
  Do you need a whistle?
  What is the procedure in the event of accidents?
- Work with a colleague if possible. This can make a potentially lonely time pass more quickly.
- Make sure you get the refreshment you need.
- Use the opportunity to get to know pupils on a more informal basis. It could be a time to chat about music, TV or holidays etc. You'll be surprised how useful such conversations can be.
- Try not to let anything get in the way of your duties. Other members of staff will soon get annoyed if they have to cover for you.

Covering for absent staff

The dreaded cover timetable – many a teacher's face drops at the sight of it as it's posted on the staffroom notice board. Yet another free period gone and you have to spend it with someone else's year 11 on a Friday afternoon. Great!

While the general rule is that you still have to teach the class to the best of your ability (and you may be observed doing this in an OFSTED inspection) the absent teacher will usually have made arrangements for the lesson, especially if their absence was planned. The lesson plan should be achievable for a teacher not familiar with the subject and rely more on individual work than a teacher-led session.

Use these points to help:

- Find out if there is a system for the posting of set work for cover lessons. Will instructions be in the relevant room or in the staffroom? Where are books left? Will paper be supplied or will you need to take some? What happens if no work is set? Answers to these questions can help to ease a potentially stressful situation.

- If you know you will be covering a certain class, try to get as much information as possible in advance.

- Be strict about behaviour but don't have very high expectations of what pupils may achieve. Think back to when you were at school and your attitude to lessons when your teacher was absent.

- If you manage to get some of your own work done during a cover lesson, treat it as a bonus. Strictly speaking, you should be teaching. If you don't *try* to get anything done, you won't be annoyed when pupils' interruptions prevent you from achieving.

- If no work has been set, your skills of management will be put to their greatest test. There should be a head of department hovering to make sure that you are coping if you have not spoken before the lesson but, if not, send a pupil to his/her room for further instructions. In the meantime you will have to get the class in order and keep them occupied. Above all, keep calm and controlled.

- If the department has no contingency plans in the event of staff absence, you are on your own. For this reason it is worth having some general lessons planned that will challenge pupils and be a worthwhile use of their time. Perhaps base such lessons around a cross-curricular theme such as citizenship. Don't feel you have to teach a lesson of the subject you are covering if no work has been set.

- Take the opportunity to get to know pupils you don't teach. This can do great things for your reputation in the school. Also observe the pupils you do teach. Do they behave differently in another classroom?

- Feed back to the class teacher what happened in the lesson and any information you feel he/she should know. You could simply leave a note in his/her pigeonhole if you don't get a chance to speak.

SETTING COVER WORK YOURSELF

Aim to prepare some interesting lesson plans for cover teachers to follow with your classes in the event of your absence. You could have them ready in a file for the teacher to select on the day. This means that you don't have to think about what your classes can do when you have phoned in with a crippling migraine at 8 am! Tell colleagues in advance where your lesson plans are (perhaps keep them in a file in the staffroom) and if your room is kept tidy it will be easy for other teachers to find resources such as paper etc. Make your instructions easy to follow – put yourself in the reader's position – and include any photocopied sheets that may be needed (don't expect a colleague to do this as they probably won't have time before the lesson begins).

Organising school visits

Taking on the organisation of a school visit is something that even the most experienced teachers find time-consuming and potentially troublesome. Your school should have clear guidelines for teachers to follow when organising visits, and if you do find yourself at the helm, take as much advice as you can.

The DfEE document, 'Health and Safety of Pupils on Educational Visits' (1998) states that:

Pupils can derive a good deal of educational benefit from taking part in visits with their school. In particular, they have the opportunity to undergo experiences not available in the classroom. Visits help to develop a pupil's investigative skills and longer visits in particular encourage greater independence.

Although, as a new teacher, you probably won't be landed with the task of organising a school visit from scratch, and certainly should not be asked to lead a residential visit, you will almost certainly be involved in them at some level. Before organising a school visit, make sure you read a copy of the above document, which is available on request from the DfEE Publication Centre. Your school may also have a copy. It contains all the information you need regarding the legality of different kinds of school visits as well as health and safety considerations for all on the visit. It also has an extensive list of useful contacts.

CHECKLIST FOR PLANNING A VISIT

The first stage of planning a visit is convincing your headteacher that the trip is worth doing; that it fits into the curriculum you are teaching and that it carries minimum risks. This is because your employer is still responsible for the health and safety of its employees (who carry a duty of care for pupils) when out on visits, as well as having to account for the way time is spent in their schools. Go no further than this at first, because if you don't get approval of the idea in principle as well as permission from your headteacher, the trip cannot go ahead.

When you present the idea to your headteacher (or head of department) have your justifications for the trip well rehearsed. It's a good idea to have a printed sheet ready to leave with the head-teacher. On the sheet you should include:

- where you propose to take the children
- whom you propose to take (including staff, supervisors and children)
- why the trip is necessary
- what aspect of the curriculum you would be covering
- how you would link it into work before and after the trip
- how much you estimate the trip will cost.

Once you get the go ahead to start the planning, use this checklist:

1   Find out if your school has guidelines for planning a visit (head of department, induction tutor/mentor or headteacher should be able to confirm this). If it has, use it, otherwise, use the following checklist:

2   Carry out a risk assessment. The DfEE document mentioned above suggests basing a risk assessment on the following considerations:

- What are the hazards?
- Who might be affected by them?
- What safety measures need to be in place to reduce risks to an acceptable level?
- Can the group leader put the safety measures in place?
- What steps will be taken in an emergency?

The document also states that:

A risk assessment for a visit need not be complex but it should be comprehensive ... Pupils must not be placed in situations which expose them to an unacceptable level of risk. Safety must always be the prime consideration. If the risks cannot be contained then the visit must not take place.

The document suggests that teachers consider these factors when assessing the risks:

- *the type of visit/activity and the level at which it is being undertaken*
- *the location, routes and modes of transport*
- *the competence, experience and qualifications of supervisory staff*
- *the ratios of teachers and supervisory staff*
- *the group members' age, competence, fitness and temperament and the suitability of the activity*
- *the special educational or medical needs of pupils*
- *the quality and suitability of available equipment*
- *seasonal conditions, weather and timing*

- *emergency procedures*
- *how to cope when a pupil becomes unable or unwilling to continue*
- *the need to monitor the risks throughout the visit.*

Once you have completed your risk assessment, make sure all those involved in the trip (but not pupils) have a copy.

3   If possible, go on an exploratory visit to:

- *ensure at first hand that the venue is suitable to meet the aims and objectives of the school visit*
- *obtain names and addresses of other schools who have used the venue*
- *obtain advice from the manager*
- *assess potential areas and levels of risk*
- *ensure that the venue can cater for the needs of the staff and pupils in the group*
- *become familiar with the area before taking a group of young people there.*

If you can't go on an exploratory visit, get the necessary information from telephone calls. You also need to make sure you have identified good places to delegate as meeting points, especially for lost pupils.

4   Think about joining up with another teacher for the trip. Perhaps another year group would benefit from the visit, or you could link with pupils from another subject area.

5   Talk through the financial arrangements with your head of department or headteacher. State schools cannot charge for visits that take place during school hours, but they can ask for voluntary contributions. There may be some money available from the school to subsidise the trip in which case you will be able to adjust the figure you request in donation accordingly. Many schools overestimate the size of the donation to allow for some parents not being able to pay the full amount. This is perfectly acceptable under current law.

6   Make sure you know who will be responsible for first aid on the trip. You will have to have a first aid box with you (your school

will provide this) and it is a good idea to find out where the nearest hospital will be.

7   Work out the best form of transport (which may not necessarily be the cheapest). If the group is small enough, a mini-bus may do, but usually a coach is the best option. Also consider walking (if appropriate) and going by train. All mini-buses and coaches that carry children between 3 and 15 years of age must be fitted with a seat belt for each child. Check this when booking. Work out what would be the best pick up and drop off points.

8   Decide on the exact timing of the day, including toilet and lunch breaks. Prepare one itinerary for pupils and one for adults.

9   Who would be the group's leader? It is important to appoint one person (usually the organiser) to whom all other staff and supervisors may refer.

10 Work out how many adults need to go on the trip. Your LEA may have set ratios, otherwise, the DfEE document (cited earlier) has set the following as an example guideline for local (non-swimming) visits:

● *one adult for every six pupils in years 1 to 3 (under fives reception classes should have a higher ratio)*

● *one adult for every 10–15 pupils in school years 4 to 6*

● *one adult for every 15–20 pupils in school year 7 upwards.*

However, even if the group you are taking out is small enough to warrant only one adult, think of the implications if you are taken ill. Never go on a trip as the only adult. Parents, volunteers and non-teaching assistants may be used instead of teachers to boost the supervision ratio but, before you ask for such help, keep in mind that many schools like to have police checks performed on all adults who will have access to pupils. Make sure you plan the roles of each adult attending the visit and convey those roles to them. Your plans for supervision should also take into account the sex and ability of the pupils.

11 Prepare a letter informing parents of the trip. Many schools have a standard format for this. Aim to give sufficient information for parents to make an informed decision on whether their child should attend, but not be swamped with detail. Make yourself available for parents to ask you questions if necessary. You will

also need to mention what clothing (if different) children will need, food that should be provided by parents and if any extra money should be taken (perhaps for spending in a gift or souvenir shop etc.). It can be worth mentioning the standard of behaviour that is expected of pupils on the trip.

12 Think about whether you want to ban carbonated drinks, glass bottles, personal stereos etc.

13 Keep equal opportunities issues in mind, especially when you arrange sub-groups.

14 If possible, involve pupils in the planning of work to be completed on the trip. This helps to ensure that they understand the relevance of the trip and can place it clearly in the context of the curriculum they are following. It also encourages them to complete the work.

15 Get a list of any children with medical needs. Their parents should supply information on any medication that their child needs as well as give their consent (in writing) for you to administer it. Some teachers like to take a list of each child, the names of their GPs and next of kin and emergency contact numbers. This is usually unnecessary, as most trips are in school hours and, in the event of any emergency, you would contact the school, where all this information is held, as soon as possible.

16 Sort out insurance in good time. Your headteacher will be able to do this for you. You may think it appropriate to make copies of the insurance schedule available to parents before the trip.

17 Discuss the standards of behaviour that you expect. It is particularly important that pupils realise how identifiable they are in school uniform.

18 Think about how travelling time might be used constructively. Perhaps give pupils a quiz to do based on what they might see on the journey.

19 Write a list of everything you will personally need on the day, from lunch to worksheets, waterproofs to registers.

20 Think about how pupils will complete their work on the day. Will they have time to do tasks? Will clipboards be necessary? Will they use exercise books, paper, or worksheets with gaps to fill in?

COLLECTING MONEY FOR A TRIP

Your school should have arrangements in place for the collection of monies for a trip. Speak to your bursar about this. If you find you have some money left over you could perhaps allocate this for tips for any guides and drivers you have. Always seek advice from your headteacher when it comes to charging for a visit, as he/she will have to follow guidelines from the LEA and DfEE.

21 Inform any colleagues who would have taught the pupils you are taking off-site of the exact details of the trip. It can be extremely annoying if they have planned an exam or assessment for your group and half of them are not there.

22 Arrange work for a cover teacher to set for any classes you are unable to teach.

23 Inform catering staff of the numbers you will be taking off-site. They will need to adjust the amount they cook for the day and plan any free lunches in advance.

24 Create a contingency plan for arriving back late. Who will you phone? Will they be able to contact parents?

25 Make sure there is someone who is able to deputise for you in the event of an emergency. If you are incapacitated for whatever reason, the trip should not necessarily be called off. You will have to keep them informed of all the arrangements.

Pitfalls to avoid

● Don't plan too much initially before getting firm approval from the powers that be.

● Once you have approval, pace your planning so that you don't have a last-minute rush. Remember that you will also have to perform all your other duties on top of organising the trip. Try to avoid being the sole organiser of a trip. This would be a pretty unfair expectation to make of an NQT.

THE JOURNEY

The travelling time on a trip can be potentially problematical. Children may get travelsick, become excitable, or worse, start misbehaving. Having a focus for the journey often helps to pre-empt any troubles and if you can make this light-hearted, even better. A quiz with a prize for the winner is usually great for occupying the time and creating unity in the group through a common task. Try to invoke a sense of anticipation of the day.

- Don't get saddled with the cost of an exploratory visit. You should be able to claim your expenses back. Speak to the bursar.
- Don't make arrangements over the phone without asking for written confirmation.

CHECKLIST FOR THE ACTUAL DAY

All your meticulous planning will pay off now as you enjoy a trouble-free trip! Use this list as guidance:

1 Start with a head count! It's not sufficient simply to call a register. Continue to count heads at regular intervals throughout the day.

2 Take a mobile phone (which should be provided by your school) and some spare cash (again, talk to the bursar) for emergencies.

3 Make sure that pupils are fully strapped in before the coach starts to move and that they stay strapped in throughout the journey. At least you won't have to contend with children trying to sit more than two to a seat!

4 Staff and helpers should be evenly spread throughout the group on the journey and through the day.

5 Ask helpers unknown to the children to wear name badges.

6 Make sure children know which adults are assigned to their group.

SUMMARY (FOR PLANNING A VISIT)

1 Get a copy of your school's guidelines.

2 Do a risk assessment.

3 Go on a preliminary visit.

4 Perhaps join up with another teacher/class.

5 Discuss finances with the headteacher.

6 Consider first-aid arrangements.

7 Assess transport possibilities.

8 Create an itinerary.

9 Designate a leader.

10 Decide on supervision levels.

11 Inform parents of the details of the trip.

12 Think about banned items.

13 Remember equal opportunities.

14 Allow pupils to help you plan work.

15 Find out any medical needs.

16 Sort out insurance.

17 Discuss standards of behaviour.

18 Consider using travel time.

19 Create a list of personal things you will need.

20 Consider the practicalities of how pupils will work.

21 Inform colleagues of those you will be taking out if necessary.

22 Arrange cover work if necessary.

23 Inform catering staff about those you are taking out.

24 Create a plan for late arrival back.

25 Arrange a deputy for the trip in case of an emergency.

7 Designate a central point as a meeting place in the event of children getting lost.

8 If travelling by coach make arrangements with the driver about where and when you will meet again. Make a note of the coach's registration number.

9 Note anything that works particularly well on the day.

10 Keep a record of behaviour, both good and bad. Pupils should receive feedback when they get back to school, and you will have to discuss this aspect of the trip with your headteacher when you get back.

11 Recap on the day on the journey back. You could also go over some of the work the pupils have done and explain what comes next.

12 Evaluate the day for the purposes of future trips. Is there anything you would change in the future, or anything you would never do again?

Pitfalls to avoid

- Don't forget a sick bucket/bag, a bottle of still mineral water for the vomiting child, plenty of tissues/wet wipes and some mints – they will want to be refreshed after throwing up!

- Don't think you can relax for a minute throughout the day. You will need to be more vigilant than usual.

- Don't be so concerned about how the day flows that you forget to enjoy it.

SUMMARY (FOR THE ACTUAL DAY)

1 Count heads regularly.

2 Take a phone and some money.

3 Strap pupils in on the journey.

4 Spread helpers throughout the group.

5 Give helpers name badges.

6 Explain groups to children.

7 Decide on a meeting point.

8 Arrange when and where to meet the driver.

9 Note what works well on the day.

10 Record good and bad behaviour.

11 Recap on the day on the journey.

12 Evaluate the day.

Writing reports

Whatever schools call them, there's no getting away from the fact that you will have to write thousands of these throughout your teaching career. It's an onerous job; you will need to give accurate messages in an accessible form while under a great deal of time pressure.

When considering the actual words you will use, never create a stockpile of phrases to scatter throughout your reports. Rarely will these apply to a child's work and progress. 'Tries hard', 'Could try harder', 'Makes a good effort', 'Makes no effort', 'Talks too much', 'Doesn't speak out', are all meaningless and reflect more on teaching style than

REPORT WRITING

Do	Don't
Take care over presentation. Would you mind if your reports were published?	Allow a report out of your hands with errors and corrections. Start again if necessary.
Keep to internal deadlines. Your headteacher, head of department or head of year will probably want to read them before they leave the building.	Forget that it is the written comments that parents tend to take most notice of, as opposed to test results and attainment levels.
Set yourself mini-deadlines of 5–10 reports at a time.	Attempt to do a whole class set in one go.
Consider writing drafts, or at least jotting down key words for inclusion.	Forget your accountability. Can you substantiate all you write?
Start your comments positively and focus on progress.	Express limits. Better to focus on possibilities (as opposed to predictions).
Avoid educational jargon (of which there is a plethora).	Waffle. Select apt, crisp language.
Offer constructive suggestions for improvement.	Hide the negatives, but be aware that reports are not the place to spring nasty surprises on parents.

any aspect of the child in question. As long as your comments are specific to the child and relate to the skills required of the subject, where appropriate, your reports will be valid and noted, and you will not lay yourself open to criticism from within or outside your school.

Parents' evenings

Whatever the name your school gives these (sometimes open evenings, appointment evenings etc.), you will probably have to face several throughout the school year. They can be daunting, especially if you did not get a chance to attend one during your training but, with a little preparation, the evening should present no problems.

BEFORE THE BIG DAY

- Don't save important concerns about a child until a parents' evening as you may be met with anger and defensiveness. Aim to communicate with parents sooner rather than later about behaviour or work problems.

- Prepare for the night by having pupils' books marked up-to-date, and records of attendance, homework, general participation in class etc. to hand.

- Make sure you know who is coming to see you and what their relationship is to the child. Be prepared to see older siblings in some cases and sometimes divorced or separated parents may want two appointments.

- Talk to colleagues about who is coming to see you to make sure you will not be meeting any parents known to be difficult or aggressive, either towards staff members (relatively rare) or their children. You may want to ask a member of the senior management team to hover near you when you are talking to such a parent.

- Be prepared for a long evening. Make sure you have plenty of sustenance with you, especially if you won't have time to get home before the evening begins.

- Aim to have a free evening as far as marking and preparation are concerned. You won't feel like doing much by the time you get home.

ON THE NIGHT

- It is worth making the effort to look smarter than usual when meeting parents, especially for the first time.
- Have a name card on your table.
- Stand up when greeting parents. It may feel as though you are bobbing up and down all night, but staying seated can appear rude.
- Don't use educational jargon. Explain everything, as a parent may not want to ask for clarification. These evenings can be just as daunting for parents as well.
- Let parents know exactly what you expect of their child.
- Focus on the progress the child has made. They may be top of the class, but have they improved?
- Show parents evidence of the child's achievements. Let them look through books etc.
- Record what happens at each interview. You don't need to include much detail, but it will be useful for future reference especially when writing the next round of reports. You could have a form ready to minimise work on the night.
- Don't slot extra consultations in that haven't been booked unless you have clear gaps.

SPECIMEN FORM

Parent	Pupil	Key points	Action	Target date
Mrs Barker (mother)	Kevin Barker 8DS	Civil War extension work	Give Kevin additional reading references and exercises if wanted	Start asap and review after a few weeks

- Be professional when other staff members or pupils are being discussed.
- Aim to give advice on how achievement can be improved. Make this advice easy to adopt and encourage the parent to pass the information on to the pupil.
- Do not get drawn in to making predictions about a child's future performance. Parents will hold you to what you say.
- Try to focus immediately on the task in hand. Don't get sidetracked by general conversation otherwise you'll get irretrievably behind.
- Take drink breaks whenever you need them. Most schools arrange for drinks to be brought to teachers.
- If you find yourself with some spare time during a parents' evening, ask a colleague if you can observe him/her in action.
- Don't worry if things don't go according to plan. It will be a learning process and you, your induction tutor/mentor or a member of the senior management team can deal with every situation.

BEING HEARD
- The best way to ensure that you are *heard* is to show you know how to *listen*. Demonstrate your attentiveness and empathy and the parent will be more likely to listen to what you have to say.
- Encourage parents to say what they want to say in order to keep the dialogue going. This is, after all, an opportunity for parents to speak as well as you.
- Think about your tone of voice. Always meet rising tension with calm. If the parent's voice rises, lower yours.
- Don't dilute what you want to say about a child to try to pacify a dominant parent. The key is to be truthful rather than blunt.
- Reiterate the fact that your main concern is the child and how he/she can develop their potential.

Facing a refusal to listen

Occasionally, adopting the above tips on being heard by a parent won't work and you may face a point blank refusal to listen to your reasoning. Read this chart in advance to help in such a situation:

DEALING WITH DIFFICULT PARENTS

Do	Don't
Be aware of prejudices that parents may be airing. It may be necessary to discuss what the parent has said to you with your headteacher.	Retract any statements you have made about a child simply because the parent won't accept them.
Be concise and consistent and have justifications for your views.	Try to force the parent to see your point of view but present your opinions and trust that they will be digested eventually.
Maintain eye contact as much as possible.	Focus on problems. Move towards solutions.
Focus on achievement and behaviour, both good and bad.	Focus on personality.
Explain that everyone has many facets to their character and that the child's behaviour and attitudes at school may not necessarily reflect the way they are at home.	Forget that the parent may be feeling embarrassed by and disappointed with the child.
Try to motivate the parents into joining you in working for the child. Encouraging a partnership can often work.	Struggle on with a conversation that is not moving forward positively without offering the parent the opportunity to talk to a member of the senior management team.

SEEING PARENTS AT OTHER TIMES

It is wise to have an 'open door' policy when it comes to seeing parents. If you encourage an ongoing dialogue with them, you are less likely to get into difficult situations on parents' evenings.

- Let parents know the best way for them to get in touch with you if they want to discuss anything. Do you have a good time when they can ring you or a good day when they can call in after school? Make sure you keep such arrangements contained, and on your terms.

EXAMPLE: 'The most difficult aspect of this year has been that, more times than not, my parents have perceived me as the 'enemy' and think that I really don't have their child's best interest in mind. Thankfully, I have an administration that is on top of their faculty and they know exactly what's going on in my room and support me 100%. Otherwise, if I had not had the support, I think that I would've crumbled under the pressure. It's tough being young and without children of my own when I try to give guidance on particular situations. Not only do I have to be policeman, nurse, mother, entertainer, counsellor, and teacher all in one, I am also forced to be a Dr Spock or James Dobson-type family counsellor who gives advice on child-rearing!' Katherine L. Cole, USA.

ABOUT

DOCUMENTING YOUR VIEWS

If a difference of opinion arises between you and a parent, it may be pertinent to document your views and why you hold them. This is so that you can refer to the conversation later, should you need to. You may also want to discuss what you have written with your mentor or a member of the senior management team. Place a copy in the child's records and keep a copy for yourself.

- If you have a need to talk to a parent on the telephone about their child, prepare a script and have to hand all the information you need.
- Parents are entitled to see their child's records but this is definitely a senior management matter. Pass the request on.

Other adults in your classroom

The involvement of support teachers in classrooms across the country has increased over recent years. In primary schools in particular, many teachers would not be able to function efficiently without the input of adult helpers. The head of a school appoints most helpers, both paid and voluntary. It would be unusual for you to arrange your own helpers as many schools carry out police checks on all adults with access to pupils.

If your school has a policy on dealing with adults in the classroom, use it. If not, these ideas will help.

- Make sure you know *why* the adult is helping you. Are they there for learning support for one pupil or as an extra pair of hands and eyes for you? Are they paid or voluntary?
- Inform your helpers of your classroom rules and routines and the *reasons* for them.
- Inform helpers of first-aid procedures in your school and routines for fire practice. Theyíll also need to know about tea and coffee arrangements and where to put bags and coats etc.
- Make sure your helpers understand the need for confidentiality. You don't want your pupils and lessons being discussed outside school.
- Back your helpers so pupils see you presenting a united front.

Look out for forthcoming guidance from the DfEE (keep an eye on the web site) on good practice when working with assistants.

STAYING IN CHARGE

Having extra adults in your classroom does throw some children into confusion. They will need to know exactly who is in charge and wonít necessarily understand the significance of teacher training, or that you are still in charge even if the headteacher is providing some classroom support.

The best way round this is to involve helpers in discussion on their role. You need to define what your ideal working relationship is and continue to work on it. Questions to look at are:

- What do you expect helpers to do?
- What have they been employed to do?
- What do they want to do?
- How much power of reward and sanction do you want your helpers to have (check your school's policy on this)?
- Can helpers give pupils permission to go to the toilet?
- Do you want helpers to carry any equipment or will you make sure they have access to all they may need while in your classroom?
- What do you want your helpers to tell you about their interactions with a child? If you have to spend too long on feedback, you simply lose gained time, yet you must be informed of all child protection issues at least.

Every now and then you should aim to give your helpers some positive feedback. Pinpoint what aspects of their work are particularly helpful to you and what seems to be working very well. This way, you should fall into a comfortable rhythm with your helpers, knowing how best to deploy them in your lessons.

MAKING YOUR INTENTIONS CLEAR

The only way to be clear in what you need your helpers to do is to know for yourself. What, exactly, are your learning intentions for your pupils? How can your helpers enable pupils to achieve them?

If you are fortunate enough to have regular helpers with which you can build a good relationship, they will be able to follow your lessons as you go along, without too much need for planning discussions. If not, you will need to brief your helpers so they don't have to bluff in front of pupils. Don't expect them to be familiar automatically with the intricacies of the curriculum you teach.

An interesting exercise is to place yourself in the position of a support teacher in one of your lessons. Do you know what you are doing and why? Do you know where this work is coming from and where it is going? The need for communication between you and your support teachers is great and you may have to be 'creative' in looking for opportunities to meet.

MAXIMISING THE USE OF CLASSROOM SUPPORT

The most effective way of maximising the use of other adults in your classroom is to raise the status of in-class support amongst the children you teach. This will ensure that pupils view your helpers as a valuable resource that they should make use of rather than an embarrassing reminder of their self-perceived 'inadequacies'.

You may also want to think about preparing an information sheet for helpers in your classes, or perhaps giving some brief training sessions on certain aspects of your work such as hearing children read etc. Mutual feedback is always valuable. If you don't have time to talk immediately after a lesson, ask your helpers to jot down any points they would like to raise and arrange a mutually convenient time to meet.

Support teachers can help you to mark your progress through your induction year in a way that your induction tutor/mentor cannot, simply because they will be witnessing your work on a daily or weekly basis for the full length of a lesson. They will see how your relationships with the pupils develop over time and how effectively you relax into your job in ordinary, unobserved circumstances. Support teachers can also give you valuable insight into how key pupils behave in the presence of other teachers; a perspective you couldn't possibly achieve alone.

Delegating tasks

Paid support staff will have guidelines to follow regarding their work in your lessons. However, volunteers who help in your classroom are often giving up valuable time and it is worth organising some structured tasks so that they do not feel they are surplus to requirements or wasting time. Perhaps ask helpers if there is anything they want to get involved in, or if they have any particular skills that can be utilised.

Think about how they can save you time by doing work displays or mounting, general tidying, collating worksheets, preparing materials etc. However, avoid the trap of relying on volunteers too heavily. You don't want your lessons to collapse if you find they can't be there for any reason.

ABOUT

ABOUT DELEGATING TO HELPERS

Do not ask helpers to perform duties that should only be done by a qualified teacher, tempting as it may be, e.g. marking, curriculum planning, report writing etc. You are ultimately responsible for what goes on in your classroom. You could, however, keep a notebook of ongoing tasks in your classroom to which helpers could refer.

Inspections

A fact of teaching life is that you will be inspected, probably by your headteacher, your head of department, your induction tutor/mentor, an advisor and anyone else involved in your induction period. In addition to this, you may be inspected by OFSTED during your first year of teaching.

Inspections can seem totally daunting experiences, requiring preparation beforehand and recovery afterwards. Yet they do have clear purposes. The OFSTED document, *Framework for the Inspection of Schools*,[5] states that:

The purpose of inspection is to identify strengths and weaknesses so that schools may improve the quality of education they provide

and raise the educational standards achieved by their pupils ...
The inspection process, feedback and reports give direction to the
school's strategy for planning, review and improvement by
providing rigorous external evaluation and identifying key issues
for action.

In order to do this the inspectors must be able to report on:
- *the quality of the education provided by the school*
- *the educational standards achieved in the school*
- *whether the financial resources made available to the school are managed efficiently*
- *the spiritual, moral, social and cultural development of pupils at the school.* [6]

OFSTED

The word 'OFSTED' is enough to strike fear into the hearts of many teachers, but as an NQT, you should remember that a little knowledge about the inspection process and the reasons for inspection could help to alleviate any concerns you may have. There have been changes made to the way OFSTED operates over the years since its inception and it is not always useful to listen to tales of inspections that took place several years ago.

The following section has been designed to give you a solid background to any OFSTED inspection you may face with the intention that it should assist in your preparation and place inspections in a helpful context.

The Office for Standards in Education, officially the Office of Her Majesty's Chief Inspector of Schools in England, was set up in 1992. It is a non-ministerial government department and is independent from the DfEE.

The reason for OFSTED's existence is to improve standards of achievement and quality of education through inspection and subsequent public reporting. Teams of inspectors led by a registered inspector carry out inspections. The size of the team varies according to the size and needs of the school.

OFSTED summarises the key aspects of its school inspection system in this way:

- *all schools are inspected regularly*
- *every inspection leads to a public report*
- *inspections conducted by independent inspectors*
- *inspection contracts won by competitive tendering*
- *every team has one lay member*
- *inspection carried out to a published national framework*
- *parents involved by being invited to pre-inspection meeting and sent summary of final report*
- *quality control for whole system in hands of independent government department – OFSTED.*[7]

OFSTED also inspects independent schools, LEAs (including aspects of youth and adult education) and teacher training institutions.

The Registered Inspector of an OFSTED team must ensure that inspections are of an extremely high quality. According to the *Framework for the Inspection of Schools*, [8] their judgements must be:

- **secure**, *in that they are rooted in a substantial evidence base and informed by specified quantitative indicators*
- **first-hand**, *in that they are based largely on direct observation of pupils' and teachers' work*
- **reliable**, *in that they are based on consistent application of the evaluation criteria in the inspection schedule contained in this Framework*
- **valid**, *in that they accurately reflect what is actually achieved and provided by the school*
- **comprehensive**, *in that they cover all aspects of the school set out in the inspection schedule and in the inspection contract specification*
- **corporate**, *in that conclusions about the school as a whole reflect the collective view of the inspection team.*

The Framework also outlines a code of conduct for inspectors, stating that they should:

- *carry out their work with professionalism, integrity and courtesy*
- *evaluate the work of the school objectively*
- *report honestly and fairly*
- *communicate clearly and frankly*
- *act in the best interests of the pupils at the school and*
- *respect the confidentiality of personal information received during the inspection.*

When a team of OFSTED inspectors visits your school, they will base their findings on evidence gathered under the following headings in the Framework:

- attainment and progress
- attitudes, behaviour and personal development
- attendance
- teaching
- the curriculum and assessment
- pupils' spiritual, moral, social and cultural development
- support, guidance and pupils' welfare
- partnership with parents and the community
- leadership and management
- staffing, accommodation and learning resources
- the efficiency of the school.

As an NQT, you should be particularly interested in the following sections. Think about how aspects of your teaching might be judged and how *you* can impact such judgements. What influence can you have on these areas? More often than not, you will already be focusing on these issues either directly or indirectly in your teaching, but you will need to *show* that you are.

Attitudes, behaviour and personal development

[Note: the following text concerning OFTSTED inspections is taken directly from the *Framework for the Inspection of Schools*.]

Inspectors must evaluate and report on pupils' response to the teaching and other provision made by the school, highlighting strengths and weaknesses as shown by:

- *their attitudes to learning*
- *their behaviour, including the incidence of exclusions*
- *the quality of relationships in the school, including the degree of racial harmony, where applicable*
- *other aspects of their personal development, including their contributions to the life of the community.*

Judgements should be based on the extent to which pupils:

- *show interest in their work and are able to sustain concentration and develop their capacity for personal study*
- *behave well in and around the school, are courteous and trustworthy and show respect for property*
- *form constructive relationships with one another, with teachers and other adults, and work collaboratively when required*
- *show respect for other people's feelings, values and beliefs*
- *show initiative and are willing to take responsibility.*

Attendance

Inspectors must evaluate and report on:

- *pupils' attendance and punctuality, analysing reasons for absence where attendance is poor or where patterns of absence affect particular groups of pupils.*

Judgements should be based on the extent to which:

- *pupils' attendance exceeds 90% and they come to school and lessons on time.*

Teaching

Inspectors must evaluate and report on:

- *the quality of teaching and its contribution to pupils' attainment and progress, highlighting:*
  - (i) *overall strengths and weaknesses in the teaching of pupils under 5, in each key stage, in the sixth form and in the different subjects or areas of learning inspected*

(ii) *factors which account for effective and ineffective teaching; and*

(iii) *the extent to which teaching meets the needs of all pupils, paying particular attention to any pupils who have special educational needs or for whom English is an additional language.*

Judgements should be based on the extent to which teachers [or other staff involved in teaching or providing learning-support]:

● *have a secure knowledge and understanding of the subjects or areas they teach*

● *set high expectations so as to challenge pupils and deepen their knowledge and understanding*

● *plan effectively*

● *employ methods and organisational strategies which match curricular objectives and the needs of all pupils*

● *manage pupils well and achieve high standards of discipline*

● *use time and resources effectively*

● *assess pupils' work thoroughly and constructively, and use assessments to inform teaching*

● *use homework effectively to reinforce and/or extend what is learned in school.*

Pupils' spiritual, moral, social and cultural development

Inspectors must evaluate and report on:

● *the strengths and weaknesses of the school's provision for the spiritual, moral, social and cultural development of all pupils, through the curriculum and life of the school: the example set for pupils by adults in the school; and the quality of collective worship.*

Judgements should be based on the extent to which the school:

● *provides its pupils with knowledge and insight into values and beliefs and enables them to reflect on their experiences in a way which develops their spiritual awareness and self-knowledge*

● *teaches the principles which distinguish right from wrong;*

● *encourages pupils to relate positively to others, take*

responsibility, participate fully in the community, and develop an understanding of citizenship

- teaches pupils to appreciate their own cultural traditions and the diversity and richness of other cultures.

Support, guidance and pupils' welfare

Inspectors must evaluate and report on:

- strengths and weaknesses in the school's provision for the educational and personal support and guidance of pupils and its contribution to educational standards achieved, taking account of individual needs
- the steps taken to ensure pupils' welfare
- the school's arrangements for child protection
- any matters which, in the view of inspectors, constitute a threat to health and safety.

Judgements should be based on the extent to which the school:

- provides effective support and advice for all its pupils, informed by monitoring of their academic progress, personal development, behaviour and attendance
- has effective measures to promote discipline and good behaviour and eliminate oppressive behaviour, including all forms of harassment and bullying
- has effective child protection procedures
- is successful in promoting the health, safety and general well being of its pupils.

Partnership with parents and the community

Inspectors must evaluate and report on

- the effectiveness of the school's partnership with parents, highlighting strengths and weaknesses, in terms of:
  - (i) the information provided about the school, and about pupils' work and progress through annual and other reports and parents' meetings
  - (ii) parents' involvement with the school and with their children's work at home.

- *the contribution which the school's links with the community make to pupils' attainment and personal development.*

Judgements should be based on the extent to which:
- *links with parents contribute to pupils' learning*
- *the school's work is enriched by links with the community, including employers, and provision for voluntary service and work experience for pupils of secondary age.*

The final report following an OFSTED inspection will include details on the characteristics of the school including information about the pupils and the area it serves, and the aims and priorities of the school. It will also look at key indicators, which summarise the attainment of boys, girls and all pupils at the end of each key stage, attendance and will state the percentage of teaching observed which is:
- very good or better
- satisfactory or better
- less than satisfactory.

Each teacher will be awarded a grade (1 to 7, with grades 1 and 2 being excellent or very good, grades 3 and 4 being good or satisfactory, and grades 5, 6 and 7 being less than satisfactory), and descriptor for their teaching. It is worth reading the OFSTED document, 'Inspection '98, Supplement to the Inspection Handbooks containing New Requirements and Guidance', as it includes detail on *how* teaching will be observed. You may find the following useful when thinking about how *your* teaching may fare against inspection – it has been taken from the above document.

Pupils should be:
- ***learning the right things.*** *The pupils should be acquiring or consolidating one or more of the key competencies that underpin the subject at a level appropriate to their age.*
- ***challenged*** *in relation to their earlier work. Pupils should be able to understand and cope successfully with lesson content, but only with intellectual, physical or creative effort.*

- **productive.** *Pupils should be working at the optimum pace – not too slow (off task, marking time) or too quick (failing to 'keep up').*
- **motivated.** *Pupils should be seeking help when needed, asking questions, learning from their mistakes, learning from each other, and so on.*

The DfEE Circular, 2/98, 'Reducing the Bureaucratic Burden on Teachers', highlights concerns that excessive time is spent preparing for OFSTED inspections. It recommends that schools facing inspection should concentrate on the essentials. Always keep this in mind when you are involved in an OFSTED inspection.

Regardless of the opinion of OFSTED that it is judge and jury of the teaching profession, it is here to stay. Use the following ideas as support in the event of an inspection.

BEFORE THE INSPECTORS ARRIVE

Although the prospect of an OFSTED inspection will probably send your school into a frenzy of preparation tinged with more than a hint of anxiety, it is important to keep a perspective of your role in all this. As an NQT, you will be inspected on *your* teaching and the way you manage *your* job.

It can be helpful to remember the three main principles underpinning the inspection and reporting of teaching as presented in the OFSTED document, 'Inspection '98, Briefing for Schools on the New Inspection Requirements':

- *to give as much **value** as possible to teachers and the school from inspection*
- *to be **sensitive** to the pressure that inspection brings to the staff in schools*
- *to maintain **confidentiality** of information.*

Inspectors are well aware of the potential trauma of an inspection. Don't think of them as ogres who are detached from life in schools.

- Your headteacher will be given the opportunity to hold a meeting where staff can meet the registered inspector. If you are asked to

EFFECTIVE AND INEFFECTIVE LEARNING

(Taken from the OFSTED document, 'Inspection '98, Supplement to the Inspection Handbooks Containing New Requirements and Guidance')

Pupils are likely to be learning effectively and therefore making more progress than expected (grades 1–3) when they are:	Pupils are likely to be ineffective in their learning and therefore making less progress than expected (grades 5–7) when they are:
● clear about what needs to be done	● unsure about what they are supposed to be doing
● engaged and informed by good teaching or in activities in which they are learning the right things suitable for their age	● occupied by purposeless teaching activities from which they cannot improve their standards in key competencies
● clear about what they are trying to achieve and how their work can be improved	● finding work unduly hard, or too easy or restricting
● understanding what they are doing and finding tasks demanding but achievable with sustained effort	● not knowing what to do to improve
● seeking and getting help when needed	● working at too slow or too fast a pace
● staying on task throughout, and maintaining a good work rate when set challenging tasks to do	● poorly motivated.
● well motivated.	
Over a period of time, new, relevant and appropriately challenging learning acquired at a very good rate in relation to what the pupils had achieved previously would be evidence of highly effective learning. Pupils can be learning effectively when acquiring or consolidating their knowledge, skills and understanding.	Over a period of time, repeated failure or undue repetition of work which is always correct, inappropriately slow rate of developing new knowledge, skills or understanding in relation to what they have already achieved or over-concentration on too narrow a range of the curriculum, would be evidence of ineffective learning.

OFSTED INSPECTIONS

Even though you are an NQT, an inspection should not happen *to* you. There are valid contributions for all teachers to make and you should allow yourself to feel empowered by that. The OFSTED document, 'Making the Most of Inspection' (1998), suggests that all teachers should:

- get to know the OFSTED 'Framework' and the criteria on which teaching will be judged
- make sure that they are involved in the school's normal review and development activities, particularly in relation to planning, teaching and use of assessment
- accept that inspectors will wish to see them working as normally as possible
- teach as they would normally teach. Inspectors will not expect to see particular methods of teaching except where schools have committed themselves to particular approaches such as the literacy framework of the National Literacy Strategy. Inspection is concerned with the effect of teaching on educational standards and in promoting pupils' learning and does not prejudge what works best.

attend such a meeting, make sure you go because it will allay many of your anxieties. Don't forget that as an NQT you are probably one of the few teachers in your school who has not already been through an OFSTED inspection. Prepare some questions before the meeting or talk to your headteacher about any fears you might have. He or she will be able tactfully to present your questions to the registered inspector. After the meeting, you should at least know how the lesson observation forms will be used and how your teaching will be evaluated.

- Avoid panic and stress by talking about your concerns. Lean on your induction tutor/mentor and try to contact NQTs in other schools who have been through an OFSTED inspection. Internet

INSPECTION AS AN NQT

- No allowances are made for the fact that you are an NQT. However, inspectors are told exactly how long each member of staff has been teaching and will not expect new entrants to the profession to be experts.
- You cannot be held responsible for what has happened in your school in the past.
- As someone in their first year of teaching, you are in an excellent position to develop your skills as a teacher using any conclusions from the inspection. Use the inspection as an indicator of progress made since qualifying.
- Get support from other NQTs. There are heaps of inspection jokes around to lighten your thoughts!
- Don't prepare excessively. If you do you will certainly pay afterwards in terms of post-OFSTED apathy and fatigue which could undo your hard work. Keep a steady, realistic pace.

newsgroups can be excellent for networking.
- Take heart from the fact that NQTs, being used to having their work observed, generally perform well in OFSTED inspections.
- Recognise that you may have a need for increased relaxation during the weeks leading up to the inspection.
- Spend time talking to pupils about the inspection. The high media profile of OFSTED inspections means that they can be well aware of what is going on.
- If there is a class or child you are particularly concerned about try talking to them in advance. Express your concerns and visualise your best possible scenario. Is there anything you can do to ease the situation? Take care not to over-prime; an inspector will detect this with ease.
- Aim to be totally prepared for the inspection week so that you

don't have to work on lesson plans too much while the inspectors are at your school. You should have copies of lesson plans for inspectors to pick up as they enter your room, or leave them on the seat you would like them to use (preferably next to some 'angels'!)

- Give the inspector any additional information he/she may find useful, for example, if a child in the class is going through a particular difficulty such as bereavement.
- Script certain parts of each lesson so that you know exactly what you will say.
- Look at your pupils' exercise books and replace any that are too damaged by graffiti.

ACTION: Consider these questions when you are facing an inspection:

- *What was your immediate reaction to hearing about the impending inspection?*
- *What are your greatest fears about the inspection?*
- *Do you have any unanswered questions about the inspection?*
- *Do you want to focus on any aspect of your work before the inspection?*

Discuss your answers with your induction tutor/mentor and other NQTs. Make sure you find answers to your concerns in good time.

DURING THE INSPECTION

'The worst thing you can possibly do is worry about what you could have done.' Lichtenberg.

- Don't change the way you teach; trying new things out for your audience is not a good idea. Don't worry that your lessons may seem unexciting. You should be given the opportunity to discuss with inspectors the *context* of the work you were observed doing and your rationale for the work.

- One inspector compared inspection with the driving test. You know how to teach/drive, but you have to *show* the inspector/examiner that you do. There will be many aspects of your teaching/driving that you do subconsciously, but you must make sure that the inspector/examiner *knows* you are doing them. The best analogy for this is looking in the rear-view mirror during a driving test. If you don't physically move your head, the examiner may not realise you have performed this crucial task and fail you. *Show* or *tell* the inspector all aspects of your teaching, especially your attention to detail; make explicit the implicit.

- It will come as no surprise that drama teachers tend to do well in inspections. Being able to rise to the occasion with a little acting will certainly serve you well.

ABOUT

OBSERVATIONS

According to the OFSTED document, 'Making the Most of Inspection, a Guide to Inspection for Schools and Governors' (1998), during the inspection the inspectors will 'observe pupils and teachers at work' and, 'note and evaluate what they see.' These notes will include:

- what the lesson is about
- what is being taught, how, and the impact of that teaching
- evidence and evaluation of pupils' attainment, progress and interest and involvement in the lesson
- information about factors such as resources, accommodation and use of support staff.

The inspector observing your lesson will be filling in an observation form. He/she will make evaluations according to a seven point scale ranging from excellent (1) to very poor (6–7). Inspectors may talk to pupils about their understanding of the work and whether what they are doing is normal practice. Any such discussions should be totally unobtrusive.

- If a lesson seems to fall apart, stop what you are doing and start another activity. You will then be able to demonstrate your flexibility and originality when it comes to problem solving.
- At least 60% of inspectors' time will be spent in lesson observations. However, inspectors have a responsibility to monitor the amount of time that each teacher is inspected. The document, 'Inspection '98, Briefing for Schools on the New Inspection Requirements', states that:

    Teachers should not normally be observed teaching for more than half of a teaching day and apart from exceptional circumstances must not be observed for more than three quarters of the day. The underlying principle is that inspectors must take a proper professional responsibility to ease the pressure on teachers.

- You should be given an indication of how the inspector feels your lessons are going. The days of icy glares not cracking until feedback time have thankfully long gone!
- If you have any concerns about the way that the inspection of your teaching is going, talk to your headteacher. He/she will be meeting the registered inspector on a daily basis so will be able to raise your concerns. For example, you may feel that you are being inspected too frequently.
- Make sure you indulge in some quality relaxation during inspection week. Perhaps some early nights or a massage?

EXAMPLE:
'When the task is done beforehand, then it is easy.' Ch'an Master Yuantong.
Although Louise was exhausted from the anticipation of the inspection she actually found the week quite exhilarating. Being so thoroughly prepared meant that her lessons flowed more smoothly than usual and she even found herself feeling pleased when an inspector arrived at her door to observe a lesson.

- Try to enjoy the week! This may seem impossible, but you will be more prepared than usual and more clued up on the work of your school, so ride that wave as much as you can.

ABOUT

THE INSPECTION

According to the document, 'Making the Most of Inspection', the inspectors will do the following during an inspection:

- *look for evidence to make judgements on all the criteria in the Framework*
- *observe teachers teaching*
- *discuss work with pupils*
- *look for evidence of planning and recording*
- *look for evidence of standards of attainment, how well pupils are learning and the quality of teaching*
- *fill in lesson observation forms to provide evidence of what works and what does not in lessons and how well pupils are learning*
- *offer feedback to teachers on the strengths and weaknesses of their teaching and on their management responsibilities*
- *provide informal feedback to the headteacher and other senior managers and to the governors.*

Feedback

You will be offered oral feedback on the quality of your teaching towards the end of the inspection. The aim of this feedback is to explain the strengths and weaknesses of your teaching *as indicated by the snapshot of your skills that the inspection provided.* Inspectors must 'spell out for teachers what works and what does not work, drawing from the evidence [you have] collected.'[9] The most important thing to remember here is that inspectors will be commenting on what they have observed *during the inspection*. It is not a judgement on your teaching in the past or on your expected future progress in the profession. You may be sent a statement of your grade a few days after the inspection, but this varies as inspection teams do work differently in this respect. If possible, ask your induction tutor/mentor to attend such feedback – it can be easy to hear the negative, ignore the positive and feel that you have to change *all* aspects of your teaching. If someone else is listening to what is said, they can elicit the important points for discussion afterwards.

AFTER THE INSPECTION

Within five weeks of the inspection, a final report will be sent to the headteacher and governors of your school. They will then have ten days to send the summary report to parents and make the report public in libraries. They may even want to contact the press (depending on the outcome of course). It is at this point that the work really starts. An action plan for school improvement must be written in response to the inspection report and this usually involves all members of staff.

Think about these points when the inspection is over:

- Don't cling on to the grade you are given too firmly. In an independent survey of schools' views by Market and Opinion Research International (MORI) during the summer term 1998, just under half of the schools who responded most valued inspection as an independent diagnosis of strengths and weaknesses. *Few felt that the teaching grades were important.* The grade you are given is not an absolute judgement but a snapshot at that time.
- There is often a collapse of morale after the inspection regardless of the outcome. Keeping the momentum going until the end of term can be a chore, but this is the same in most schools. If you feel tired or 'flat', ease up on your planning and try to take some time out for relaxation and hobbies.
- If you are very unhappy about the way you were treated during the inspection, there is now the opportunity to make a complaint.

The complaints procedure is sent to all schools when they are advised of an imminent inspection. Your school should also have set up a forum for the airing of concerns related to the inspection. If your concerns have not been heard by the time the inspection has ended, contact your union for advice before complaining to OFSTED. There are basically six steps that can be taken, but it is best not to take any without advice. Your union will be able to advise you.

- Many schools mark the end of an inspection with some form of celebration. This is important as you have collectively reached a milestone in a school's life and to ignore this fact can be a missed opportunity to give each other the proverbial pat on the back. You could also aim to treat yourself in some way when the dust has settled and your energy has returned.

OTHER OBSERVATIONS

As an NQT you will have other teachers observing your lessons as part of your induction. This can be daunting, but is mostly very constructive. However, in order for the observations to hold value for you, aim to:

- spend time beforehand talking to your observer about the lesson you plan to teach, its place in the scheme of work and what it will lead on to
- give your observer all the necessary documents for the lesson, e.g. lesson plan (if applicable) and any work sheets or textbooks used
- decide where would be the best place for your observer to sit
- decide how much of the lesson will be observed
- decide when you can meet to discuss the lesson and hear the feedback
- listen to the feedback carefully and accept any tips that may be offered while justifying your actions when appropriate.

Utilising the feedback

It can be tiresome when you have completed your training, to listen to yet another review of your teaching skills. However, think of these positive aspects:

- your observer may not have seen you teach before so will be looking at you through fresh eyes
- you will be observed in the context of *your* school, therefore feedback should be specific to your job.

EXAMPLE: 'I was due to be observed by my mentor and she was late for the lesson. I had introduced to the class what I had planned for them so when she finally turned up she had missed the crucial part. In her feedback she kept talking about what I could have done differently when, if she had looked at my scheme of work, she could have seen my rationale for doing what I did. I was really angry that I had spent so much time preparing for the observation in vain.' NQT, Greenwich.

After each observation you should be given some constructive feedback. This should reflect on what happened in the lesson, what was learnt by the children and how effective your teaching appeared to be. The discussion should be two way. Don't feel you have to sit and listen to what your observer has to say without being able to interject and explain your actions and decisions.

You may want amend your Career Entry Profile. This will help you to glean the most from the observations and to feel that you are not working alone by involving your induction tutor/mentor. Often, additional support and training is blocked by lack of money. If there isn't any money for you to go on courses etc., there needs to be some other form of affordable follow-up care, which can be written into your action plan. Try not to let any amendments be forgotten until the next observation, inspection or appraisal when it is likely that the same points will be picked up. If the appropriate support is not forthcoming, talk to your induction tutor/mentor.

Computer-related ICT and the NQT

This is quite a controversial area of teaching, with daunting expectations of ITT courses combining with the mixed bag of resources available in schools (with some still being described as 'information poor').

A starting point for NQTs must be the document outlining the requirements of the ITT national curriculum for the use of ICT in subject teaching. A copy of this can be downloaded from the Teacher Training Agency website. It is a very comprehensive document covering all the expectations of NQTs regarding effective teaching and assessment methods, and knowledge and understanding of, and competence with, information and communications technology. Make sure you read this document; it not only outlines what you have to know, but also makes some useful suggestions on the applications of ICT.

The purpose of this section is to highlight just some of the opportunities for NQTs to receive support and information about useful applications for ICT rather than to focus on detailing the knowledge that NQTs are supposed to have. There could well be a gap in skills that NQTs must fill once in post, especially if the ITT institution passed responsibility for ICT training on to a hard-pressed teaching-practice school. When you consider that the long-term goal is that, by 2002, all of those in service must 'feel confident and are competent to teach using ICT within the curriculum',[10] knowing how to seek support is going to be crucial.

Clearly it is going to take time to get everyone up to the expected standards and key issues about the use of ICT in schools will have to be addressed (issues to do with equality of opportunity and financing to name a few). Nevertheless, ICT in schools is being given 'massive priority' and the emphasis is on an ICT culture in all schools, at all ages and in all subjects.

ONLINE SUPPORT

Internet support for teachers is growing literally every day, from individual teachers sharing their schemes of work and lesson plans to commercial organisations providing a rich selection of resources. And, of course, there's the government support too in the form of the National Grid for Learning (NGfL) at www.ngfl.gov.uk.

The National Grid for Learning

There are three main elements of the National Grid for Learning (NGfL):

- a structure of useful educational material on the Internet which is administered by the British Educational Communications and Technology Agency (BECTA)
- a programme for ensuring access for schools etc.
- a programme of ICT training for those involved in education.

It aims to 'connect the learning society' and be a major part of the way teachers use the Internet both for teaching and preparation as well as being a resource for other members of the learning society. It would be well worth reading BECTA's information sheets on the NGfL as well as their documents 'Making the Most of the NGfL' (available for primary, secondary and FE teachers).

The development of the 'Grid' is ongoing so the resource links already in existence will grow. At the time of writing, it has over 60 000 different pages of information. The sites within the Grid are all safe and appropriate for teaching as they are closely monitored by 'web-keepers'. Have a good look at the Virtual Teacher Centres (VTCs) as they are designed to support your work as a teacher.

Future support

Hundreds of millions of pounds have been allocated to the training of serving teachers using money from the National Lottery, and the use of ICT in schools is now one of the most important focuses of today's curriculum. While it is expected that this will be directed towards those already in the profession in order to bring them up to the standards of the ITT curriculum for ICT, it is important for NQTs to be heard in their requests for further ICT training. This is especially so as some of the Lottery-funded courses will be modular and could count towards masters degrees. Don't miss out.

ABOUT

LOTTERY-FUNDED ICT COURSES

Contracts are being awarded to ICT companies to provide computer-based training for serving teachers as well as needs identification materials and skills audits. In some cases, this training may be modular (leading to certificates and perhaps contributing to a masters degree) and is likely to include generic ICT skills, subject-specific applications, pedagogical and management issues and legal, moral and ethical issues associated with ICT.[11]

There are many other initiatives such as the BBC's 'Computers Don't Bite for Teachers'. Talk to your ICT co-ordinator to find out what you are entitled to in your school. Even if you are fully competent, there are always improvements that can be made and skills learnt. Do also read about ICT in the education press. *The Times Educational Supplement* produces its ONLINE supplement regularly which focuses on computers in education.

You may well have a role in training serving teachers but be sure to prevent this from becoming an additional burden. You should always be given time and choices when asked to take on additional duties and there may even be some payment for such a task. Check with your union if you have been asked to undertake such training.

APPLICATIONS OF ICT FOR NQTS

There are many possible applications of ICT here, and only two initial questions to ask of any application you may have for ICT in the course of your work:

- Will it improve the quality of education I deliver?
- Will it ease my workload?

Both are equally valid questions to ask.

Don't forget the other forms of ICT that have traditionally had a role to play in education, such as radio, TV and video. They can all add to the breadth of your lessons when used appropriately and are simply tools to aid the delivery of the skills you must teach.

Using ICT within your curriculum area

This is where subject-specific INSET will be invaluable. The key is to know the best situations in which to use ICT and when not to use it.

- When will it add to the quality of your teaching?
- When is ICT the *best* resource to use?
- Are there explicit links between the subject matter and the application of ICT in each circumstance?
- Is it possible for children to identify what they have learnt from the application of ICT in your lesson?

Use your links with NQTs in other schools to find out what software and CD ROMs they are using and what web sites they make use of, as well as taking advice from your curriculum leader(s) and the advisor responsible for NQTs in your LEA (who will be able to talk to the relevant advisors/inspectors for your curriculum area). Any schemes of work that you follow should have ICT opportunities highlighted, especially where they may benefit the way you teach children with special educational needs.

With such a rapidly changing market, there will be new resources available on a daily basis and it's virtually impossible to keep your finger on every pulse, so lean on the support that's there.

Communication

This may at first appear to be of limited use to NQTs, but this is not the case.

E-mail

This is an excellent form of communication for teachers. You can keep in touch with former colleagues and your training institution and access your mail on your terms. It is much less demanding than using the telephone.

> *EXAMPLE: One NQT decided to make as much use of the e-mail system as possible. He asked pupils to e-mail questions to him. The only proviso was that the questions had to be on topics covered recently and prizes were introduced for the most ingenious. It sounds like a lot of work, but it certainly encouraged the use of ICT. If pupils at your school have e-mail addresses you could e-mail individual homework questions to pupils as a novelty, but tell them when to check their mail.*

Newsgroups

The use of newsgroups as a teacher's aide is only just beginning to be recognised. They are an excellent way of sharing ideas, gaining answers to questions that would previously have taken valuable time to research and linking with teachers overseas. It is a good idea to 'lurk' for a while to get an idea of the nature of the group before posting your own message. Don't be surprised by the goodwill out there. There are many people willing to spend time helping you problem-solve.

As a starting point, look at:

- uk.education.staffroom
- uk.education.teachers
- uk.education.governors

Do also search for other education newsgroups as this is a growth area and it is likely that more specific groups will appear before long (e.g. a subject-based group for a particular LEA etc.). You could even set one up. The NGfL, BECTA and DfEE also have discussion groups. See:

- http://vtc.ngfl.gov.uk/vtc/meeting/meeting.html
- http://www.standards.dfee.gov.uk/discussion
- http://www.becta.org.uk/senco/sources/senfor.html

Also look at the electronic mailing lists hosted at:

- http://www.mailbase.ac.uk
- http://www.zola.ngfl.gov.uk/cgi-bin/majordomo

Newsgroups can help to guard against the isolation that some teachers experience. You can also use them to pass on skills that you have learnt and share *your* resources. You are in a profession that can only thrive in a culture of give and take. There is simply no need to keep reinventing the wheel.

Resource preparation

Gone are the days when a hastily cobbled worksheet will suffice. ICT is being used ingeniously by teachers around the country to produce excellent class-specific, and even pupil-specific resources. There may be hard work involved initially, but with the time-saving properties of ICT, they can be readily adapted with ease.

Word processing and desktop publishing

Use clipart to add eye-catching graphics to worksheets. Vary the font and font size as appropriate and remember that, if you are using ICT to create acetates for overhead projectors, you will need to use large print.

When asking pupils to use word-processing skills, encourage them to take advantage of the creative/design aspects of the task. Whatever their subject, all documents should have at least some element of this in their production.

The Internet

Not only can this help with your own research and in teaching research skills to pupils (crucial in any subject), but some teachers are now taking advantage of their own free space from home connections and creating their own web pages. There are some great examples around; look at the teachers' newsgroups for links.

By creating your own web site, you are providing direct access for pupils and parents to the work of the classes you teach. You could use it to post extra snippets of work and puzzles etc. and to display pupils' work. You could also include information for parents on the way you teach, homework polices, classroom rules etc. See Appendix 8 for information on books to guide you through web page design.

Although the number of homes with Internet access is still relatively small, you could encourage pupils to use the site while at school and invite parents to browse it on parents' evenings or other occasions when they are in school.

Record keeping

Put an end to scrappy mark books filled with blobs of correction fluid! Use ICT to store records of pupils' attainment and of progress through schemes of work. However, you will probably still want to make use of a daily planner unless you have a computer *for personal use* in your classroom.

Be aware of how you can link databases and spreadsheets with word-processed documents. This can make report writing easier if you are keeping an ongoing record of achievement of each child in, for example, Word, as well as records of the group's marks in a spreadsheet.

One word of caution. Think about the content of information you keep on a computer that pupils may have access to. Your ICT co-ordinator will be able to give you advice on data protection/confidentiality considerations.

Databases

Databases are excellent for the storage of schemes of work and information on classes. They can help in the organisation of most aspects of your work as a teacher and cut down on the amount of paper you need to accumulate.

Spreadsheets

Spreadsheets have applications for teachers of all subjects. They are particularly useful for keeping track of coursework, forecasting and 'what if' scenarios. Use them in conjunction with ongoing records of achievement and your task at report-writing time is easy!

HEALTH AND SAFETY ISSUES

It is important to be aware of health and safety with ICT. Much will, of course, be commonsense; nevertheless, repetitive strain injury (RSI) and eyestrain in particular need to be guarded against. You also have a responsibility to ensure that ICT equipment is used safely.

- Make sure you are familiar with your school's policy on health and safety when using ICT.
- Think about workstation design and encourage pupils to make changes to their seating arrangements where possible.
- Teach good postures for sitting (forearms horizontal and parallel with thighs) and encourage children to be aware of the distance between the screen and their eyes.

The BECTA information sheet, 'Health and Safety with IT'[12] suggests that teachers should be aware of these issues:

Electrical safety

Watch out for:
- stray leads – re-route, secure and cover
- trailing flexes – secure and cover
- frayed leads – replace
- damaged plugs – replace
- overloading/power surging

- *coiled cables – where the heat generated could be sufficient to start a fire*
- *accidental damage – from dust, spilt liquid, users etc.*

The information sheet also mentions a number of other hazards:

- **Noise** Think about ways of reducing background noise of ICT equipment by switching off the sound on software packages where appropriate and the machines themselves when they are not in use.
- **Heat** Be aware of the heat that ICT equipment builds up – ventilate the area well.
- **Light** Use blinds to reduce the glare of screens (dim them if necessary) and keep them clean.
- **Space** Keep workstations free from clutter and allow for more than one person to access each machine at a time.
- **User comfort** Adjust the height of screens and the brightness/colour when needed. Also think about the hygiene of headphones etc. Think about using glare guards, wrist rests, footstools and copy holders.

Useful web sites

The following web sites may be useful. Follow the links once in as these sites are being updated all the time and relevant new universal resource locators (URLs) are being added frequently. Time your surfing sessions though. Linking from site to site can be addictive and it is easy to lose track of time.

For information about:

- NGfL: http://www.ngfl.gov.uk
- BECTA: http://www.becta.org.uk
- VTCs: http://www.ngfl.gov.uk, http://www.svtc.org.uk, http://www.vtccymru.ngfl.wales.gov.uk
- DfEE: http://www.dfee.gov.uk (Superhighways and Multimedia Unit can be reached at: super.highways@dfee.gov.uk). Also look at: http://www.standards.dfee.gov.uk and http://www.dfee.gov.uk/teachers
- Scottish Council for Educational Technology (SCET):

http://www.scet.org.uk

- tips on searching the web: http://www.monash.com/spidap.html
- SEN: http://www.becta.org.uk/senco/sources/senorgs.html
- ICT training and support providers:
http://www.becta.org/projects/support/services/

Also try these for education resources:

- http://www.yahoo.co.uk/education
- http://www.uce.ac.uk/tapin
- http://www.spartacus.schoolnet.co.uk/teachers.html
- http://www.nine.org.uk (the Northern Ireland Network for Education)
- http://www.argosphere.net
- http://www.bbc.co.uk/education/schools/
- http://www.schools.channel4.com
- http://www.yearofreading.org.uk
- http://www.askjeeves.com

ABOUT

PROTECTING YOUR COMPUTER

With so much conflicting information about the extent of the virus problem, it is important to take the risk of damage seriously. There are over 20,000 viruses in existence (with 100 new viruses being identified each month) but only a few cause 98% of the damage.[13] Take preventative measures by installing anti-virus software on your own machine and restricting the amount of data you transfer from one machine to another. Only use machines allocated for teachers' use when working at school, back up all your work on paper and disk and only accept files from trusted sources. However, it is impossible to reduce the risks of infection completely if you are going to take advantage of the Internet, e-mailing and newsgroups. For information about hoax viruses and useful links try:

http://www.pa.msu.edu/services/computing/virus-info.html

Looking ahead

As you reach the successful conclusion of your induction year you can look ahead to a career in which you will face many challenges, changes and triumphs. There are so many directions you could take and ways you can make a positive impact on the lives of your pupils in a society that now demands creativity and resourcefulness. Here are just some ideas to consider:

THE CHANGING FEATURES OF TEACHING

Performance-related pay is not the only changing feature of teaching at present. There are also:

Multiple intelligences

Multiple intelligences, whether we love them or hate them, are creating quite a stir both in the UK and in the USA, where Multiple Intelligence (MI) schools seem to be popular. While some may be arguing for these ideas to be jettisoned, others have successfully incorporated aspects of the MI theory into their teaching. Thankfully we are not at the stage of prescribing philosophies of education so you are free to reach your own conclusions.

The MI theory, formulated by Howard Gardner in the 1980s, has been described as 'a pluralised way of understanding the intellect'.[14] Gardner breaks down the concept of 'intelligence' into eight categories:

- musical intelligence
- bodily-kinaesthetic intelligence
- logical-mathematical intelligence
- linguistic intelligence
- spatial intelligence
- interpersonal intelligence
- intrapersonal intelligence
- naturalist intelligence.

According to the theory, everyone has different profiles of intelligence and education must take this into account. A favourite question of Gardner to teachers is, 'If you had one hour a term to teach your pupils, what would you teach them?' Some of these ideas have been built on by the organisation, **Re:membering Education**, which believes that children need (and aren't necessarily getting) an education which will enable them to have:

- *a strong sense of self and an empathetic awareness of others*
- *an awareness of the role and power of emotions in decision-making*
- *a sound basis for their values and morality*
- *a tolerance of diversity and difference*
- *a sense of meaning and purpose in their lives.*

The five-term year

The five-term year is an idea being piloted in some areas and thought about in others. The basic aim is to change the structure of school year from one which allowed children in the past to help their parents with the harvest to one more in line with the needs of today's society.

There would be five eight-week terms with two-week holidays in mid-October, Christmas, early March and late May and four weeks' holiday in the summer. This would cover the last weeks of July and the first weeks of August.

The five-term year would have a considerable impact on the flow and pace of each term, much reducing the risk of teachers suffering from near burn-out at the end of long terms (especially when the half-term break has been used to catch up on administration and marking). However, the jury is still out, but it would be worth considering whether you would like to work in this way.

The shift from teaching to learning

'Education today, more than ever before, must see clearly the dual objectives: education for living and education for making a living.'
James Mason Wood.

What does 'the shift from teaching to learning' actually mean? Is it just rhetoric? We are told about life-long learning, learning through doing (or experiential learning) and that learning is not only happening in the classroom. This recognition of the fact that we learn from all contexts of life is opening up possible directions of change for schools.

In Birmingham Education Authority, the University of the First Age and the Children's University provide community-based, interest-led accelerated learning for children outside school hours. This is an admirable initiative when you consider that even if a child spends every possible minute throughout childhood in school, in other words has no time off for events such as sickness, he/she will only be there for 9 minutes out of every 60 minutes of waking time.

Computer-assisted learning

Perhaps, in the near future, pupils will be able to link in to expert teachers supplying remote tutorial support. As computer-based ICT transforms opportunities for learning and teaching (with some software so sophisticated it diagnoses problems in learning), what is the role of the teacher of the future? The views of educators are needed as a guide through this important time. It would appear that teachers will be managing a learning environment far larger than the classroom. It's something to ponder.

POSSIBLE FUTURE DIRECTIONS

Although continuing professional development is largely your responsibility, your school should be ensuring that you have the opportunities to undertake appropriate, valuable development and that you are motivated in this.

There are many opportunities for the teacher with a little spare cash. Here are just some ideas from the Institute of Education, University of London:

- **Advanced Diploma in Education** This is a stepping stone between ITT and an MA.

CONTINUING PROFESSIONAL DEVELOPMENT

A sad fact about teaching is that much professional development must be undertaken in your own time and at your own expense. Here are some points to consider:

- If you want to stay in your present school, make sure that any course you do has specific application to the needs of the school. Talk to your headteacher about your proposals. In the meantime, take every opportunity to attend INSET and perhaps run an INSET course, if you are asked.

- If you will want to move on to a different school in the near future, select a course that is specific to where you want to go in education. Simply going for the qualification (i.e. an MA) is not enough any more. Read the education press for ideas and talk to colleagues.

- Think about funding issues. It would be extremely unusual for your school or LEA to pay for the course but sometimes agreements can be reached.

- Find out exactly how a specific course would suit you and your work.

- Ask whether you will be given any time to complete the course, even if it is only a couple of hours of non-contact time. Again, this would be very unusual.

- **Specialist Advanced Diploma** This is an opportunity to specialise in a particular area such as educational psychology or management.
- **Advanced Diploma in Professional Studies** This is a flexibly structured course in which you can choose from a selection of modules.
- **Master's courses** These are run in just about any subject.
- **Research degrees** These are more suitable once you are firmly into your career. Degrees awarded include Master of Philosophy and Doctor of Philosophy in Education.

Your local university will be able to give exact details of appropriate courses in your vicinity and the VTCs also offer ideas on professional development. You may also want to consider teacher-exchange programmes. There are huge personal and professional benefits involved. For example, you could get direct experience of another education system, different teaching methods and strategies and access to new materials, not to mention an insight into another culture.

Pacing your targets

As the induction year is so busy, it probably won't be until your second year at the earliest that you start to think about your own target setting for additional qualifications. When you do get round to this, pacing is crucial. Expect too much of yourself and your performance will suffer, not enough and you risk stagnation.

If possible, don't depend on future study for anything ('I must complete this MA in two years otherwise I won't be able to go for … by my deadline'). This will keep harmful stress at bay and allow you to work at a pace most suitable for you. If you can possibly do a modular course with the option of self-planning, this may be more appropriate to combine with a full-time job.

Above all, make sure that any further professional development you do above the INSET you are offered responds to issues raised by your induction and Career Entry Profile and serves to fuel your enthusiasm for your career.

1   Rechtschaffen, S. (1996). Rider Books, London.
2   Wilson, P. *Calm at Work*. (1997). Penguin Books, London.
3   *Statistics of Education* (1997). The Stationery Office, London.
4   Mindell, E. (1985). *The Vitamin Bible* (2nd edition). Arlington Books.
5   *Framework for the Inspection of Schools* (1995). The Stationery Office, London.
6   Ibid.

7   'Background Briefing on OFSTED'. Document available from OFSTED (see Appendix 7).

8   *Framework for the Inspection of Schools* (1995). The Stationery Office, London.

9   'Inspection '98, Supplement to the Inspection Handbooks Containing New Requirements and Guidance'. OFSTED, 1998.

10 'The Government's Commitment' http://www.dfee.gov.uk/grid/challenge/govern.htm

11 Maxim Training, Brighton, in partnership with the University of Western England.

12 http://www.becta.org.uk/info-sheets/HandS.html

13 TES ONLINE, 16 October 1998.

14 'MI – The Theory' http://edweb.cnidr.org/edref.mi.th.html

CHAPTER 5

Frequently asked questions

'A teacher affects eternity; he can
never tell where his influence stops.'
Henry Brooks Adams.

Before gaining employment

**I have been asked to attend an interview and have been told that I
may have to teach part of a lesson. Should I be given more detail
before the day?**

It would be extremely poor practice if you arrived on the day and had
not been told exactly whom you were going to be teaching and for
how long. You should certainly be given more detail before the day.
The purpose of practical sessions in interviews is for members of the
panel to assess how well you interact with pupils, whether you ask
probing, stretching questions and if you can judge the ability of pupils
and adjust your delivery accordingly. The usual format for this is for
the interviewee to take a small group of pupils for approximately 20
minutes.

I have attended several interviews without success and feel sure that my nerves affect my performance. How can I remedy this?

Preparation can help to relieve anxiety. Find out as much about the school as you can before the interview. Pay attention to your diet for the few days prior to the interview and aim to avoid stimulants such as caffeine, chocolate, alcohol, sugar and nicotine, as these can make you feel 'hyped' and contribute to feelings of anxiety. Use positive self-talk so that negative thinking doesn't take hold. Affirmations such as, 'I perform very well in interviews' or 'I answer the questions I am asked with ease' can work wonders, as can visualising yourself being successful. Keep a bottle of Bach 'Rescue Remedy' (available at many wholefood outlets) in your pocket and take as directed; it is extremely calming. A massage the day before an interview will also help to relax you.

If this doesn't work, ask your tutor from college or a trusted friend or relative to take you through some mock interviews.

I have not managed to secure employment for September. Will this affect my career prospects?

Not at all, providing you use the time gaining additional experience. Once your financial position is sorted out (you could get a temporary part-time job, or sign on), you could organise some voluntary work in a local school. If there is a 'Small School' near you, voluntary work there would give you valuable insight into the alternatives available. You could also look into special schools. Add any additional experience you gain while job seeking to your CV and Career Entry Profile. When you do find a job and start mid-year, find out *at the interview* what the implications will be for your induction year – when will you be deemed to have completed your induction? Will you be given any additional support? Sometimes delays like this can be a blessing in disguise. You may not be in full-time employment, but what additional experience has it allowed you to get? You will probably find you will go for very different jobs as a result.

I have been offered a job but, as a mature entrant to the profession with ten years experience in industry, I am not happy with the salary I have been offered.

You have a mandatory entitlement to two points for a good honours degree (second class and above) and one full point for every year in which you have completed at least 26 weeks as a teacher in employment, up to a combined total of nine points. Your school will have a salaries policy that will cover the award of points for non-teaching experience and it really is at the discretion of your employers as to what points you will be awarded. However, your union will be able to offer advice on what you should be paid and may also offer to negotiate an improved salary on your behalf. This is probably your best option. If you feel you are the victim of ageism, contact the Association of Teachers Against Ageism as they would be interested in hearing about your experiences.

Having completed my training, I am not sure whether I want to enter the teaching profession. What are my options?

Having got this far, it would be a good idea to complete successfully an induction year. At least you won't have that ahead of you in future if you subsequently decide to teach. This would also give you a greater insight into the profession, as being a teacher in your own right is very different from being a student. Aim to get a job in a school other than where you did your training for a greater breadth of experience.

However, if you are *sure* that teaching is not for you, there would be little point in forcing yourself to pursue a path that is so obviously wrong. Take some careers guidance from your training institution for ideas on what could be your next step. Above all, view your decision *positively*. If you have cause for regret, perhaps it would be better to complete an induction year.

I am having to broaden my job search to include LEAs and areas I am unfamiliar with. Will this cause problems if and when I start work?

LEAs do have different ways of working, but you will be told about anything that is relevant to you and your work as part of your induction process. Don't let the fact that you are unfamiliar with an LEA stop you from applying for a job. It is your colleagues, your school and its pupils who will be your main concerns, once you are in post.

I have been offered a job but have another interview in a school in which I think I would rather work in a few days. What can I do?

This is a difficult situation. It is unlikely that the school that offered you a job will wait for you to be offered another and then weigh up the odds! You can ask for time to consider the first offer, or be totally honest and explain your dilemma. Unfortunately, the most likely outcome of this sort of situation involves taking an empty-handed leap of faith and rejecting the first offer in the hope that you will pass the second interview. With so much resting on the induction year, it is really important that you choose your first post wisely. Take heart in the fact that you have been successful at one interview.

I have just had an interview and was asked about my plans for having a family in the future. I answered that I was committed to my career at the moment, but did not feel happy about being probed in this way. Can interviewers do that?

No. There are many areas that interviewers cannot question on during an interview to protect the interviewee against discrimination. If that happens again in an interview you can always say, 'I believe I don't have to answer that question.' Better still, answer along the lines of, 'I don't have any plans to start a family now' and seek advice from your union immediately after the interview, whatever the outcome. You may also like to think of the implications of working for a senior management team that so openly flouts the law!

I have been asked to undertake a significant amount of preparation during the summer holiday before my first term. Is this normal?

The expectations of newly qualified teachers regarding preparation before they begin their first term vary tremendously from school to school. A general 'rule' to follow is that at least 75% of any holiday should be just that, pure holiday, *once you have started work*. You will probably not be paid for the holiday before your first term so if you need to earn money during that period you may not have time for schoolwork. However, you may feel more relaxed about starting your new job if you have done some preparation. The key is balance. If you feel uncomfortable about the demands that have been made of you *before* you are on the pay role, simply say that you have had to arrange other work commitments but will make sure you have read and digested all the necessary handbooks. You do need to think about the implications for your future workload if you are prepared to work for free!

I have accepted a job in my teaching practice school and will be teaching a class that I taught while I was training. I am concerned that pupils will not take me seriously as a 'proper teacher'.

This is a common concern, but one that is not necessary. Pupils have remarkably short memories regarding such things and, once the summer holidays have passed, you will not be in their 'student' pigeonhole! However, you will still need to spend time asserting your classroom rules and systems of reward and sanction so that they know how *you* work and what it will be like to have *you* as their teacher. Don't feel as though you have to do things in the same way as their previous teacher. This can be more tempting if you actually *worked* with their last teacher and you may even find yourself mimicking him/her subconsciously. Simply focus on asserting yourself.

I would like to work in a sixth-form college as I prefer to teach A level classes. Will this affect my induction period?

You will not be able to serve an induction period in a sixth-form college (or any other establishment that is not a maintained school, a non-maintained special school or a participating independent school), *but you do not need to do so in order to work in one*. However, if you were to leave sixth-form teaching to work in a school, you would have to serve an induction period then, even if you have several years of teaching experience. For this reason, it is best to serve your induction period as soon as possible after gaining QTS, even if that means you have to shelve your ambition for a year. At least you will then be a fully qualified teacher with the freedom to work in virtually any setting. Your induction period can include experience in a sixth-form college and if this is what you would like to do, talk to your induction tutor/mentor about the possibilities early in your induction period.

I would like to do some supply teaching when I qualify as I am not sure where I want to work. Will this count towards my induction period?

Supply work can complicate your induction period and it is best to avoid it in this important year if at all possible. However, if you do take on supply engagements, they need to be of a term or more in length to count towards your induction period. If you take a series of short-term engagements that are less than a term in length, this experience cannot count towards your induction period *and you may only do this for a year and a term*. Thereafter, all engagements must count towards induction.

Supply teachers should be treated as permanent employees for the purposes of induction. Advice to NQTs must therefore be to avoid supply teaching until the induction period has been satisfactorily completed if this is possible.

Once in post

I will be moving to a new area but have been unable to find suitable accommodation. Where can I go for help?

Your first port of call should be the education personnel department of your LEA. They are very familiar with the difficulties faced by NQTs moving to new areas and some even have county or borough accommodation available for rental. Another alternative is to speak to your regional union representative.

I can't afford the deposit for my accommodation. What can I do?

This is extremely common and it is no secret that teachers in their first few years struggle financially, as they try to juggle student loans with living and professional costs. Most banks are sympathetic to this plight and will arrange for a loan. Some, particularly thoughtful, LEAs will give an advance on salary for this purpose, but they are in the minority. Your LEA's education personnel department is a good place to start.

My school doesn't seem to have an induction programme set up. Does this matter?

Your induction into your new job and the profession generally is vitally important. You should be receiving extensive support and training to ensure that you pass your induction year. If you are not receiving a formal induction this will have implications for your future in the profession and you should contact your union representative and the named person at your appropriate body as soon as possible. It would also be a good idea to document your concerns for future reference. Talk to your induction tutor/mentor and your tutor from your training institution for more ideas about improving your situation and contact some teaching newsgroups for experiences of other NQTs. Do not let this situation go on. Your school has a statutory responsibility to provide the support that will give you the best possible opportunity to pass your induction year.

I do not have a good relationship with my induction tutor/mentor. Does this matter?

This is a problem for several reasons. Your aim should be to build good working relationships with *all* your colleagues. Also, an induction tutor/mentor is often the gatekeeper to additional INSET training and support and can make or break an NQT's experience of joining the teaching profession. With so much resting on the induction year, it simply isn't worth not having an excellent working relationship with your induction tutor/mentor! That said, if you really don't get on, perhaps your induction tutor/mentor does not have the skills (or time) necessary to perform the job to professional standards. Do talk to your induction tutor/mentor about your concerns, or, if that seems inappropriate, talk to a trusted colleague. If there are other NQTs at your school who share your induction tutor/mentor, talk to them about how they feel. It may be necessary to mention this to the person (usually a deputy headteacher) who has responsibilities for all NQTs. Again, do not let the situation go on indefinitely; it needs to be resolved as soon as possible.

A pupil/parent has made a complaint about me. What should I do?

This is a relatively common occurrence so don't feel inadequate in any way, unless there really is cause for complaint about your actions. The usual explanation is a misunderstanding and a skillful headteacher will be able to discern this and resolve the situation with no ill feeling. As soon as you are told of the complaint, take some time to jot down exactly what you perceive the situation to be. If possible, talk to your union about the complaint. You should be given the opportunity to relate your interpretation of events to an impartial listener.

If your headteacher does have cause to talk about your conduct, you're not the first new teacher and certainly won't be the last that this has happened to. There is a great deal to become familiar with in the first few years of teaching and you should treat such a pep talk as a learning experience – one that may even enable you to become a better teacher. If you feel disgruntled, talk to your headteacher – he/she should be able to explain the situation to your satisfaction. If not, talk to your union representative again.

My head of department seems to be making unfair demands of me.

This is a common complaint and one that can be easily remedied. First, keep a record of the expectations that have been made of you for future reference. It would also be a good idea to talk to other NQTs at your school to find out what their experiences are, and of course, talk to your induction tutor/mentor. This will help you to gain some perspective on the situation, as it can be easy to feel 'put upon'. Next, employ some skills of assertion! Explain to your head of department that you feel that if you take anything else on at the moment you will not be performing your tasks to adequate standards. You feel the need to consolidate what you have to do and focus on fewer tasks. If this doesn't help to relieve the pressure on you, talk to your induction tutor/mentor or a trusted colleague to see if they will take up your case for you. Try your union as a last resort.

I teach many children with special educational needs and there does not seem to be adequate learning support in place for them. This is putting a great deal of pressure on me. What can I do?

The first thing to do is identify exactly who has extra needs in your classes (this should have been done for you by your SENCO). Next, jot down some ideas on why support is needed in *your* lessons in particular. Do you rely on the use of a lot of equipment? Does your subject require heavy emphasis on writing and reading? You are expected to do a certain degree of differentiation in your lessons, but if this means you are writing additional schemes of work simply to accommodate the children with learning difficulties, you will soon burn yourself out. Talk to your SENCO about the problems. He/she will be able to give you some ideas on how to manage the extra needs in your classes and is also the person able to allocate additional non-teaching support to particular classes. Lean on your SEN department for help differentiating materials etc. By raising this issue, you have shown your commitment to all the abilities in your classes and have opened up the possibilities of a more extensive working partnership with colleagues in the SEN department.

One particular child is making my lessons a misery. How can I deal with this?

Whatever the age of the child, talking to them and explaining what it is about their behaviour that you find unacceptable is always a good place to start. You need to establish clear expectations of the child and even clearer consequences for misbehaviour. Discuss with the child the rewards and sanctions you have in mind (and every opportunity for praise must be taken) and arrange a trial period of a week, after which you will have another talk. When you are getting to the point of hating a child, you need to take a step back and focus on finding solutions. It would be a good idea to talk to your induction tutor/mentor or head of department about your difficulties and the ways that you are attempting to resolve them. There may be established systems in your school for dealing with such situations that you can lean on. Never underestimate the effectiveness of being honest with children about *their* behaviour and *your* disappointment. You could also involve their parents by writing to them and outlining your expectations for improvements in the child's behaviour (clear this with your head of department or induction tutor/mentor first). However, do something sooner rather than later, before you reach the point of just wanting the child removed from your lessons. Teachers who also teach or have taught the child will be a good source of support too.

I feel as though I am drowning under a sea of paperwork and have just been given a batch of reports to write. I simply don't have time to do everything. What can I do?

It can be very difficult to pace your work in your first year. Time management skills will develop as you get used to the rhythm of each term, but it is no failure to find yourself swamped from time to time. You will have to lean on others for a while. Ask your induction tutor/mentor if anyone can help you with marking and preparation to free up some time to focus on the reports. Some headteachers recognise the added pressures that report time brings and arrange for additional (or some) non-contact time. Ask your induction tutor/mentor if this is a possibility for you. At very busy times, you are perfectly justified in minimising the amount of written work you ask classes to do and making sure that any homework you give will not require you to mark it outside lesson time. It is also worth remembering that at such times you may need to look after yourself a little more so that you don't fall ill when it all dies down.

I don't have a classroom base and have to carry a great deal of books and equipment from room to room. Can I ask pupils to help me?

There is nothing wrong with asking pupils to help you. This encourages a sense of community and responsibility. However, it is far better to have many pupils carrying small amounts than one pupil carrying a heavy load. You really do need to cover yourself in case of injury to a child in your care, so the best way round this is to give a pupil half the amount you think they could manage to carry. Always stay in charge of such activities and monitor the amount a child is carrying – there may be some macho pupils wanting to prove their strength to you!

The best way around this is to ask for improvements to be made to your existing arrangements so that you do not have to put yourself and pupils at risk from injury. Having to teach under these circumstances adds greatly to your stress levels not to mention the time you waste having to move your resources for each lesson. Express your difficulties to the person who arranges the room timetable, highlighting the fact that valuable teaching time is being lost.

A group of children in my tutor group has been boasting about their drug-taking antics. What should I do with this knowledge?

While the children could well be bluffing, especially as they don't seem to want to hide what they are doing, you must take this seriously. Talk to your head of year about what you have heard and take any advice you are given. It may be that the parents will be contacted or some drugs awareness counsellors brought in to focus on the issue. The key here is to share the knowledge you have with someone of higher authority than you.

I have been asked to take on additional responsibilities and have only just completed my first two terms. I know I shouldn't take anything else on just yet, but don't want to adversely affect my career prospects. What can I do?

There are many issues here. Firstly, if your seniors have asked you to take on the work they clearly believe you can achieve it. However, if you want to focus on your induction year, you should not be put under undue pressure to take on extra responsibilities. Talk to your induction tutor/mentor about the situation, as he/she will probably have been consulted in the first place. Do also find out how much of a financial incentive is going to be provided. This shouldn't sway your decision, but it will give you insight into the way that your management team is working. As for fears for future career progression at the school, it would be perfectly reasonable to decline the offer of extra responsibilities in your first year and extremely unreasonable for this to affect your career prospects. If you express your desire to consolidate the vast amount you are learning in your first year for the sake of improving your teaching, and that you would be happy to consider the proposition again in the near future (perhaps six months time), there should be no problem. If you feel that a tense atmosphere has been created, talk to your union representative. It may be necessary to document any conversations you had in case of a future need to refer to them.

I am coming to the end of my induction year and wonder if I should be looking to change schools to broaden my experience.

There is no law stating that teachers must keep moving from school to school, otherwise their experience will be severely limited, but it is worth thinking about the benefits of not teaching at the same school for years and years. A consolidation period of two or three years is perfectly acceptable and advisable in many cases, especially if you are happy in your school. Beyond that you may want to start thinking about promotion and additional responsibilities and, unless there are openings at your school, you will have to move on. Comfortable as it may seem to stay put, your next school may be a vast improvement on your first, and the simple fact that it is a different institution will mean that you will broaden your experiences. The decision is yours.

I am often asked to take part in fundraising activities. This is beginning to drain my time and I feel that the main focus of my school is gathering money rather than educating. Can I excuse myself from such activities?

This is awkward, as extra money in the coffers benefits the entire school community, yet if fundraising is taking you away from your teaching duties, something is wrong. Aim to get a balance between appearing sympathetic to your school's cause and not compromising the quality of education you offer your classes. Don't excuse yourself entirely, but perhaps limit your involvement to high-profile fundraising events such as the summer fair. You could also give yourself the role of 'ideas generator' as this involves more thinking and less doing!

I would like to be able to lend materials and equipment freely to pupils, but so much is being stolen. What can I do?

The best approach is to have a formal system of lending things out. Use a book to record exactly who has what, when, and remember to note when the item is returned. This may seem complicated, but it will allow you to see who can be trusted and who needs reminding to return your property. It would be wonderful to be able to trust everyone but using a system like this helps to avoid disappointment.

Personal issues

After teaching in my school for nearly a term, I still feel like a newcomer. What can I do?

It is likely that you will feel 'new' until another NQT joins your school. If this really bothers you, talk to your induction tutor/mentor about ways you can establish yourself more firmly in your position in the school. Another alternative is to enjoy the feeling – as soon as you get into your second year you'll be treated as part of the furniture and colleagues won't be able to remember if you've been at the school one year, two years or ten years! What's more, neither will you!

My schoolwork has taken over my life and I don't seem to have a social life any more. What can I do?

This is actually more serious than it seems. All work and no play makes Jack extremely dull, not to mention Jack's lessons. It also has grave implications for mental and physical health. Sit down with your induction tutor/mentor and work out where you can ease up on your planning, preparation and marking. The first year of teaching is difficult and time-consuming, but you should be able to have at least one full day off at the weekend and one evening during the week. Not only that, but you should aim to limit the time you spend working in the evenings and stick to that limit. Long hours lead to increased stress levels, which lead to reduced performance and health problems. Get friends and family to keep an eye on you and aim to go on at least one social outing a week. You may also like to join a relaxation class, as this will mean you are not only 'off duty' but learning a valuable skill as well.

I am thinking of opting out of the teachers' pension scheme to help free up some money for bills. Is this wise?

Not under any circumstances! It is not the place of this book to offer financial advice, but it is generally accepted that teachers should pay in to the superannuation scheme as soon as they start in the profession and pay additional voluntary contributions (AVCs) as soon as possible after. Your union will be able to offer pension ideas and may be able to put you in touch with a financial advisor. Don't take advice from someone who is not a financial advisor – the world of pensions is extremely complex and there is a tremendous amount of misinformation floating around. Opting out of a pension scheme is usually interpreted as being misguided and short-termist.

My headteacher has told me that my clothing is inappropriate. Do I have to accept it?

There are several issues here. First, you need to establish whether your clothing really is inappropriate or whether your headteacher simply doesn't like your style. Take some advice from the relevant union representative in your school. He/she will be familiar with the dress code of the school and will be able to help you discern whether or not your headteacher is being unreasonable. Secondly, how important is it to you that you wear clothes that upset your boss? Perhaps, in the interests of making a good impression, you should conform to your school's standards. Don't worry that your head-teacher has had cause to correct you – that is part of the job after all!

I am pregnant in my first year of teaching. Am I entitled to maternity leave?

As long as you have given your employer proper notification of your pregnancy you are entitled to time off with pay to attend antenatal classes (including parentcraft and relaxation classes) and 14 weeks maternity leave. You may also be entitled to statutory maternity pay (contact your union for information relating to your circumstances). You can arrange your leave to begin any time after the beginning of the eleventh week before the baby is due as long as you give three weeks notice. If your baby is premature, your leave starts on the day your baby is born.

You may request that your induction period be extended. Talk to your induction tutor/mentor about whether this would be appropriate for you. It would also be a good idea to look at the publication, *New and Expectant Mothers at Work.*[1]

I seem to be catching every cough and cold that's around. What can I do?

The sheer number of people you are interacting with as a teacher means that your body has to fight off millions of germs every day. The fact that you are succumbing to so many of them indicates that your immune system is not as effective as it could be. Aim to boost immunity by taking care of your diet (emphasis on fresh fruit and vegetables), getting plenty of early nights, drinking fresh filtered water as opposed to caffeinated drinks and taking 'Echinacea' supplements, available from a good chemist or health food shop. You should also aim to restrict your working time so that you can increase the amount of rest you get. Doing this over a period of a few weeks should see great improvements in your health and energy levels.

One of the colleagues I have to work with constantly undermines me, resulting in me feeling inadequate. How can I tackle this behaviour?

It would be a good idea to talk to your induction tutor/mentor about this as it sounds as though this colleague is employing bullying tactics when s/he communicates with you. Explain what your concerns are and document any conversations you have with the colleague, which result in you feeling inadequate. Make sure you refute all unfair claims made against you and contact Redress[2] for further advice. It is important that you take steps to improve this situation as persistent criticism can seriously affect your performance and add unnecessarily to stress and anxiety levels.

I suspect I am being unfairly discriminated against. Is there anything I can do?

The first thing you should do is document any situations that cause you to feel discriminated against. Write everything down so that when you talk to someone about it you have actual examples to refer to with dates and times. Next, read some of the Department of Trade and Industry factsheets about discrimination to help you determine whether or not that is what you are suffering. You may be interested in 'Disability Discrimination in Employment', 'Racial Discrimination in Employment' and 'Sex Discrimination and Equal Pay'.[3] Your union will also be able to give you advice on how to tackle your situation, as will your induction tutor/mentor. Try not to let this affect your work, although this can be unavoidable. By talking to colleagues you may gain some valuable support.

I am a smoker who has been told I can't smoke on the school premises any more. Is there anything I can do about this?

No, your employer is acting within the law in disallowing smoking on school premises. If you need to smoke during the school day and your school does not have a smoking room, find somewhere off site where pupils won't observe you.

I have been reprimanded about drinking water in my classroom. Is this unreasonable?

There are some frightening statistics about the number of teachers who develop the need for speech therapy after permanent voice damage through over-use. If taking a sip of water helps to keep your throat comfortable, then this should be accepted and promoted by your management and any attempts to prevent you from drinking in class could be interpreted as foolish. However, you may like to discuss any need to have a glass or a bottle of water with you in your classroom with your headteacher or induction tutor/mentor so that any objections can be raised. If your school has a strict 'no drinks in the classroom' policy, perhaps raise the issue at a staff meeting.

---

1 *New and Expectant Mothers at Work* (1995). The Stationery Office, London.

2 Redress is the Bullied Teachers' Support Network and it can offer excellent advice to teachers suffering from this type of behaviour. Contact details are given in Appendix 7.

3 These are available from the Department of Trade and Industry by phoning their order line. See Appendix 7.

Standards for the Award of Qualified Teacher Status

(Annex A of DfEE Circular 4/98)

Taken from the TTA document, 'Standards for the Award of Qualified Teacher Status'.

A. KNOWLEDGE AND UNDERSTANDING

1. Secondary

Those to be awarded QTS must, when assessed, demonstrate that they:

a) have a secure knowledge and understanding of the concepts and skills in their specialist subject(s) **at a standard equivalent to degree level to enable them to teach it (them) confidently and accurately at:**

   i. **KS3 for trainees on 7–14 courses;**

   ii. **KS3 and KS4 and, where relevant, post-16 for trainees on 11–16 or 18 courses; and**

   iii. **KS4 and post-16 for trainees on 14–19 courses;**

b) **for English, mathematics or science specialists,** have a secure knowledge and understanding of the subject content specified in the relevant Initial Teacher Training National Curriculum;[1]

c) have, for their specialist subject(s), where applicable, a detailed knowledge and understanding of the National Curriculum programmes of study, level descriptions or end of key stage descriptions for KS3 and, where applicable, National Curriculum programmes of study for KS4;

d) **for Religious Education (RE) specialists,** have a detailed knowledge of the Model Syllabuses for RE;

---

e) are familiar, for their specialist subject(s), with the relevant KS4 and post-16 examination syllabuses and courses, including vocational courses;[2]

f) understand, for their specialist subject(s), the framework of 14–19 qualifications and the routes of progression through it;[3]

g) understand, for their specialist subject(s), progression from the KS2 programmes of study;[4]

h) know and can teach the key skills required for current qualifications relevant to their specialist subject(s), for pupils aged 14–19, and understand the contribution that their specialist subject(s) make (s) to the development of the key skills;[5]

i) cope securely with subject-related questions which pupils raise;

j) are aware of, and know how to access, recent inspection evidence and classroom-relevant research evidence on teaching secondary pupils in their specialist subject(s), and know how to use this to inform and improve their teaching;

k) know, for their specialist subject(s), pupils' most common misconceptions and mistakes;

l) understand how pupils' learning in the subject is affected by their physical, intellectual, emotional and social development;

m) have, for their specialist subject(s), a secure knowledge and understanding of the content specified in the ITT National Curriculum for Information and Communications Technology in subject teaching;

n) are familiar with subject-specific health and safety requirements, where relevant, and plan lessons to avoid potential hazards.

2. Primary

For all courses, those to be awarded QTS must, when assessed, demonstrate that they:

a) Understand the purposes, scope, structure and balance of the National Curriculum Orders as a whole and, within them, the place and scope of the primary phase, the key stages, the primary core and foundation subjects and RE;

b) Are aware of the breadth of content covered by the pupils'

National Curriculum across the primary core and foundation subjects and RE;

c) Understand how the pupils' learning is affected by their physical, intellectual, emotional and social development.

d) **For each core and specialist subject**[6] covered in their training:

   i. have, where applicable, a detailed knowledge and understanding of the relevant National Curriculum programmes of study and level descriptions or end of key stage descriptions across the primary age range;

   ii. for RE specialists, have a detailed knowledge of the Model Syllabuses for RE;

   iii. cope securely with subject-related questions which pupils raise;

   iv. understand the progression from SCAA's *Desirable Outcomes for Children's Learning on Entering Compulsory Education* on KS1, the progression from KS1 to KS2, and from KS2 to KS3;

   v. are aware of, and know how to access, recent inspection evidence and classroom-relevant research evidence on teaching primary pupils in the subject, and know how to use this to inform and improve their teaching;

   vi. know pupils' most common misconceptions and mistakes in the subject;

   vii. have a secure knowledge and understanding of the content specified in the ITT National Curriculum for Information and Communications Technology in subject teaching;

   viii. are familiar with subject-specific health and safety requirements, where relevant, and plan lessons to avoid potential hazards;

e) **for English, mathematics and science**, have a secure knowledge and understanding of the subject content specified in the ITT National Curricula for primary English, mathematics and science;[7]

f) **for any specialist subject(s)**, have a secure knowledge of the subject to at least a standard approximating to GCE Advanced level in those aspects of the subject taught at KS1 and KS2;

g) **for any non-core, non-specialist subject covered in their training**, have a secure knowledge to a standard equivalent to at least level 7 of the pupils' National Curriculum. For RE, the required standard for non-specialist training is broadly equivalent to the end of key stage statements for Key Stage 4 in QCA's Model Syllabuses for RE.[8]

3. **Additional standards relating to early years (nursery and reception) for trainees on 3–8 and 3–11 courses**
Those to be awarded QTS must, when assessed, demonstrate that they:

a) have a detailed knowledge of SCAA's *Desirable Outcomes for Children's Learning on Entering Compulsory Education*

b) have a knowledge of effective ways of working with parents and other carers;

c) have an understanding of the roles and responsibilities of other agencies with responsibility for the care of young children.

B. **PLANNING, TEACHING AND CLASS MANAGEMENT**
This section details the standards which all those to be awarded QTS must demonstrate, when assessed, in each subject that they have been trained to teach. For primary non-core, non-specialist subjects, trainees being assessed QTS must meet the required standards but with the support, if necessary, of a teacher experienced in the subject concerned.

1. **Primary English, mathematics and science**
For all courses, those to be awarded QTS must, when assessed, demonstrate that they:

a) have a secure knowledge and understanding of, and know how and when to apply, the teaching and assessment methods specified in the ITT National Curricula for primary English, mathematics and science;[9]

b) have a secure knowledge and understanding of, and know when to apply in relation to each subject, the teaching and assessment methods specified in the ITT National Curriculum for Information and Communications Technology in subject teaching.

2. Primary and secondary specialist subjects

For all courses, those to be awarded QTS must, when assessed, demonstrate that they have secure knowledge and understanding of, and know how and when to apply, in relation to their specialist subject(s), the teaching and assessment methods specified in the ITT National Curriculum for Information and Communications Technology in subject teaching.

3. Secondary English, mathematics and science

To be awarded QTS specialists in secondary English, mathematics or science must, when assessed, demonstrate that they have a secure knowledge and understanding of, and know how and when to apply, the teaching and assessment methods specified in the relevant ITT National Curriculum.[10]

4. Primary and secondary for all subjects

Planning

For all courses, those to be awarded QTS must, when assessed, demonstrate that they:

a) plan their teaching to achieve progression in pupils' learning through:

   i.   identifying clear teaching objectives and content, appropriate to the subject matter and the pupils being taught, and specifying how these will be taught and assessed;

   ii.   setting tasks for whole class, individual and group work, including homework, which challenge pupils and ensure high levels of pupil interest;

   iii.   setting appropriate and demanding expectations for pupils' learning, motivation and presentation of work;

   iv.   setting clear targets for pupils' learning, building on prior attainment, and ensuring that pupils are aware of the substance and purpose of what they are asked to do;

   v.   identifying pupils who:

      • have special educational needs, including specific learning difficulties;

      • are very able;

- are not yet fluent in English;

and knowing where to get help in order to give positive and targeted support;

b) provide clear structures for lessons, and for sequences of lessons, in the short, medium and longer term, which maintain pace, motivation and challenge for pupils;

c) make effective use of assessment information on pupils' attainment and progress in their teaching and in planning future lessons and sequences of lessons;

d) plan opportunities to contribute to pupils' personal, spiritual, moral, social and cultural development;

e) where applicable, ensure coverage of the relevant examination syllabuses and National Curriculum programmes of study.

Teaching and Class Management

For all courses, those to be awarded QTS must, when assessed, demonstrate that they:

f) ensure effective teaching of whole classes, and of groups and individuals within the whole class setting, so that teaching objectives are met, and best use is made of available teaching time;

g) monitor and intervene when teaching to ensure sound learning and discipline;

h) establish and maintain a purposeful working atmosphere;

i) set high expectations for pupils' behaviour, establishing and maintaining a good standard of discipline through well-focused teaching and through positive and productive relationships;

j) establish a safe environment which supports learning and in which pupils feel secure and confident;

k) use teaching methods which sustain the momentum of pupils' work and keep all pupils engaged through:

   i. stimulating intellectual curiosity, communicating enthusiasm for the subject being taught, fostering pupils' enthusiasm and maintaining pupils' motivation;

   ii. matching the approaches used to the subject matter and the pupils being taught;

iii. structuring information well, including outlining content and aims, signalling transitions and summarising key points as the lesson progresses;

iv. clear presentation of content around a set of key ideas, using appropriate subject-specific vocabulary and well-chosen illustrations and examples;

v. clear instruction and demonstration, and accurate well-paced explanation;

vi. effective questioning which matches the pace and direction of the lesson and ensures that pupils take part;

vii. careful attention to pupils' errors and misconceptions, and helping to remedy them;

viii. listening carefully to pupils, analysing their responses and responding constructively in order to take pupils' learning forward;

ix. selecting and making good use of textbooks, ICT and other learning resources which enable teaching objectives to be met;

x. providing opportunities for pupils to consolidate their knowledge and maximising opportunities, both in the classroom and through setting well-focused homework, to reinforce and develop what has been learnt;

xi. exploiting opportunities to improve pupils' basic skills in literacy, numeracy and ICT, and the individual and collaborative study skills needed for effective learning, including information retrieval from libraries, texts and other sources;

xii. exploiting opportunities to contribute to the quality of pupils' wider educational development, including their personal, spiritual, moral, social and cultural development;

xiii. setting high expectations for all pupils notwithstanding individual differences, including gender, and cultural and linguistic backgrounds;

xiv. providing opportunities to develop pupils' wider understanding by relating their learning to real and work-related examples;

l) are familiar with the Code of Practice on the identification and assessment of special educational needs and, as part of their responsibilities under the Code, implement and keep records on individual education plans (IEPs) for pupils at stage 2 of the Code and above;

m) ensure that pupils acquire and consolidate knowledge, skills and understanding in the subject;

n) evaluate their own teaching critically and use this to improve their effectiveness.

5. Additional standards relating to early years (nursery and reception) for trainees on 3–8 and 3–11 courses

For all courses, those to be awarded QTS must, when assessed, demonstrate that they:

a) plan activities which take account of pupils' needs and their developing physical, intellectual, emotional and social abilities, and which engage their interest;

b) provide structured learning opportunities which advance pupils':

    i. personal and social development;

    ii. communication skills;

    iii. knowledge and understanding of the world;

    iv. physical development;

    v. creative development;

c) use teaching approaches and activities which develop pupils' language and provide the foundations for literacy;

d) use teaching approaches and activities which develop pupils' mathematical understanding and provide the foundations for numeracy;

e) encourage pupils to think and talk about their learning and to develop self-control and independence;

f) encourage pupils to concentrate and persevere in their learning for sustained periods, to listen attentively and to talk about their experiences in small and large groups;

g) use teaching approaches and activities which involve planned adult intervention, which offer opportunities for first-hand experience and co-operation, and which use play and talk as a vehicle for learning;

h) manage, with support from an experienced specialist teacher if necessary, the work of parents and other adults in the classroom to enhance learning opportunities for pupils.

C. MONITORING, ASSESSMENT, RECORDING, REPORTING AND ACCOUNTABILITY

This section details the standards which all those to be awarded QTS must demonstrate, when assessed, in each subject that they have been trained to teach. For primary non-core, non-specialist subjects, trainees being assessed for QTS must meet the required standards but with the support, if necessary, of a teacher experienced in the subject concerned.

For all courses, those to be awarded QTS must, when assessed, demonstrate that they:

a) assess how well learning objectives have been achieved and use this assessment to improve specific aspects of teaching;

b) mark and monitor pupils' assigned classwork and homework, providing constructive oral and written feedback, and setting targets for pupils' progress;

c) assess and record each pupils' progress systematically, including through focused observation, questioning, testing and marking, and use these records to:

   i.   check that pupils have understood and completed the work set;

   ii. monitor strengths and weaknesses and use the information gained as a basis for purposeful intervention in pupils' learning;

   iii. inform planning;

   iv. check that pupils continue to make demonstrable progress in their acquisition of the knowledge, skills and understanding of the subject;

d) are familiar with the statutory assessment and reporting requirements and know how to prepare and present informative reports to parents;

e) where applicable, understand the expected demands of pupils in relation to each relevant level description or end of key stage description, and, in addition, for those on 11–16 or 18 and 14–19 courses, the demands of the syllabuses and course requirements for GCSE, other KS4 courses, and, where applicable, post-16 courses;

f) where applicable, understand and know how to implement the assessment requirements of current qualifications for pupils aged 14–19;

g) recognise the level at which a pupil is achieving, and assess pupils consistently against attainment targets, where applicable, if necessary with guidance from an experienced teacher;

h) understand and know how national, local, comparative and school data, including National Curriculum test data, where applicable, can be used to set clear targets for pupils' achievement;

i) use different kinds of assessment appropriately for different purposes, including National Curriculum and other standardised tests, and baseline assessment where relevant.

D. OTHER PROFESSIONAL REQUIREMENTS

Primary and Secondary
For all courses, those to be awarded QTS should, when assessed, demonstrate that they:

a) have a working knowledge and understanding of:

    i. teachers' professional duties as set out in the current School Teachers' Pay and Conditions document, issued under the School Teachers' Pay and Conditions Act 1991;

    ii. teachers' legal liabilities and responsibilities relating to:

- the Race Relations Act 1976;
- the Sex Discrimination Act 1975;
- Section 7 and Section 8 of the Health and Safety at Work etc. Act 1974;
- teachers' common law duty to ensure that pupils are healthy and safe on school premises and when leading activities off the school site, such as educational visits, school outings or field trips;
- what is reasonable for the purposes of safeguarding or promoting children's welfare (Section 3(5) of the Children Act 1989);

- the role of the education service in protecting children from abuse (currently set out in DfEE Circular 10/95 and the Home Office, Department of Health, DfEE and Welsh Office Guidance *Working Together: A guide to arrangements for inter-agency co-operation for the protection of children from abuse 1991*;

- appropriate physical contact with pupils (currently set out in DfEE Circular 10/95);

- appropriate physical restraint of pupils (Section 4 of the Education Act 1977 and DfEE Circular 9/94);

- detention of pupils on disciplinary grounds (Section 5 of the Education Act 1997);

b) have established, during work in schools, effective working relationships with professional colleagues including, where applicable, associate staff;

c) set a good example to the pupils they teach, through their presentation and their personal and professional conduct;

d) are committed to ensuring that every pupil is given the opportunity to achieve their potential and meet the high expectations set for them;

e) understand the need to take responsibility for their own professional development and to keep up to date with research and developments in pedagogy and in the subjects they teach;

f) understand their professional responsibilities in relation to school policies and practices, including those concerned with pastoral and personal safety matters, including bullying;

g) recognise that learning takes place inside and outside the school context, and understand the need to liaise effectively with parents and other carers and with agencies with responsibility for pupils' education and welfare;

h) are aware of the role and purpose of school governing bodies.

1   This does not apply until September 1999.

2   This does not apply to trainees on 7–14 courses.

3   This does not apply to trainees on 7–14 courses.

4   This does not apply to trainees on 14–19 courses.

5   This does not apply to trainees on 7–14 courses.

6   A specialist subject may be one of the core subjects.

7   For primary science this does not apply until September 1999.

8   Where providers offer more limited coverage of subjects than the required non-core, non-specialist subjects, *e.g. a few hours of taster training in a foundation subject, safety training in PE and/or design and technology*, the nature and extent of such training can be recorded on the newly qualified teacher's TTA Career Entry Profile.

9   For primary science this does not apply until September 1999.

10 This does not apply until September 1999.

The Induction Standards

In order to meet the Induction Standards, the NQT should demonstrate that he or she:

PLANNING, TEACHING AND CLASS MANAGEMENT

(a) sets clear targets for improvement of pupils' achievement, monitors pupils' progress towards those targets and uses appropriate teaching strategies in the light of this, including, where appropriate, in relation to literacy, numeracy and other school targets;

(b) plans effectively to ensure that pupils have the opportunity to meet their potential, notwithstanding differences of race and gender, and taking account of the needs of people who are:

- underachieving;

- very able;

- not yet fluent in English;

making use of relevant information and specialist help where available;

(c) secures a good standard of pupil behaviour in the classroom through establishing appropriate rules and high expectations of discipline which pupils respect, acting to pre-empt and deal with inappropriate behaviour in the context of the behaviour policy of the school;

(d) plans effectively, where applicable, to meet the needs of pupils with Special Educational Needs and, in collaboration with the SENCO, makes an appropriate contribution to the preparation, implementation, monitoring and review of Individual Education Plans;

(e) takes account of ethnic and cultural diversity to enrich the curriculum and raise achievement;

MONITORING, ASSESSMENT, RECORDING, REPORTING AND ACCOUNTABILITY

(f) recognises the level that a pupil is achieving and makes accurate assessments, independently, against attainment targets, where applicable, and performance levels associated with other tests or qualifications relevant to the subject(s) or phase(s) taught;

(g) liaises effectively with pupils' parents/carers through informative oral and written reports on pupils' progress and achievements, discussing appropriate targets, and encouraging them to support their children's learning, behaviour and progress;

OTHER PROFESSIONAL REQUIREMENTS

(h) where applicable, deploys support staff and other adults effectively in the classroom, involving them, where appropriate, in the planning and management of pupils' learning;

(i) takes responsibility for implementing school policies and practices, including those dealing with bullying and racial harassment;

(j) takes responsibility for their own professional development, setting objectives for improvements, and taking action to keep up-to-date with research and developments in pedagogy and in the subject(s) they teach.

Telephone numbers of LEAs in England

Barking and Dagenham	020 8592 4500
Barnet	020 8359 2000
Barnsley	01226 770 770
Bath and North East Somerset	01225 477 000
Bedfordshire	01234 363 222
Bexley	020 8303 7777
Birmingham	0121 303 2872
Blackburn with Darwen	01254 585 585
Blackpool	01253 476 555
Bolton	01204 522 311
Bournemouth	01202 456 219
Bracknell Forest	01344 424 642
Bradford	01274 751 840
Brent	020 8937 3190
Brighton and Hove	01273 290 000
Bristol, City of	0117 922 2000
Bromley	020 8464 3333
Buckinghamshire	01296 395 000
Bury	0161 253 5000
Calderdale	01422 357 257
Cambridgeshire	01223 717 111
Camden	020 7911 1525
Cheshire	01244 602 424
Cornwall	01872 322 000
Corporation of London	020 7332 1750
Coventry	024 7683 3333
Croydon	020 8686 4433
Cumbria	01228 606 060
Darlington	01325 380 651
Derby, City of	01332 293 111
Derbyshire	01629 580 000
Devon	01392 382 000

Doncaster	01302 737 222
Dorset	01305 251 000
Dudley	01384 818 181
Durham	0191 386 4411
Ealing	020 8579 2424
East Riding of Yorkshire	01482 887 700
East Sussex	01273 481 000
Enfield	020 8366 6565
Essex	01245 492 211
Gateshead	0191 477 1011
Gloucestershire	01452 425 300
Greenwich	020 8854 8888
Hackney	020 8356 5000
Halton	0151 424 2061
Hammersmith and Fulham	020 8748 3020
Hampshire	01962 841 841
Haringey	020 8975 9700
Harrow	020 8863 5611
Hartlepool	01429 266 522
Havering	01708 772 222
Herefordshire	01432 260 000
Hertfordshire	01992 555 555
Hillingdon	01895 250 111
Hounslow	020 8862 5352
Isle of Wight	01983 821 000
Isles of Scilly	01720 422 537
Islington	020 7226 1234
Kensington and Chelsea	020 7361 3334
Kent	01622 671 411
Kingston-upon-Hull, City of	01482 610 610
Kingston-upon-Thames	020 8546 2121
Kirklees	01484 221 000
Knowsley	0151 489 6000
Lambeth	020 7926 1000
Lancashire	01772 254 868
Leeds	0113 234 8080
Leicester City	0116 254 9922
Leicestershire	0116 232 3232
Lewisham	020 8695 6000
Lincolnshire	01522 552 222

Liverpool	0151 227 3911
Luton	01582 548 001
Manchester	0161 234 5000
Medway	01634 306 000
Merton	020 8543 2222
Middlesborough	01642 245 432
Milton Keynes	01908 691 691
Newcastle-upon-Tyne	0191 232 8520
Newham	020 8555 5552
Norfolk	01603 222 300
North East Lincolnshire	01472 313 131
North Lincolnshire	01724 297 241
North Somerset	01934 888 888
North Tyneside	0191 200 5151
North Yorkshire	01609 780 780
Northamptonshire	01604 236 236
Northumberland	01670 533 677
Nottingham, City of	0115 915 5555
Nottinghamshire	0115 982 3823
Oldham	0161 911 4260
Oxfordshire	01865 792 422
Peterborough, City of	01733 563 141
Plymouth, City of	01752 307 400
Poole	01202 633 633
Portsmouth	023 9282 2251
Reading	0118 939 0900
Redbridge	020 8478 3020
Redcar and Cleveland	01642 444 000
Richmond-upon-Thames	020 8891 1411
Rochdale	01706 647 474
Rotherham	01709 382 121
Rutland	01572 722 577
Salford	0161 832 971/8
Sandwell	0121 525 7366
Sefton	0151 933 6003
Sheffield	0114 272 6444
Shropshire	01743 251 000
Slough	01753 552 288
Solihull	0121 704 6000
Somerset	01823 355 455

South Gloucestershire	01454 863 333
South Tyneside	0191 427 1717
Southampton	023 8022 3855
Southend-on-Sea	01702 215 000
Southwark	020 7525 5050/5001
St Helens	01744 546 000
Staffordshire	01785 223 121
Stockport	0161 480 4949
Stockton-on-Tees	01642 393 939
Stoke-on-Trent	01782 236 100
Suffolk	01473 584 800
Sunderland	0191 553 1000
Surrey	020 8541 9501
Sutton	020 8770 5000
Swindon	01793 463 000
Tameside	0161 342 8355
Telford and Wrekin	01952 202 100
Thurrock	01375 652 652
Torbay	01803 208 208
Tower Hamlets	020 7364 5000
Trafford	0161 912 3251
Wakefield	01924 306 090
Walsall	01922 650 000
Waltham Forest	020 8527 5544
Wandsworth	020 8871 8013
Warrington	01925 444 400
Warwickshire	01926 410 410
West Berkshire	01635 519 723
West Sussex	01243 777 100
Westminster	020 7841 6000
Wigan	01942 244 991
Wiltshire	01225 713 000
Windsor and Maidenhead, Royal Borough of	01628 798 888
Wirral	0151 666 2121
Wokingham	0118 974 6000
Wolverhampton	01902 556 556
Worcestershire	01905 763 763
York, City of	01904 613 161

Telephone numbers of LEAs in Wales

Blaenau Gwent CBC	01495 350 555
Bridgend CBC	01656 668 126
Caerphilly CBC	01443 815 588
Cardiff CC	029 2087 2000
Carmarthenshire CC	01267 234 567
Ceredigion CC	01545 570 881
Conwy CBC	01492 574 000
Denbighshire	01824 706 000
Flintshire CC	01352 752 121
Gwynedd Council	01286 672 255
Merthyr Tydfil CBC	01685 725 000
Monmouthshire CC	01633 838 838
Neath Port Talbot CBC	01639 763 333
Newport CBC	01633 244 491
Pembrokeshire CC	01437 764 551
Powys CC	01597 826 000
Rhondda-Cynon-Taff CBC	01443 424 000
City and County of Swansea	01792 636 000
Torfaen CBC	01495 762 200
The Vale of Glamorgan Council	01446 700 111
Wrexham CBC	01978 292 000
Isle of Anglesey CC	01248 750 057

Telephone numbers of LEAs in Scotland

Aberdeen City	01224 522 000
Aberdeenshire	01224 664 630
Angus	01307 461 460
Argyll and Bute	01369 704 000
Clackmannanshire	01259 452 435
Dumfries and Galloway	01387 260 427
Dundee City	01382 433 088
East Ayrshire	01563 576 000
East Dunbartonshire	0141 942 9000
East Lothian	01620 827 631
East Renfrewshire	0141 577 3430
Edinburgh, City of	0131 469 3322
Falkirk	01324 506 600
Fife	01592 414 141
Glasgow City	0141 287 2000
Highland	01463 702 000
Inverclyde	01475 712 824
Midlothian	0131 271 3718
Moray	01343 563 134
North Ayrshire	01294 324 411
North Lanarkshire	01236 812 336
Orkney Islands	01856 873 535
Perth and Kinross	01738 476 211
Renfrewshire	0141 842 5663
Scottish Borders	01835 825 095
Shetland Islands	01595 744 000
South Ayrshire	0192 612 201
South Lanarkshire	01698 454 545
Stirling	01786 443 322
West Dumbartonshire	01389 737 000
West Lothian	01506 776 000
Western Isles	01851 703 773

Telephone numbers of education and library boards in Northern Ireland

Belfast	028 9056 4000
Western	028 8241 1411
North Eastern	028 2565 3333
South Eastern	028 9056 6200
Southern	028 3751 2200
Council for Catholic Maintained Schools	028 9042 6792

Useful addresses

JOB SEEKING

Gabbitas Educational Consultants
Carrington House
126–130 Regent Street
London W1R 6EE
Tel: 020 7734 0161
E-mail: reccon@gabbitas.co.uk
Website: http://www.gabbitas.co.uk

The British Council
Overseas Appointment Section
Bridgewater House
58 Whitworth Street
Manchester M1 6BB
Tel: 0161 957 7383
E-mail:
mark.hepworth@britcoun.org

Voluntary Services Overseas (VSO)
317 Putney Bridge Road
London SW15 2PN
Tel: 020 8780 7200
E-mail: via website
Website: http://www.vso.org.uk

Association of Teachers against Ageism
Carole Hawkins
19 The Grange
London N20 9EB
Tel: 020 8445 0088

PROFESSIONAL ASSOCIATIONS (UNIONS AND REDRESS)

Association of Teachers and Lecturers
7 Northumberland Street
London WC2N 5DA
Tel: 020 7930 6441
E-mail: info@atl.org.uk
Website: http://www.atl.org.uk

National Association of School Masters/Union of Women Teachers
Hillscourt Education Centre
Rose Hill
Rednal
Birmingham B45 8RS
Tel: 0121 453 6150
E-mail: nasuwt@nasuwt.org.uk
Website:
http://www.teachersunion.org.uk

National Union of Teachers
Hamilton House
Mabledon Place
London WC1H 9BD
Tel: 020 7388 6191
Website: http://www.teachers.org.uk

Professional Association of Teachers
2 St James' Court
Friar Gate
Derby DE1 1BT
Tel: 01332 372337
E-mail: hq@pat.org.uk
Website: http://www.pat.org.uk

Redress: The Bullied Teachers Support Network
Bramble House
Mason Drive
Hook
Near Goole
East Riding of Yorkshire DN14 5NE
Tel: 01405 764432

GOVERNMENT DEPARTMENTS AND AGENCIES

Commission for Racial Equality
Elliott House
10–12 Allington Street
London SW3 4RR
Tel: 020 7828 7022
E-mail: info@cre.gov.uk
Website: http://www.cre.gov.uk

Department of Trade and Industry
1 Victoria Street
London SW1H 0ET
Tel: 020 7215 5000
Publication order line:
  0845 6000 925
E-mail: dti.enquiries@imsv.dti.gov.uk
Website: http://www.dti.gov.uk

Teacher Training Agency
Portland House
Stag Place
London SW1E 5TT
Tel: 020 7925 3700
E-mail: teaching@ttainfo.demon.co.uk
Website: http://www.teach-tta.gov.uk
Publication order line: 0845 6060323

Department for Education and Employment
Sanctuary Buildings
Great Smith Street
Westminster
London SW1P 3BT
Tel: 020 7925 5000
Publication order line:
  0845 6022260
E-mail: info@dfee.gov.uk
Website: http://www.dfee.gov.uk

Office for Standards in Education (OFSTED)
Alexandra House
33 Kingsway
London WC2B 6SE
Tel: 020 7421 6744
Publications order line:
  020 7510 0180
E-mail: via website
Website: http://www.ofsted.gov.uk

**National Assembly of Wales
Education Department**
Cathays Park
Cardiff CF10 3NQ
Tel: 029 2082 5111
Website: http://www.wales.gov.uk

**Scottish Executive Education
Department**
Area 2A
Victoria Quay
Edinburgh EH6 6QQ
Tel: 0131 556 8400
E-mail: via website
Website: http://www.scotland.gov.uk

**Department of Education for
Northern Ireland**
Rathgael House
Balloo Road
Bangor
Co. Down BT19 7PR
028 9127 9279
E-mail: deni@nics.gov.uk
Website: http://www.deni.gov.uk

SUBJECT ASSOCIATIONS

These associations offer a wealth of specialist information, resources and publications. NQTs usually benefit from savings on the cost of membership in their first year.

The Geographical Association
160 Solly Street
Sheffield S1 4BF
Tel: 0114 296 0088
E-mail: GA@geography.org.uk
Website: http://www.geography.org.uk

**The Physical Education
Association of the United
Kingdom**
Ling House
Building 25
London Road
Reading RG1 5AQ
Tel: 0118 931 6240
E-mail: pea.uk@cableol.co.uk
Website:
http://www.teleschool.org.uk/PEA

**The National Association for
Special Educational Needs**
NASEN House
4/5 Amber Business Village
Amber Close
Amington
Tamworth B77 4RP
Tel: 01827 311500
E-mail: welcome@nasen.org.uk
Website: http://www.nasen.org.uk

**The Association of Teachers of
Mathematics**
7 Shaftesbury Street
Derby
DE23 8YB
Tel: 01332 346599
E-mail:
atm_maths@compuserve.com

The Mathematical Association
259 London Road
Leicester LE2 3BE
Tel: 0116 221 0013
E-mail: HwhitbyMA@aol.com
Website: http://www.m-a.org.uk

The Schools Music Association
Maxwell Pryce
Educamus
71 Margaret Road
New Barnet
Hertfordshire EN4 9NT
Tel: 020 8440 6919

**The Design and Technology
Association**
16 Wellesbourne House
Walton Road
Wellesbourne
Warwickshire CV35 9JB
Tel: 01789 470007
E-mail: DATA@data.org.uk
Website: http://www.data.org.uk

**The Association for Language
Learning**
150 Railway Terrace
Rugby CV21 3HN
Tel: 01788 546443
E-mail:
langlearn@languagelearn.co.uk
Website:
http://www.languagelearn.co.uk

**The Association for Science
Education**
College Lane
Hatfield
Hertfordshire AL10 9AA
Tel: 01707 266532
E-mail: ase@asehq.telme.com
Website: http://www.ase.org.uk

Christian Education Movement
Royal Buildings
Victoria Street
Derby DE1 1GW
Tel: 01332 296655
E-mail: cem@cem.org.uk
Website: http://www.cem.org.uk

The Historical Association
59A Kennington Park Road
London SE11 4JH
Tel: 020 7735 3901
E-mail: enquiry@history.org.uk
Website: http://www.history.org.uk

**The National Society for
Education in Art and Design**
The Gatehouse
Corsham Court
Corsham
Wiltshire SN13 0BZ
Tel: 01249 714825
E-mail:
113662.770@compuserve.com
Website: http://www.nsead.org

**National Association for the
Teaching of English**
50 Broadfield Road
Sheffield S8 0XJ
Tel: 0114 255 5419
E-mail: nate.hq@campus.bt.com
Website: http://www.nate.org.uk

**National Association for Pastoral
Care in Education**
c/o Institute of Education
University of Warwick
Coventry CV4 7AL
Tel: 024 7652 3810
E-mail: napce@warwick.ac.uk
Website:
http://www.warwick.ac.uk/wie/napce

ORGANISATIONS CONCERNED WITH EMOTIONAL LITERACY AND/OR SMALL SCHOOLS

Antidote: Campaign for Emotional Literacy
5th Floor
45 Beech Street
London EC2 8AD
Tel: 020 7588 5151
E-mail:
antidote@geo2.poptel.org.uk
Website under construction

The Self-esteem Network
32 Carisbrooke Road
London E17 7EF
Tel: 020 8521 6977
E-mail: titus@gci.org.uk
(Membership joint with Antidote)

Re:membering Education
66 Beaconsfield Villas
Brighton BN1 6HE
Tel: 01273 239311
E-mail: remember@mcmail.com
Website:
http://www.remember.mcmail.com

Human Scale Education
96 Carlingcott
Bath BA2 8AW
Tel: 01972 510709
E-mail: hse@clara.net
Website: http://www.hse.clara.net

MISCELLANEOUS

National Foundation for Educational Research in England and Wales
The Mere
Upton Park
Slough
Berkshire SL1 2DQ
Tel: 01753 574123
E-mail: enquiries@nfer.ac.uk
Website: http://www.nfer.ac.uk

National Confederation of Parent Teacher Associations
2 Ebbsfleet Estate
Stonebridge Road
Gravesend
Kent DA11 9DZ
Tel: 01474 560618

Equal Opportunities Commission
Overseas House
Quay Street
Manchester M3 3HN
Tel: 0161 833 9244
E-mail: info@eoc.org.uk
Website: http://www.eoc.org.uk

National Society for the Prevention of Cruelty to Children
National Centre
42 Curtain Road
London EC2A 3NH
Tel: 020 7825 2500
E-mail: via website
Website: http://www.nspcc.org.uk

**Royal Society for the Prevention
of Accidents**
Edgbaston Park
353 Bristol Road
Birmingham B5 7ST
Tel: 0121 248 2000
E-mail: help@rospa.co.uk
Website: http://www.rospa.co.uk

**General Teaching Council for
Scotland**
Clerwood House
96 Clermiston Road
Edinburgh EH12 6UT
Tel: 0131 314 6000
Website: http://www.gtcs.org.uk

*Anyone wanting to teach in a local
authority school in Scotland should
contact the General Teaching
Council for Scotland.*

Further reading

A browse through a good bookshop or the URLs listed in this book will undoubtedly open up more possibilities for further reading. The books chosen here are good starting points.

PERSONAL ISSUES

Stress management
Hare, B. (1988). *Be Assertive*. Vermilion. London.

Hindle, T. (1998). *Manage your Time*. Dorling Kindersley. London.

Peiffer, V. (1996). *Principles of Stress Management*. Thorsons, London.

Rechtschaffen, S. (1996). *Time Shifting*. Rider Books.

Shapiro, D. and Shapiro, E. (1999). *Ultimate Relaxation*. Quadrille, London.

Wilson, P. (1997). *Calm at Work*. Penguin, London.

Well-being
The Body Shop Book of Wellbeing (1998). Ebury Press, London.

Golten, R. (1999). *The Owner's Guide to the Body*. Thorsons, London.

Levy, E. and Monte, T. (1997). *The 10 Best Ways to Boost your Immune System*. Bantam Books, London.

Mindell, E. (1985). *The Vitamin Bible* (2nd edition). Arlington Books, London.

Tobias, M. and Sullivan, J.P. (1992). *The Complete Stretching Book*. Dorling Kindersley, London.

Workplace bullying
Adams, A. (1992). *Bullying at Work: How to Confront and Overcome it*. Virago.

Field, T. (1996). *Bully in Sight*. Success Unlimited.

Miscellaneous
Goleman, D. (1996). *Emotional Intelligence*. Bloomsbury, London.

Goleman, D. (1998). *Working with Emotional Intelligence*. Bloomsbury, London.

Pease, A. (1997). *Body Language*. Sheldon Press, London.

TEACHING ISSUES

Rights and responsibilities

The Bristol Guide (1998). Document Summary Service, University of Bristol, Graduate School of Education.

The Bristol Guide is available from the Document Summary Service, University of Bristol, Graduate School of Education, 35 Berkeley Square, Bristol BS8 1JA. Enclose a cheque with your order for £5.00 for one copy. Orders for 2–15 copies cost £3.50 per copy and 16–24 copies cost £3.00 per copy. All prices include postage and packing.

Web page design and ICT

Freedman, T. (1999). *Managing ICT.* Hodder and Stoughton.

Salkind, N. (1998). *Microsoft Office 97 for Windows for Teachers.* IDG.

Holzschlag, M. (1998). *HTML4 in 24 Hours.* Sams.

Smith, B. (1999). *Creating Web Pages for Dummies.* IDG.

Behaviour management

Watkins, C. (1998). *Managing Classroom Behaviour: A Bit Like Air Traffic Control.* ATL.

This is available from the Association of Teachers and Lecturers despatch section (020 7782 1584). There is a charge for non-members.

Charles, C.M. (1996). *Building Classroom Discipline.* Longman.

Green, Dr C. and Chee, Dr K. (1997). *Understanding ADHD.* Vermilion, London.

Cooper, P. and Ideus, K. (1996). *Attention Deficit/Hyperactivity Disorder (A Practical Guide for Teachers).* David Fulton Publishers, London.

Teaching and schools

Bennett, V. (1996). *Making Dreams Come True: visualisations and practical exercises to help children set and achieve their goals.* Gazebo, Stratford-upon-Avon.

Bentley, T. (1998). *Learning Beyond the Classroom.* Routledge.

Carnie, F. *et al.* (eds) (1996). *Freeing Education: Steps towards Real Choice and Diversity in Schools.* Hawthorn Press, Stroud.

McCarthy, K. (1998). *Learning by Heart: the role of emotional education in raising school achievement.* Co-ordinated by Re:membering Education. Available from Re:membering Education (01273 239311).

Petty, G. (1998). *Teaching Today.* Stanley Thornes, Cheltenham.

Smith, L. and Vickers, A. (1995). *Supply Teachers.* Scholastic (Bright Ideas series).

The Education Authorities Directory and Annual (published annually). The School Government Publishing Company Ltd. *A good resource for addresses of public offices, examinations organisations, schools, careers centres etc. It is available in most libraries.*

Prime-Ed Publishing has a good selection of photocopiable resources, merit stickers and CD-ROM etc. available from Prime-Ed Publishing, Kelsey Close, Attleborough Field Industrial Estate, Nuneaton, Warwickshire CV11 6RS. Tel: 024 7635 2002. E-mail: sales@prime-ed.com. Website: http://www.prime-ed.com

Tutoring

Marland, M. and Rogers, R. (1997). *The Art of the Tutor.* David Fulton Publishers, London.

Tattum, D. and Herbert, G. (eds) (1997). *Bullying: Home, School and Community.* David Fulton Publishers, London.

Smallwood Publishing Group has a good selection of books for teachers on emotional literacy and self-esteem etc. Available from The Old Bakery, Charlton House, Dour Street, Kent CT16 1ED. Tel: 01304 226800. E-mail: information@smallwood.co.uk. Website: http://www.smallwood.co.uk.

DfEE publications

Have a look at the DfEE website (http://www.dfee.gov.uk) for a full list of available publications. The following list is good to start with. DfEE publications are available from the publication centre (0845 6022260).

CIRCULARS (available to download from the DfEE website or from the publication centre)

2/98 Reducing the Bureaucratic Burden on Teachers

4/98 Teaching: High Status, High Standards (in particular annex B, Initial Teaching Training Curriculum for the Use of Information and Communications Technology)

9/98 School Teachers' Pay and Conditions of Employment 1998

5/99 The Induction Period for Newly Qualified Teachers

Curriculum IT support publications (second edition 1998).
       A useful booklet listing curriculum IT support subject by subject.

Health and Safety of Pupils on Educational Visits. DfEE (1998).

Supporting Pupils with Medical Needs. DfEE (1996).

Guidance on First Aid for Schools. DfEE (1998).

Meet the Challenge: Education Action Zones. DfEE (1999).

OFSTED publications

Have a look at the OFSTED website (http://www.ofsted.gov.uk) for a full list of available publications. The following list is good to start with. OFSTED publications are available from the order line (020 7510 0180).

Equal Opportunities Commission and OFSTED (1996). *The Gender Divide: Performance Differences between Boys and Girls at School.* HMSO, London.

Weston, P. (1999). *Homework: Learning from Practice.* The Stationery Office, London.

OFSTED (1995). *Framework for the Inspection of Schools.* The Stationery Office, London.

OFSTED (1998). Making the Most of Inspection.

OFSTED (August 1998). Inspection '98: Briefing for Schools on the New Inspection Requirements.

OFSTED (July 1998). Inspection '98: Supplement to the Inspections Handbooks Containing New Requirements and Guidance.

Index

Page numbers in *italics* refer to tables and boxes.

non-teaching duties *2, 3*, 59, 209–12, 241 *see also* extra-curricular activities

non-teaching staff 84, 87

non-verbal communication *32*, 161–3, *191, 240*

nosebleeds 207–8

observing
    by classroom support 261
    colleagues 122, 129, 174–5, 192
    by colleagues 120, 128, 279–80

OFSTED
    after inspection 278–9
    background 263–4
    code of conduct 264–5
    complaints procedure 278–9
    feedback *275*, 277–8
    Framework 262–3, 265–9, *271*
    during inspection 274–7
    making the most of *272, 273, 276*, 277–8
    preparation 270, 272–4
    publications 62–3, 194, 262–3, 269–70, *271*, 276, 346
    purpose 262–4
    report 269–70, 278
    requirements 165, 179, 192, 262–3, 265–71
    worries about 270, 272, 275–6

organising yourself 212–19, 221–2, 224–5, 234–5, 295, 307–8

overhead projectors *168*

overwork 216–19, 221, 234–5, 305–6, 307–8, 311–12

panic attacks 222–3, *235*

parent governors *86*

parent–teacher associations 108–9

parental involvement 3, 254–8

parents' evenings 254–7

part-time teaching 11, 50

pastoral care *see* tutoring

paternity leave 74, *75*

pay 2, 5, 7, 11, 15, 57, 70–2, 299

pay scales 2, 4, *14, 21*, 70–1

pensions 2, 4, 12, 312

period pain 208

personal issues 175–8

personal property 68–9

personality clashes *99*, 304–5

personnel in school 83–8

physical contact 66–7, *68*

police checks *40*

post-16 colleges *see* sixth-form colleges

power structure 2, 3, 4, 76, 78–87, 97

praise *see* rewards

pre-appointment preparation *38*, 128, 301

preparation
    classroom 225
    interviews 26–9
    lesson 166, 215–16, 241, *243*
    for OFSTED 270, 272–4
    pre-appointment 38, 128, 301

prioritising your work 214–15

private tutoring 15

problem children 155–60, 306–7

professional development 42–4, *45*, 111–14, 115, 293–5

progressive education 6–8

project work 16

promotion 45–6